THE

Mind

OF A

Child

MARSHANNE MISHOE

20 Twenty
Literary Group

The Mind of a Child
Copyright © 2023 by Marshanne Mishoe

ISBN
978-1-961250-56-7 (Paperback)
978-1-961250-57-4 (eBook)
978-1-961250-55-0 (Hardcover)

THE
Mind
OF A
Child

Chapter 1

May, 1940, Junction Point,
South Carolina

Jessa lay on her side, panting roughly. It was quiet except for the rain hitting the windowpane and the wind chimes tinkling in the pecan tree outside her bedroom window. The sun had been setting– was it an hour ago or two already?– as Raymond had taken Danny to their elderly neighbor's, Mrs. McGraff's. Danny had been a real trooper all day but both she and Raymond knew it was time to pass him off for the night. He didn't need to witness all that would come.

Jessa's blue eyes darted around the room as she tried to focus on something...anything. They fell on the bedside picture of Danny. He smiled at her from the black and white photo, taken at his second birthday party last month. She pushed a golden lock of hair out of her face and smiled back weakly. He was worth it. This one would be, too.

Jessa could hear Raymond, far off somewhere, banging pots and pans. As her eyes trailed down, they stopped on her stomach. It looked as if it had a life of its own. First it contorted, then a tiny bump thrust itself out in a protrusion to her side. Moving, though…all the time, it was moving. Jessa closed her eyes, blocking out the alien sight and breathed in deeply. Nausea began its wave over her and she clutched the sheet, trying to prepare herself for that paralyzing grip that would inevitably come again.

Raymond came into the room with a bowl and washcloth and tried to place it on his wife's forehead. She swatted it away, agitated, and then moaned as panic seized her face.

"Jessa, look here," Raymond commanded, trying to make eye contact with this wild, wounded beast that was his wife. "I need you to breathe…in, slowly, out slowly, in…"

Jessa swept her hand around, trying to sit up, and spilled the water from the bowl. Raymond ran his fingers through his thick, red hair and yelled out loud, "Damn it! This isn't how it was with Danny! It went quicker, it wasn't so hard. Woman, you need to tell me. Can you do this here or do I need to take you to County?"

Jessa's groans became more hysterical as the pressure, the pain increased. Raymond suddenly realized she couldn't tell him. She wasn't able. He would have to make the call himself. Screwing up all the self-discipline it had taken to get him through basic training at Parris Island, Raymond stuffed down his own panic. He went back over the day.

* * *

Things had been slow and annoying for her at first, starting at about 4:30 in the morning. By midday, the pain increased; it came more often. He'd had to keep Danny playing in the kitchen so the boy wouldn't worry about his mother. Then, all afternoon things had stayed about the same, with labor pains just grinding away at his wife, her strength, his nerves.

Then it all had really picked up again at suppertime. He had been feeding Danny oatmeal in the kitchen when he heard Jessa cry out for him from the bedroom. It was all he could do to keep Danny from scrambling out of his high chair to follow him.

Raymond had come into the bedroom to find Jessa clinging to the post of their rice bed, her face pasty and grimaced.

"I need you with me!" she cried.

So, putting his arm around her waist and practically lifting her, Raymond had helped his wife back to bed. She had fallen back into the feather pillows and begged, "Please don't leave me!"

"Jessa, hon, I have to take care of Danny. Then I'll be right back. I promise."

He had kissed her forehead, then turned and ran to the boy's room. He had grabbed up Danny's pillow and blanket from his crib and rushed back to the kitchen.

He found his son smiling his dimpled grin, as usual. *He is always so cheerful*, Raymond had thought absently. Danny immediately started scooting out of his chair, saying, "I see Momma!"

"Not now, son," Raymond had replied as he scooped him out of his chair and wrapped him in the blanket. "Mommy is sleeping, but Mrs. McGraff has just baked one of her chocolate layer cakes and she says if you are a good boy, you can have a piece."

He had clutched the boy to his chest as he ran out of the side door into the rain. It was getting dark, so he had stepped in every puddle between his yard and the McGraffs'. The little boy laughed at the drops of water running down his face. When he reached the porch, Mrs. McGraff had come to the door and said, "Come on in, little fella. I have a cobbler in the oven."

"Choc-it cake." Danny replied.

Mrs. McGraff's eyes had met Raymond's anxious ones, and she said, "Well, come on in and let's see about that." She held out her arms and took the boy. As Raymond turned to run off the front stoop, Mrs. McGraff had stopped him.

"Listen, son, it's 1940. Women do not have to give birth at home every time. She's been going a long time now. If things don't happen shortly, I'd get her to County."

"Right," he'd replied and then run back out into the rain.

* * *

Now it was time to decide. He looked at his wife's face. He listened to her laboring screams. He'd never felt more helpless. He knew another one was coming. He had about three or four minutes to move her. As she collapsed back into the pillows, exhausted from the latest round, Raymond gingerly worked his arms under her neck and knees. As he lifted, Jessa folded in half at the waist and let out a scream.

"Unbend me! Please!" she shrieked.

He straightened her out the best he could, as he carried her, sheet, blanket and all, to the front door. *Of course, the rain and wind had picked up*, he thought to himself. He'd just make a run for it.

For the second time this horrible night, he held one of the two…almost three…most important people in his life to his chest and dashed out into the storm. He used the fingers of his left hand to open the back door of the Buick. The next part was tricky. He turned and put Jessa's head in first, working her across the backseat as best he could. The end of the blanket dropped into the rain water on the ground and Raymond threw that part on the floorboard. He ran around to the other back door and tried to fashion a pillow from part of the sheet. He shoved it under Jessa's head, slammed the door and patted his pockets. No keys!

"I'll be right back!" he yelled to no one listening. He scrambled up the back steps, reached inside the kitchen door and felt along the wall in the dark. His hands stumbled onto the key hook and his fingers gripped the car keys. *Thank the Lord*, Raymond mumbled. Racing back to the car, he started it up, threw it in reverse and backed out of the driveway, just in time to hear Jessa start to scream again.

* * *

Smoke billowed out of Raymond's nostrils as he lit up a Lucky Strike. Filterless. The only way this former Marine would smoke. Jessa hated his smoking, but she never nagged. She just looked at him with her knowing blue eyes and he knew what she was thinking.

Raymond stared through his reflection in the waiting room window, out into the wet darkness. The rain had stopped, finally. They'd made it to the hospital two or more hours ago. Nurses, doctors, everyone in the ER it seemed, all came out to help get Jessa on the gurney. One of them, an orderly, had asked him, "Why'd you wait so long?" He hadn't answered the question, even though he had also been asking it of himself.

Now everything was quiet. *It's enough to drive you mad,* Raymond thought. First, he was swarmed by activity, questions about Jessa; how far along was she, how often were the labor pains coming, was this her first birth? As the gurney worked its way down the hall, he'd held Jessa's hand. But when they arrived at the labor room doors, a nurse planted herself in front of him.

"I'm sorry, Mr. Bland. This is as far as you can go. We'll take good care of your wife and baby. You can wait on the second floor in the room to the left of the elevator. We'll let you know something shortly."

Shortly! He hadn't heard a word since then and he was trying very hard to control his impatience.

The doors of the elevator opened around the corner. Raymond turned from the window and walked across the room just in time to meet a doctor at the door.

"Mr. Bland?" the doctor asked.

Raymond nodded.

"I'm Dr. Joseph. You're the only one in here at this hour, I see."

Raymond stepped aside so the doctor could enter the room.

"Let's sit down, shall we?" Dr. Joseph asked gently.

Raymond obeyed, but his patience was at its breaking point, so he blurted, "My wife, Doctor. How's my wife? Did I get her here in time?"

"Well, yes. You two pushed it to the limit. But she's fine! Exhausted but okay."

Relief washed over Raymond's face. "Can I see her? Can I see them?" he asked.

Dr. Joseph set his jaw for a moment and said, "Mr. Bland, I'm afraid there might be some complications."

Raymond's eyes shot back to the doctor's, giving him full attention. "What do you mean? Was it a boy or a girl? Is it all right?"

"A boy," the doctor stated flatly.

A boy! Another son! Raymond's mind tried to get around this fact. Jessa had wanted a girl. They would have named her Jessica, after her mother. But a boy was fine. Danny needed a playmate. But wait…the doctor had said "complications."

"What did you say about complications?" Raymond asked, fighting through the fatigue to understand.

"Yes, well, I want you to know that we had to use forceps to get the baby out," the doctor explained. "He was not quite full breech, but rather sideways. I was able to turn him but he and your wife needed help getting him out of the birth canal. That's when I saw that he was blue. The nurses took all the steps to get him breathing, clearing the mucus, suctioning his nose and mouth. They worked quite a while. Anyway, he is weak. That could be explained by the long labor. But we'll need to keep him under close observation for a while. We will do some tests on him in the morning. Your son doesn't seem able to suckle. So, first things first. We've got to get some nourishment into him."

"Then what?" Raymond interrupted. "Will he be okay then?"

Dr. Joseph hesitated before responding. "Mr. Bland, sometimes with labors like this, well, there is a chance that your son's mental or physical abilities might have been impacted. We'll know more after we run some tests. Right now, it is important for you to be strong. We've tried to make your wife comfortable. We've given her something to help her sleep. But in the morning, she will need you to help her grasp the findings of the tests. You need to get some sleep yourself and then be back here first thing in the morning."

While the doctor had been talking, Raymond's head had dropped into his hands, with his eyes toward the floor. Now he looked up. "Doctor, are you saying my son might be crippled or... retarded?" He choked on the last word.

"Mr. Bland, there is that chance. But we just don't know anything right now. It's been a long night for all of you. Go home, get some rest and we will talk again in the morning."

With that, the doctor stood up, put his hand on Raymond's shoulder momentarily and turned to go, leaving Raymond more confused than ever.

CHAPTER 2

September, 2007, Deerfield County, North Georgia

Oh good grief! Willa yelled at herself silently. She had managed to run the front tire of her minivan up on the curb as she tried to park in front of Gold Mine Elementary. *Once again, you've pushed it to the limit, leaving no time for error, and now you park like a 15-year old driver's ed student,* she continued her silent scolding. She often said no one could be harder on her than she was on herself.

Willa's watch said 10:00 on the dot. So, she quickly decided to leave the van jacked up on the curb. She threw the door open only to hear the skin-crawling sound of metal scraping cement. Willa cursed under her breath and grabbed the folder with her resume in it. Tossing her pocketbook over her shoulder, she jumped out and threw her weight against the door. Again the ear-splitting scraping. After three tries, the door finally freed itself of the curb and slammed shut.

Willa rolled her eyes to heaven, hoping the principal's office didn't overlook the front parking lot.

In the school lobby, the woman at the front desk was busy checking in parent volunteers.

"I'm sorry it's taking so long," she explained, "but we've just installed a new security system, county-wide, and everyone must have their driver's license scanned before they are allowed in any school building. Then we take your photo and keep it stored here for future visits. Next time you come, you'll just swipe in and get a printed security badge. So it won't take this long again."

Great! fumed Willa, as she forced a pressed-lipped smile. She was fourth in line. The clock on the check-in desk said 10:03. The woman at the front of the line produced her license, had it scanned, stepped to the side to have her photo taken and was on her way. The man behind her was just as efficient. But the woman directly in front of Willa was balancing a large plate of cupcakes and a plastic grocery bag of juice boxes in one hand and a boy about two-and-a-half years-old on the opposite hip.

"Jackson, I gotta put you down," the woman said.

The little boy held onto his mother's shoulder as she tried to lean over and put him down.

"Jackson, put your feet down, honey. Mommy needs to sign in so we can go to Rachael's class."

But the little boy stubbornly kept his legs latched around his mother's waist. The woman put the cupcakes on the counter, dropped the bag from her reddened fingers and tried to pry the kid off her. Now, apparently, he decided that while he was losing the battle of physical strength, he'd try a temperamental method of resistance. He went limp, flopped on the floor and wailed like an ambulance siren.

"Jackson, you stand up this minute!" his mother commanded.

But Jackson would have nothing of it.

"All right, young man, you stand up right now or you won't get any of Rachael's birthday cupcakes," she threatened.

The woman glanced up at Willa as she continued to try and get the jelly-boy to his feet. "I'm so sorry. It's the terrible two's.

He's just got a mind of his own and he's out to prove it," she smiled wearily. "

"Come on, son," she said as she scooped him up off the floor.

The woman behind the counter said, "Well, we won't be able to take your picture like that. Do you think he will let me hold him?"

"Who would snap the photo then?" the mother asked. Both women turned and looked at Willa.

Willa thought fast, but not fast enough. As she protested that she had an interview with the principal scheduled for that very minute, the mother passed the lump of boy to her.

"But…" Willa objected. And then she just sighed and gave in. The little boy was kind of cute and he was looking right into her face with his big, brown eyes. "Oh, you're not so bad," Willa began as the other two women got the necessary photograph. "You're just a cutie and need somebody to notice…" At that very moment the boy drew in a huge breath, flung his head back and sneezed with all his might, right in her face.

The mother quickly ran over and took her son back, grabbed a tissue out of her purse and started dabbing at Willa's shirt.

"Please, please, it's okay. Can I just get checked in? I really am running late." Willa's impatience was showing, despite her best effort.

"Oh, of course, why didn't you say so?" the mother asked sheepishly.

When Willa's temporary badge was printed out with her photo on it, she noticed the large dots of kid snot all over her silk blouse. *So much for first impressions,* Willa grouched, once again, to nobody but herself.

* * *

Finally, Willa found herself sitting stiffly in a small waiting chair in the school's administrative office. She felt no less nervous than the time in 6th grade when she got sent to the principal's office for smoking in the bathroom. She tried to psych herself up. *Now Willa, you're a grown woman,* she told herself. *You used to eat people like this guy for lunch when you were a branch manager for the Savings and Loan. Just because you've been home raising three kids for the past decade doesn't mean you've lost your edge.* Willa bit her lip, trying to believe what she was thinking.

A petite, attractive woman came out of an inner office and held out her hand. She was impeccably dressed from her quaffed hair to her trendy shoes. Willa felt clumsy as she rose from her chair. She was just glad it didn't stick to her ample fanny and rise up with her.

"Hello. I'm Cathy Cook, Mr. Johnson's assistant," the woman said crisply. "He's ready to see you now."

Great!" replied Willa as she shook the tiny woman's tiny hand. Ms. Cook had the unfortunate luck to have a rather pinched, upturned nose, so she appeared to be snooty, whether she really was or not.

"Right this way," Ms. Cook instructed.

Willa followed along, trying to balance in her high heels, which she usually wore only to church. Tennis shoes were her typical foot attire for the part time nob she held at her kids' preschool. She had earned peanuts in salary, but the reduced tuition had really helped. And she enjoyed seeing her kids, even in passing, during their school day. Daniel had moved on to elementary school several years ago, followed a few years later by Ray.

Willa would have loved to have spent one more year being with Bella in that more relaxed preschool setting. But Joel's layoff last year had really put a dent in their savings. His new job didn't offer medical benefits. So, both of them knew that even though he was working again, the time had come for Willa to go back to a "real job." Now Bella was enrolled full time in Georgia Pre-K for four year olds. She'd been attending since school started a few weeks ago. They'd been lucky to get her in the free program, because there was a waiting list.

Willa's goal was simple…but not easy. She needed full time work, plus benefits, plus a schedule that would closely match her kids' so they could avoid more child care costs. That ruled out going back into banking. When she heard about an opening at Gold Mine Elementary for a Paraprofessional, the politically correct term these days for Teacher's Aid, she'd called right away for an interview.

"This is Mr. Johnson's office," Ms. Cook explained as she swept the door open. Willa was taken aback by the fact that there were three people…one man and two women…in the room.

"Good Morning," Willa enthused cheerfully, as she walked into the roomy office. "I'm Willa Grizzard." She held out her hand. The short, stout man stood from behind his desk and shook her hand. "I'm Paul Johnson," he said, not bothering to introduce the two women, who had also stood up during Willa's entry. "Nice to meet you," Willa replied as she nodded first in his direction then toward the women. Everyone sat back down in their chairs, which were pulled up around the man's desk He was younger than Willa had expected.

"Grizzard…" the principal mused. Are you any relation to that newspaper columnist who wrote for the AJC for so many years? What was his name?"

"Lewis Grizzard," said one of the two Anonymous Women.

"That's right, Lewis Grizzard. Didn't he die a while back?" Mr. Johnson replied.

"Oh no, no relation," Willa answered. "My husband's family is from South Carolina. We both call that home. My maiden name was Bland. Anyway, Mr. Grizzard had a high-falutin' way of pronouncing his name. You know, he always portrayed himself as so down home in his columns, but he said Gri-ZARD', with the emphasis on the last syllable. Like he was from England or something. Anyway, we South Carolina Grizzards must have southernized the name somewhere along the way. We say Griz-zerd. Rhymes with 'blizzard.'" Willa stopped as she realized she'd kind of gone on a bit too long.

"Griz-zerd," Mr. Johnson repeated. "Well, Mrs. Grizzard, you're applying today for the Parapro position we have open. We're anxious to fill the spot because we are already five weeks into the school year. But we do want to get the right person in there. Tell us a little bit about yourself."

He'd lobbed the ball to her. She remembered how the interview game worked from when she was the one doing the hiring.

"I have lived here in Goshen for over 10 years now. My husband and I have three children." She knew it would have been illegal for him to ask her about her family, but she wanted him to know about them right up front. Nothing was more important to her than her family.

"I got my degree in Business Management from the University of South Carolina in 1985. Then I spent 12 years working my way up in the banking industry." She passed a copy of her resume across the desk to him. "You can see my work history right here," she indicated with a French manicured nail. "Anyway, when I had my first child I decided to stay home with him full time. But during the interim while I wasn't employed, I have continued to use my management skills in a volunteer capacity. I headed up my neighborhood homeowners' association. I started a Mothers' Morning Out program at the local Rec. Center. I have been in charge of our church's Vacation Bible School for the past three summers. I've also taught swim lessons at the YMCA. Then two years ago, I took a position with Goshen Community Church Preschool. It was part time, just three mornings a week. But I was the lead teacher in the three-year olds' class." Willa paused to let what she had said sink in. She really believed the skills she'd gained in her volunteer and part time work should not be undervalued.

"What did you do as a lead teacher?" asked Nameless Woman Number One.

Willa turned toward her. "Well, I was responsible for lesson plans. I tried to focus the curriculum on engaging the children's five senses as much as possible. Research shows that young children learn best through play. Academics come naturally when you let them build with blocks, pour rice from one container to another, squish play dough between their fingers." Willa knew she had a sing-song drawl and southern way of expressing herself. She just hoped it wouldn't get in the way of her knowledgeable experience and love for children.

"Now, that's not to say that we didn't have a schedule with an outline for reaching certain goals. We had Welcome Time, Circle Time, Movement Class, Music, Reading, Story Time, Recess, and Snack Time. It was always a busy morning. I worked directly with the children, focusing on developing social skills, like sharing, helping them develop both their fine and gross motor skills, as well as teaching them classroom skills, such as listening and following directions, walking in line and sitting quietly for a period of time."

"Were you in the classroom alone or did you have an assistant?" asked Nameless Woman Number 2.

"I had an assistant. I was responsible for directing my assistant in implementing the curriculum. For instance, while I was talking about the day's weather during Circle Time, I would have her sit with the children on the floor to help them focus their attention, to teach them to sit 'crisscross applesauce.' That sort of thing." Willa used her fingers to make quotation mark signs when she used teaching jargon.

"Well, you're used to being the lead teacher. Would you have a problem being in the assistant position here at Gold Mine Elementary?" the principal questioned.

"Oh, heavens, no," Willa replied. "I feel I have developed skills that will make me a useful assistant in working with the students here. I know that a certified teacher has the training and skills to lead the class. I would welcome the opportunity to come alongside her and reinforce what she's teaching. I would hope to learn a lot along the way."

"Good, good," Mr. Johnson said supportively. "You know Mrs. Grizzard, we are lucky here at Gold Mine Elementary. Our community is a wealthy one. Demographics show that ours is one of the richest suburbs in the nation. Median income here is in the high 80's. But there are many who make so much more than that."

And so much less than that, Willa thought.

"The economic downturn just doesn't seem to have hit us as hard as it has the schools down in Atlanta, at least not yet," he continued.

Willa looked down, feeling embarrassed, even though there was no way this principal could possibly know the financial straits she and Joel were in.

"That gives us the benefit of having a whole lot of volunteers who come on campus every day," Mr. Johnson went on. "We have plenty of other applicants who would like to work here at our school, just to be near their children, just to have something to do during the day. Why should we consider you above all the others?"

Oh, it's the what-sets-you-apart question, Willa thought. "Well, sir, I can tell you that I truly love working with children. Watching their growth over a school year is so rewarding! I have always been interested in the education of young children and even though I don't have a degree in Early Childhood Education, I do a lot of reading on the subject and try to follow the trends. I have three children in Deerfield County Schools right now. I would love an opportunity to become a part of this school system and to help in the education of children here." Quite a speech, if she did think so herself.

That's when things took a turn...a very unexpected, life-changing turn.

"How do you feel about working with children with special needs?" asked Woman One.

Special needs? Did she mean handicapped? Children who had learning disabilities? What did she mean?

"What do you mean by 'special needs'?" asked Willa. There went the air quotes again.

"Well, we have a classroom with children who have developmental delays. They are the age of kindergarteners, but are not ready for the typical kindergarten classroom," the lady explained. "We have them follow a kindergarten curriculum but they move at a slower pace."

"Oh," said Willa. "I see." She didn't see. "Do they just need a little bit of extra help learning their numbers and the alphabet?" she asked.

"Well," said Woman Number Two, "That's part of it. Some of them also have behavior issues that would keep them from succeeding in a regular class. You'd work with a teacher who has gone to school and gotten her degree in Special Education. Ms. Smith is also certified to teach Special Ed. She's new to our school this year, but she finished her first year of teaching at Granger Elementary last year. The county moved her position here for this school year. I think you'll like her. What she lacks in experience, she more than makes up for with her passion for her work and her students."

"What kind of things would be my responsibility?" Willa asked carefully. The teacher's experience level just skipped right over her at this point.

"In our school, parapros assist the teacher in whatever he or she needs," the principal explained. It's really impossible to tell you exactly what you would be doing every day. You'd need to follow the teacher's lead. The best skill you can bring to a job like this if flexibility."

"I agree with Mr. Johnson," Woman Number One chimed in. "If you can come in with an open mind, jump right in and help in whatever way necessary, and be flexible, you will be very successful in this position."

"I'm sorry," Willa scratched her head in a little bit of a frenzied way. "But I missed your name. Are you the head of the Special Education Department here?" She could no longer put up with this rude oversight.

"No, no. I'm sorry Mrs. Grizzard. This is Carol Harper and Patty Long, our two assistant principals here at Gold Mine," Mr. Johnson said. Willa got an inkling that this guy was learning the ropes of being the boss right before her eyes.

"Oh, well, nice to meet you," she replied. Somewhere in the back of her mind, Willa felt a little alarm going off. Something was up here. Was it the old "bait and switch" routine? She thought she was interviewing for a job working with kindergartners. At no time had anyone mentioned "special needs." Until now. And where were the slew of applicants the principal had mentioned a moment ago? Willa's guess was they heard "special needs" and bolted. Just like she was going to do.

"Um, well, I really have no experience in Special Education. I don't know anything about it. All three of my children have been in regular ed so far. I'm sure that could change at any moment, if their grades keep dropping," she joked lamely. "But I really would feel very unprepared."

Willa was trying to say something that wouldn't turn them off from her completely. She really needed a job like this. Just one that wasn't so "special."

"Mrs. Grizzard, we really would like to have you spend a day in the class we are talking about. Work with the lead teacher. See how it goes. Everything you said you were doing to help prepare the three year olds you worked with, the social skills, the classroom skills, that's what you would bring to this class. These children are older, chronologically, but developmentally they are closer to three-year-olds. Some of them maybe are more like two-year-olds. We like what you've said about your classroom. You won't have to know all the answers. That's what the teacher is for. You will just assist, similar to the way your assistant helped you," Mr. Johnson leaned forward intensely in his chair.

Willa's hazel eyes met his. For a moment she almost felt the presence of desperation. Was it his or hers? She couldn't tell. Anyway, before she knew what she was saying, her mouth opened and she gave her answer. Again, a life-changing one.

"Okay."

CHAPTER 3

J essa sat quietly in her hospital bed the morning after she gave
birth, but her thoughts were anything but silent. She had
wanted to spare Raymond the cost of a hospital birth this time,
too. But she had just been hurting so much. And exhaustion had
overtaken her. She couldn't even argue with him when he decided
to bring her here. She was still weak and overly tired, having gotten
only a few hours of sleep last night. The doctor had stitched her
up and had given her an I-V with fluids in it. It must have had
something else in it too, because she didn't remember much after
they inserted the needle in her arm. She had seen her baby...a
boy...for only a few moments before she fell asleep. His hair was
so fair, almost translucent. He looked different from Danny, she
did remember that. And they had kept him away from her for
quite a while, before bringing him in, all swaddled in blankets,
to see if he would nurse. He was just as worn out as she was, Jessa
reasoned, so he had been unable to latch onto her breast. She'd love
to try again, if they would just bring him to her! She was dying to
unwrap the blankets and examine her new son from head to toe,
counting fingers, all that sort of thing.

Jessa fidgeted with her covers and was trying to plump the
pillows behind her when the door opened and a colored woman
brought in a tray with breakfast on it. She was hungry but

anxiously looked past the woman to see if anyone was following. She wanted to see her baby!

"Good mornin'!" the woman announced as she rolled the tray up to Jessa's bedside. "How you feeling dis mornin'? All tuckered out?"

Jessa smiled politely and gingerly raised herself up to a sitting position. "Yes. I just kind of lost control of the whole situation and wore myself out."

"Honey, ain't no such thing as a woman who is in control during childbirth. I worked here at County for going on 12 years and I ain't met one yet. Hit's da' only time we women are allowed to lose complete control, so dat part you should enjoy." She put the tray before Jessa.

"Thank you," Jessa replied, and she noticed the eggs were runnier than she liked. "Hey, have you seen Dr. Joseph? I am really feeling up to seeing my baby and I haven't had anyone come in and check on me yet this morning." She took a nibble of a wedge of toast.

"Oh, I just work in da kitchen…Takin' patients they food and collecting they trays afterwards. But I did see two nurses workin' they way down da hall. We had a busy spell here. Three births yesterday, 'sides yours. Dere's 'nother lady laborin' right now. So I guess they tied up wit her. I'm sure they be here shortly. Now just enjoy yo' breakfast and relax," she smiled kindly. "You'll have dat baby witch you full time soon 'nuff. Dis may be yo' last moment of peace and quiet."

A little too much peace and quiet, Jessa worried.

Meanwhile, Raymond stood just outside his wife's hospital room, clutching a vase containing a bunch of daisies. Jessa loved flowers. He took his empty hand and ran it down his face. He was exhausted. He had gotten only a few hours' sleep last night. Now, he had to brace himself for whatever the doctor had found out about his son. And he had to be there for Jessa. How could he? If it weren't for him trying to save a little money on the hospital, none of this would be happening. He drew in a deep breath and pushed open the door.

"Hi," he said quietly, as he saw his wife sitting in her hospital bed. "How are you feeling?" he asked as he leaned over and kissed her cheek. He had aimed for her mouth, but she had turned away, distracted by her thoughts. Was she mad at him?

"Well, I'm 'moan leave you folks alone now. Let me know if you need anythin'," the breakfast woman said as she left the room.

Jessa waited until the door shut and she said, "Raymond, I am so glad you're here." She was clearly upset, thought Raymond. "I finished my breakfast and was hoping they would have brought in our boy by now." She stopped and looked up with a smile. "We have a new son!"

"I know, Jessa!" Raymond smiled. "I was here 'til late last night. Dr. Joseph came down and told me about you and the baby and then sent me home. He said you were sleeping. Sorry I didn't get here earlier."

"Well, it wouldn't have done much good. They just have me sitting here. I'm ready to get out of this bed and go find my son. It's not right to keep a newborn baby from its mother this long." Jessa's face had the same mother-bear expression on it that she would get whenever she felt Danny was in trouble.

Once, he and Danny had gone for a walk in the woods behind their house after supper and he'd lost track of time. They were looking at birds in the trees, bugs on the ground and everything they could see in between. The sun set and it was dark when he'd walked up the back stoop with Danny riding on his shoulders. Jessa had met him at the screened door with this same look. He knew she wasn't scared for him, but rather for the boy. "Where have you been?" she had fussed. She'd reached up and lifted Danny right off his father's shoulders and held him close to her chest. "He's been all bitten up by mosquitoes and look at the scratches on his legs." After taking a moment to see that he was all right, she had relaxed and smiled, almost apologetically, at Raymond. "I was worried," she said. Then she had kissed him.

The same look that he'd seen on Jessa's face that night had gripped it again. Something was standing between her and her baby and she wasn't going to put up with it.

"Raymond, help me up" She started to swing her legs over the edge of the bed and winced.

"Jessa, wait. You get back under the covers and let me go see if I can find out something," Raymond said as he helped her put her legs back on the bed. "No, I want to come, too," she said tiredly.

"Jessa, I promise. I'll find him." Raymond leaned onto the bed and cupped her face in his rough hands. "Please. I want you to rest while you are here. Let me take care of this. Okay?"

"Okay," she acquiesced. "Go to the nursery, will you? Just look at him. His hair is so light. He looks like an angel," her voice sounded drained.

"That's exactly what I plan to do," he said. "Now just catch a cat nap. It may take me a few minutes to locate the doctor." He smiled at her again, turned and left the room.

Raymond made his way down the hall and through some doors. Finally, he found himself staring through the glass at the nursery window. Four little bassinets were lined up front and center. Inside each one was a squinted up face peering out of its swath of blankets. Two of the faces were squalling their little lungs out. They were so red they looked like they would burst. The two trouble makers seemed to be annoying the bundle in the middle. Its face was also red and screwed up and it looked like it might join in the chorus at any time. The fourth lay blissfully sleeping while sucking on its fist, unhindered by all the noise.

Then there was the crib at the back of the nursery, pushed off to one side. Raymond could see the mound of blankets inside, but not the occupant. A nurse opened a side door and walked into the room, checked a thermostat, and started making some notes. She glanced up and saw Raymond at the window. She smiled and questioned with her mouth, "Which one?" The nurse started pointing at the bassinets, one by one. Raymond shook his head as she held up first a name tag saying, "Caldwell," then "Carter," then "Norris," and finally "Turner." The nurse's face lost a bit of its sunny expression as she turned toward the bassinet at the back. She walked over and picked up the tag out of that one and turned and faced Raymond with it. "Bland." Raymond wiped his hand down his face and nodded yes. The nurse picked up the bundle from the bassinet cradling her package carefully, she presented it at the window for Raymond to see.

His boy, his newest son. The baby's face was smaller than the others, Raymond noticed right off. He wasn't red, or crying. Or moving. He didn't seem to be sound asleep either.

It was hard for Raymond to figure out, but something seemed different about this one. He noticed his tongue peeking out of his mouth. Maybe it was his imagination. A phone with a red light rang inside the nursery. The nurse smiled apologetically and quickly returned Raymond's baby to his bassinet. She picked up the phone and exchanged a few words with whoever was on the other end. After she hung up, she carefully examined the tag on one of the screamer's bassinets. Seeming satisfied, she picked up that baby and left the room with it.

Dr. Joseph stood up the hall, watching Raymond Bland at the nursery window. He looked like a nice enough fellow. His wife was young and strong. Why had Fate been so cruel to them? They didn't seem to deserve it, any more than anyone else.

Raymond turned to go. Dr. Joseph came towards him from up the hall.

"Mr. Bland," the doctor called. "I was just coming to see you and your wife." Raymond held out his hand and shook Dr. Joseph's. The doctor continued. "I've spent the morning on the phone with two pediatric specialists in Columbia and I wanted to share what I've learned with you both."

"Doc, if it's okay, can you give me the details first? Then I'll be better prepared when you tell Jessa." Raymond looked the doctor's face over, trying to decipher whether the news was good or bad.

"Of course, Mr. Bland. I understand," Dr. Joseph responded and motioned Raymond toward a row of chairs set up across from the nursery window. The viewing section for the "happy" parents, he thought ruefully.

The two men settled into the seats. Raymond sat with his shoulders bent forward, elbows on his knees, head down. The doctor followed suit, leaning forward also. Then he began.

"Mr. Bland, we have been monitoring your son and checking his reflexes for about twelve hours now. We're concerned because he is lethargic, lacks muscle tone, is almost 'floppy.'"

"Doctor, excuse me for my ignorance, but aren't all newborns 'floppy?'" Raymond inserted. He couldn't explain it, but he felt defensive, like someone he loved was being attacked and he needed to protect him. "This is different Mr. Bland. You have an older child, correct?" the doctor asked.

Raymond nodded. "A two-year-old son."

"Well, with him, as with all normal newborns, they have inborn reflexes. They can have an amazingly strong grip when they are first born and can, in theory, hold themselves up by their grip. They can actually take steps, when supported upright, on their own two feet. These seemingly 'miraculous' reflexes usually disappear after the first few days or so, as the baby becomes able to uncurl itself and stretch out. Your baby never had these reflexes. Most newborns innately know how to suckle. Yours does not. We have managed to get some nourishment into him by slowly pouring a few drops of special formula onto the back of his tongue. But he is not strong enough yet to suck."

So, he's weak from the long labor. Can't we work with him, exercise his arms and legs, help him get stronger?" the worried father asked, still not willing to accept that these were signs of something terribly wrong.

Well, yes, Mr. Bland. The nurse will show you and your wife how to gently manipulate his limbs. This may help some. But there are other signs we are concerned about," the doctor persisted with his difficult diagnosis. "The pediatricians in Columbia have a text book and they read out symptoms to me over the phone. You son's palms, they have a singular line running across them. Look at yours." Raymond complied.

"Normal people have two transverse lines across their palms."

"So?" Raymond was still defensive.

"This difference in his palms, along with his large tongue, his low set ears, his lack of muscle tone and his slanted eyes…Well…"

"Well what, doctor?" Raymond wanted to know now. He wanted to know the truth, even if it was awful.

"The text book called it "Mongolian Idiocy," the doctor now dropped his head too.

"Mmm…mongrel? You're telling me my son's a mongrel?" Raymond's face was now as red as his hair, his blue eyes squinting back any tears. "Mongrels" is what his drill sergeant had called them during basic training. Later, in the barracks, he and the others had thrown the term around, joshing about each other's intelligence.

"No, Mr. Bland. I didn't say 'mongrel.' Mongrels are mixed breed dogs. Your son is a 'Mongoloid.' It is a distinct form of mental retardation." Dr. Joseph had been struggling to maintain his professional distance.

He continued. "It means your son will always have the mind of a child, no matter how long he lives. Which brings me to the physical problems with this condition." The doctor knew he was throwing a lot at this poor young man. Perhaps, nature would be merciful and take its course, putting the poor thing out of its misery sooner rather than later. Then maybe this family could put it all behind them and move on, perhaps have other children.

"We have detected a heart murmur," Dr. Joseph explained. "We don't know how severe it is or what effect it will have on your boy. But it could mean that he will never be very strong, physically."

The doctor looked at the distressed father. He decided to add the words that he felt would be comforting. "Mr. Bland, sometimes these things have a way of working themselves out. The physical weaknesses can overrule our best efforts. Sometimes, it's best to let Mother Nature take her course."

"What do you mean?" Raymond asked quietly.

"I mean that these forced feedings we're doing, we could stop those. Try to keep him comfortable. Give you and your wife time to say good bye. The heart murmur alone will probably do him in."

Raymond looked the doctor square in his eyes. He wanted to make sure he had understood the not-so-subtle implications. When their eyes locked, Raymond was sure he had caught the doctor's meaning. Have all this go away in a matter of days. Jessa would be wounded, but hopefully not mortally. Other women lost children and had gone on to live normal lives. Danny was so young he'd barely remember all this. As for himself…he was tired. He was unbearably sad. He could never let Jessa know just how responsible he was for what had happened to their son. Maybe he could fix it all by just agreeing to the doctor's sinister plan.

But there was a nagging question that insistently pushed its way into this private consideration Raymond was having. What if the doctor was wrong? What if his boy got stronger? What if he just was a funny-looking newborn? Something rose up inside of Raymond. Call it indignation, protectiveness, denial. Whatever. Even if the doctor was right on the money, Raymond knew he had to protect his little son. He was the only thing standing between the baby and certain death. He knew Jessa would fight like a wild animal for this boy. And he would, too.

CHAPTER 4

Willa followed closely behind the three principals. They had turned down several quiet halls and finally were coming to a stop in front of room 311.

Mr. Johnson rapped on the door softly, then entered the classroom. There were no children present and no teacher at the desk either. Willa surveyed the large, square room. She noticed right away that the overhead lights were off and the room was lit by three floor lamps scattered around in various locations. The furniture had been used to divide the room into distinct areas. There were three low, rectangular tables arranged in a horseshoe at the center of the classroom. A kidney-shaped table sat at the back. All the tables were surrounded by small chairs. Near the front of the room was a large rug, centered before a large, whiteboard, which was mounted on the wall. A smaller carpet anchored one tall bookcase, and two shorter ones. There were beanbag chairs scattered on that rug in what appeared to be a reading center. Next to that was a small play-kitchen, complete with plastic food and utensils. Willa noticed one wall held hooks for jackets and book bags. Underneath the hooks were cubbies stuffed with pillows and blankets. Four computers stood against another wall and behind them a small tent had been pitched. A glass door at the back of the classroom let in natural light and overlooked a small, grassy courtyard. Another door at the back led to what Willa assumed was the bathroom. A nice set up, she thought.

"This is Ms. Smith's DDK classroom," Mr. Johnson explained. "DDK stands for 'developmentally delayed kindergarten.'"

"Oh," said Willa. "How many students are in this class?" she asked.

Mrs. Long responded. "We have nine in here full time right now, but we can have up to twelve. There are also a couple of students who come in for brief blocks of time, to take a break from the regular ed setting. It gives them a chance to have some 'down time.'"

"Oh," Willa said again. The empty classroom gave a false sense of serenity. Willa knew adding students, any "kind" of students, would give the place a whole different dynamic. It was just impossible to get a feel for things without the children. "Where are the students?" she questioned.

"They are in Specials right now," a voice said from the doorway. Willa turned to see who was speaking. At first glance, it looked like a high school student…maybe a college co-ed. "Hi, I'm Caleigh Smith. I run the place," she joked as she stepped forward and extended her hand toward Willa.

Willa reciprocated the smile and hand shake. "I'm Willa Grizzard. Nice to meet you, Ms. Smith." This gal was probably just about half her age, Willa guessed.

"Call me Caleigh," she said as she walked over toward her desk. "We can save the formalities for when the students are here." Then she turned toward the pack of principals. "Is this our Para candidate?" she asked them.

"Yes, Caleigh. Mrs. Grizzard is here to observe for the rest of today," Mr. Johnson replied. "We really like her background and think she could be a big asset to you and your students. Just don't make the mistake of calling her Mrs. Griz- 'ZARD. It's Grizzard. Rhymes with 'blizzard.'" Mr. Johnson smiled as he repeated Willa's pronunciation.

"Well, it's all about the students here. If you like them and they like you, it's all good," Caleigh said. Willa got the impression that this youngster had some spunk. She also had a feeling that she was going to like her.

The administrators had made their introductions, and so, excused themselves to go do whatever it is that administrators do. This left Willa and Caleigh alone together in the classroom.

"So, how did you end up here?" Willa tried to ask casually. Though she smiled, Caleigh was quick with her reply.

"I didn't 'end up' here. I chose to be here. I have always been around people with special needs in my life. I have a cousin with Autism, my boyfriend's uncle has Down Syndrome, I was always drawn to students who had special needs when I was in school, especially high school. I volunteered to be a Special Olympics Buddy. I have done peer mentoring with women my age who have intellectual disabilities. So, when I went to college, I just naturally gravitated toward a degree in Special Ed. I graduated a year and a half ago from Valdosta State University and I'm proud to say I have recently taken the State-mandated tests that make me 'highly qualified' to teach Special Ed in grades K through 12."

"Wow! Sounds like your life's calling," Willa admired this young woman's commitment to her field. "By the way, I didn't mean 'end up here' the way it sounded," she said apologetically. "I was just asking how you got into teaching, really."

"Mrs. Grizzard..."

"Oh, please call me Willa," she asked, hoping to seem less middle-aged to this energetic young woman.

"Okay, when the kids aren't here, Willa it is. Anyway, this really is my life's calling. I feel like I would have no meaning in my life if I couldn't work in some way with people with special needs. I don't want to be across the hall," her pony tail shaking with her head. She continued. "This wasn't a consolation class. I have no desire to teach 'regular' kindergarteners. I really have no patience with typical students. When they act like brats, they have no excuse. My kids on the other hand can't help themselves many times. If their behavior is part of their disability, I have all the patience in the world with them."

Caleigh began to move around the room as she talked, straightening chairs, putting books back in the bookcase, and picking up blocks off the floor. "I still hold them to high standards. They will one day have to function in the real world and I try to prepare them for that. For instance, they aren't allowed to lie on top of the tables or on the floor, because their typical peers aren't allowed to do that in their classrooms. Now that doesn't mean they won't try it. But it's my job, and now possibly yours…to intervene in that behavior and correct it. I'd say 75 percent of what we do is behavior modification and 25 percent is academic." Caleigh paused and took a swig out of the water bottle on her desk. "Now tell me about you. What's your experience with children with special needs?"

Willa swallowed a lump in her throat. "I…I really don't have any. I have experience in working with children in many different settings. I also have three of my own. So, common sense and hands-on experience is what I would bring to the job. Special needs kids can't be all that different from regular ones, can they?" She finished her statement more confidently than she started.

"Well, in a sense, you're exactly right. By the way, we don't call them 'Blind kids,' or 'Autistic children,' or 'Down Syndrome children.' We say, 'a child with Autism,' or 'a child with Down's.' That way we recognize that they are children first, and their disability is secondary. Just a 'P-C' heads up." Caleigh seemed patient and willing to explain things to Willa.

"Oh, thanks. I'll need a lot of that kind of guidance. You know, as I think about it, I am just realizing that I don't have any contact or experience with people with special needs. I mean all of my own children are in regular ed. I don't have friends or relatives with special needs' kids. I really feel out of my element."

Willa paused, realizing she had already broken the label rule about putting kids before the disability description.

Caleigh still wore her smile but it seemed to Willa that she was looking at her a little skeptically now. *That's okay,* Willa thought. She'd just have to prove herself, and not just to Caleigh, but to herself, also. She kept thinking how much she really needed this job. At that moment, Willa heard a bustle of activity in the hallway. "Oh, it's time to get my class from Specials," Caleigh said urgently.

"Specials?" Willa questioned.

"Yeah, 'Specials' is what we in this county call Art, Music, P.E. and Spanish classes. They aren't part of the main academic curriculum, but enhance and provide different growth experiences for students. They go to each Special during this time, one per day. They get P.E. twice a week. They go with students from a regular ed class so they can observe how typical children interact and behave." Caleigh had been talking over her shoulder as she moved out the door and started up the hall. As Willa followed along behind her she could see several different teachers at the head of groups of about 20 students, guiding them, reminding them of hall rules.

"Hips and lips, people," one teacher called to her brood and they all obediently put their left hands on their hips and the forefinger of the other hand across their lips in a "shhh" gesture.

The little soldiers marched in a remarkably straight, quiet line, for kindergarteners, Willa thought.

The two women continued on, winding their way through the rows of children, in and out of doorways, through the cafeteria, past the stage. Finally, Caleigh stopped in front of a room with an "Art" banner above the doorway and met up with a frazzled-looking woman. "Ms. Smith," the other woman started. "We have to talk about Jon. He is causing such a commotion in class and even snatched art work away from a student in Mrs. Kindall's class, causing it to rip. I was afraid he was going to hit the other boy. I am at a loss as to what to do with him!"

Caleigh drew a deep breath, exhaled and stepped aside, talking quietly with the woman for a few minutes.

This left Willa free to look over the students standing in the Art room doorway. One was thin and tall for a kindergartener. He had two, large, bucked, front-teeth and a stock of spiky, rusty-colored hair. The concerned glances he kept casting toward the two whispering teachers gave Willa the impression he might be Jon. Another child, also a boy, appeared to be Indian. He had short, thick, black hair and long, dark eye lashes. He was even thinner than the first boy. He was doing small jumps as he waited, with an absent-minded smile on his face and his hands flapping in what looked like a bird imitation. A third boy was shorter than the others and he too had dark hair and almond-shaped eyes. His head appeared a little bit small for his body and was somewhat flat on the back. Lastly, there was another boy, a beautiful child, with huge, green eyes and blonde, wavy hair.

Caleigh walked back toward Willa, smiling wearily and said, "Well, another little fire put out. I just told her if Jon cannot control himself and keeps up with this anti-social behavior, then she can send him back to me and he'll just have to miss. Art. I hate that, because it is a great chance for him to interact with typical students. Jon's not a bad kid. He is just so hyper and has a hard time calming himself." She turned toward her students. "Come on, guys. I need you to line up. Jack is our line leader."

The boy with the green eyes suddenly came to life and elbowed his way in front of the others. "Yeah," he said. "I'm line leader. Jon, Sadar, Jeff, get behind me!" he ordered. Surprisingly, the others took their cue from him and moved to the back of the line.

"We're off to get the rest of them," Caleigh announced.

"The rest of them?" Willa asked. She'd kind of hoped this was all of them "Yes, we have five more," Caleigh called cheerfully over her shoulder. "These four are capable of attending specials without a parapro's direct supervision. The other five must be supervised by a para at all times, even though there is a lead teacher in the room. It's in their I.E.P.'s. They have bathroom needs, limited mobility, comprehension issues, trouble following directions. The para that is filling in 'till we can find someone permanent, Sue Anne Joye, stays with them in Specials."

Just then, a small, blonde woman was moving her way up the hall with a group of boys, some of whom had that unmistakable look of mental retardation. The woman was calling out to different boys, "James, Jared, Maleeke, stop and wait for us. Jason, Justin, you guys have to hurry up. Stay with us!" Willa was all too certain that this rag tag crew was the rest of Ms. Smith's class.

* * *

Caleigh Smith, Sue Ann Joye, nine boys and Willa had all made it back to the classroom. And in Willa's opinion, it was no small miracle. Two of the boys were extremely fast walkers and neither of them was the designated line leader. It would infuriate Jack every time they sped up and passed him, so they had to constantly be reminded to slow down and stay in line. Two other boys poked along at the rear of the line, walking so slowly they had to be prodded along by the parapro or they would have been left behind. In the middle, the other boys kept jockeying for position, touching each other, shoving and exchanging taunting words. Then, occasionally, someone would run off altogether, enticed by one distraction or another. All the while Ms. Smith and Mrs. Joye used their voices, their arms, even their whole bodies to herd their students in the right direction. "Herd" was the operative word, in Willa's mind, because it was like trying to lead a bunch of sheep through the school.

As they all finally filed into the classroom Ms. Smith said "Okay, boys, I want everyone except for Jon to get your chairs and come to the carpet for our Social Studies time. Jon, because you made a bad choice in Art and ripped someone else's work, you will need to sit in our Thinking Chair. You know one of the rules in Ms. Smith's class is 'We keep our hands to ourselves.' That means we don't touch our friends' work."

"But he isn't my friend," Jon asserted. "Lance was saying I couldn't have any paint and got in my way when I tried to get some."

Ms. Smith walked over to an isolated chair in a corner and firmly motioned Jon toward it. "We keep our hands to ourselves, Jon. Again, that includes keeping our hands off others' work. Understand?"

Jon reluctantly nodded and sat in the chair. It was positioned so that he could not see the whiteboard at the front of the room. Ms. Smith walked over to her desk, punched in five minutes on a hand-held timer, then picked up a remote control. She used it to turn on a projector that hung from the ceiling. Then she made a few key strokes on her laptop computer and the whiteboard filled with images.

"Now class, before we begin our lesson on apples, I want to introduce you to Mrs. Grizzard," Caleigh gestured toward Willa as she made her way to the front of the room. "Mrs. Grizzard is visiting our class today to see if she thinks she would like to work with us all the time. So be on your best behavior."

The boys all turned and stared at Mrs. Grizzard. Jon piped up from the corner, "She won't like it if we're bad."

"Jon, that's your first warning. No talking while you're in the Thinking Chair. Boys, just be yourselves and make Mrs. Grizzard feel welcome. Now, who remembers where we left off yesterday when we talked about apples?"

None of the students responded. As a matter of fact, two of the boys had left their seats and were lying on the carpet on their stomachs, legs tucked under, butts hiked up in the air. From his perch in isolation, Jon snickered, a bit hysterically in Willa's opinion.

"Jeff, Justin, back in your chairs, you have to sit up and listen."
Ms. Smith walked over to one of the boys and pointed to his chair.
"Come on," she coaxed. "Sit up and we'll get to eat apples in just
a minute."

Neither boy budged.

"Jeff and Justin, I am going to count to five. Let's see if you
can get into your chairs yourselves like big boys or if you'll need
my help."

Ms. Smith remained calm and focused on the two boys on
the floor. They both had the same slanted eyes, Willa noticed.
Even with her limited experience, and though they looked like
they came from different ethnic groups, Willa recognized their
commonality was probably Down Syndrome.

"Okay, I am going to start counting," Ms. Smith reminded
them. "One...two..." She said the numbers very slowly. The boys
still remained flopped in their positions, showing no signs of
moving.

"...Three...Four..."

Oh, this is ridiculous, Willa thought. She didn't believe in
counting for her own children. She found it just gave them an
excuse to continue their bad behavior for a few more moments.
No, she believed in quick action when there was a problem. None
of this pandering to their whims stuff.

"Five." Ms. Smith finished abruptly and immediately bent
over one boy, put her arms under his and lifted him to his chair.
"You can sleep at home, Jeff. But you have to sit up and listen in
Ms. Smith's class," she said as she placed him. Willa hadn't noticed
until right then that Mrs. Joye had moved in close to the circle on
the carpet, and she too swooped down and lifted the other boy
back into his chair. "Sit up and listen," she parroted.

With both boys back in their seats, Ms. Smith picked up
right where she left off. "Now, who can tell me where apples come
from?"

"Trees!" Jon shouted from the corner with glee.

"Jon, this is your final warning. You may join the class when you have finished your time." Ms. Smith still maintained her composure. In the meantime, Willa thought about the precious instructional time that was ticking by.

Another boy…Maleeke, as Willa recalled…jumped out of his chair and said, "Trees, trees, trees." He put one palm against his forehead and smacked himself each time he said the word. "Trees, trees, trees." He was pacing back and forth at the front of the room. Mrs. Joye moved toward him and said, "Maleeke, I am going to touch you on your shoulders." And she did just that. He flinched slightly at her touch, but allowed her to guide him back to his chair without further disruption.

"Boy, they are 'off their chains' today, huh, Mrs. Joye?" Ms. Smith smiled. "Okay, boys. We've established that apples come from trees. Can anyone tell us the three colors of apples?" Ms. Smith patiently waited for an answer.

Jeff jumped up from his chair and said, "Red. And green too!" As he answered his teacher, the boy struck a pose, which to Willa looked like someone playing an air guitar.

Ms. Smith walked over and guided Jeff back to his chair while she said. "That's right. Apples do come in red and green. But there is another color. Who can remember that one?"

Sadar raised his hand and without waiting to be called on said quietly, "Yellow."

"That's right, Sadar," Ms. Smith affirmed. "Now, when do farmers pick apples from their trees and send them to the grocery store?"

"In the fall!" Jon shouted from the corner.

"All right, Jon, you have broken one of my classroom rules: No talking in the Thinking Chair. You are no longer welcome in my classroom. Goodbye!" Ms. Smith said bluntly. Mrs. Joye held Jon's upper arm and guided him up out of the chair.

"No, Ms. Smith, I'll be good!" Jon stubbornly refused to move his feet. Ms. Smith joined Mrs. Joye in the corner and took Jon by the other arm. "Let's go!" she said.

"No, no! I don't want to!" Somehow, the two women worked the boy slowly to the classroom door and opened it. Ms. Smith looked back over her shoulder at Willa and said, "We'll be right back!"

"Right back?!" Willa thought with alarm. The hall outside the classroom got quiet as the women took Jon into the classroom next door. Willa glanced at the remaining boys.

They looked at her. She couldn't be certain, but it looked like two of them were whispering about her. She tried to judge how long it would take her to get to the door. But just then, Ms. Smith and Mrs. Joye came back into the classroom.

"I'm sorry, Mrs. Grizzard. I didn't mean to leave you, even for a few seconds. We just had to remove Jon from his 'audience.' Now, class, when do farmers pick their apples and bring them to market?"

"In the fall," three of them said together.

"That's right. Now, let's go to the back table and taste some apples in each color." She motioned to the kidney shaped table. "Don't forget to bring your chairs!" Willa obliged, picked up a chair and followed the commotion of boys to the apple-tasting.

CHAPTER 5

Raymond had joined Jessa in her hospital room again. She was steaming mad. He knew it.

"Where is our son?" she asked emphatically. It didn't help that now there was another mother holding her newborn on the other side of the semi-private room.

"Jessa, hon, I ran into Dr. Joseph and he is getting the nurse to bring the baby to you right now." Raymond and the doctor had made a plan. They would let Jessa hold the boy, and then tell her some of the issues with him. Maybe not all of them right now. But they both knew they could not put her off completely any longer.

"Raymond, why haven't they brought him before now? I was just talking to this lady and she had her baby this morning and she's already got him with her. Is something wrong? What's going..." Jessa was interrupted by the door pushing open with a baby bassinet following.

"Here we are, Mrs. Bland. Your son is right here." It was the same nurse Raymond had seen in the nursery earlier.

"Well, it's about time. I hope you people know that it is not right to keep a newborn baby from its mother. He's probably starving to death. Give him to me." Jessa reached out her empty arms. The nurse, who seemed not to take anything Jessa was saying personally, carefully lifted the bundle from the bassinet and placed him with his mother.

Jessa's demeanor changed almost instantly. Her body relaxed, her face softened and her voice cooed soothingly to her baby. She didn't seem to notice any difference between him and when Danny was a baby, Raymond thought. For a moment, Raymond allowed himself to bask in the joy passing from mother to son. He'd made the right decision. This baby needed him, Jessa and Danny. And in return they all needed this child, too. He was part of the family, no matter what.

"Russell," Jessa said. "How do you like Russell Kenneth Bland? After Daddy?" she looked up at Raymond, her eyes full of love.

"That's a fine name, Jessa. Russell Kenneth Bland it is." Raymond's voice choked. He leaned into his wife, kissing her hair and touching the baby's cheek with his huge finger. Jessa began to unwrap the sleeping infant. She expertly made a cradle with her upper legs and folded the blanket back. "Oh, look. I just love their feet at this age. So tiny. And five toes on each one," she said satisfied. "And look! Look at his hands," she marveled. "They're so delicate. Fragile, even. But all ten fingers are present and accounted for!"

She seemed so proud. Raymond wished so hard that fingers and toes were all they had to worry about. He couldn't bear the hurt that he knew was waiting outside that door. At that moment, Raymond felt an overpowering sense of protectiveness for his wife, for his new son. He just couldn't let this doctor's guesses about his baby's future steal away Jessa's happiness. Raymond knew one thing for sure. The plan was about to change. He had come up with another one. One that would shield his family, at least for a while, from the devastation he knew could come crashing down on them.

* * *

Jessa gingerly moved about her hospital room, folding the nightgown Raymond had brought from home, gathering the baby blankets that would go with them this afternoon. It had been almost a week since she gave birth to Russell. She missed Danny terribly and was ready to sleep in her own bed. Still, the hospital had given her a sense of comfort. She had round-the-clock nursing help and she had needed it. Russell just wasn't nursing the way Danny had been by this time. Sometimes it had taken her and two nurses to get the baby positioned on her breast correctly, and even then, he would unlatch with barely a few sucks. This worried her. But, her doctor, Dr. Joseph, had reassured her that the baby was still in the learning phase.

She hadn't seen Dr. Joseph very much. He had come in to check her once a day and he'd left orders with the nurses about what medicine she needed. The nurses were experts on postpartum care, so they'd really been the ones to help her get her strength back. Another doctor, Dr. Hines, had driven in from Columbia and had checked on Russell twice. He had performed the baby's circumcision. Other than that, he hadn't said much to her, so she guessed things were as they should be with her newborn. Jessa had expected Dr. Miller from right here in Florence. He was everybody's family doctor in these parts. But she figured he couldn't be everywhere so she was glad to have had an expert pediatrician come and examine Russell.

* * *

While Jessa was getting her things together, Raymond had been checking on their bill. It was going to take them about a year of payments to cover all the expenses, he figured. Normally, this alone would have caused him a great deal of stress. He didn't like taking on debt, especially in this economic depression. But now he was feeling the press of guilt in addition to stress. He felt like he'd cared too much about the cost. He should have gotten his wife and baby medical care earlier. Maybe it would have changed things for his boy. Raymond was glad they would be going home with him today. He was exhausted from running interference between Jessa and the doctors. Dr. Joseph had really fought Raymond about keeping all the medical diagnoses from Jessa. He had told Raymond that it was unethical, that Jessa was his patient and that he needed to give her all the medical information. Raymond had played upon the sympathy he sensed the doctor had for him, for Jessa and for the baby. He said he would tell Jessa himself when the time was right. He'd explained that she wasn't a strong person naturally and he felt, as her husband, that the information should come out slowly and only as she needed it. Otherwise, he told the doctor, she was the type to get hit by the baby blues so hard that she wouldn't be able to function. In the end, Raymond had managed to convince the doctor that this was the best thing for the health of both his wife and his baby. But deep down in his heart, Raymond was hoping that he'd never have to tell his wife a thing. He wanted the doctors to be wrong. And if he wanted it badly enough, maybe he could make it come true.

* * *

Smoke from the tip of his cigarette circled Carl Joseph's head. He was sitting in his office and before him lay the patient release orders for Jessica Bland and her baby. He had no problem signing the papers for the mother. She was getting her strength back and would be back to her normal self in the next couple of weeks. Normal, that is, if she wasn't taking this extremely damaged infant home with her. And she didn't even know what she had! This was his fault. He knew that. He had let the father talk him into withholding the baby's prognosis from the mother. First it was to give the man a few hours to tell his wife himself. He'd respected that the information might come easier from the husband. Dr. Joseph pinched his brow with his fingertips. Now it had been almost a week. He'd occupied Dr. Robert Hines, a pediatrician from Columbia, while he was here, under the premise of getting more information about Mongolian Idiocy. He'd kept the other doctor from meeting with the mother, explaining she wasn't up to it. He'd assured Dr. Hines that he would give the family his contact information, so that when they were ready, they could reach him.

Now, it was too late to rectify this cover up, without damaging his own reputation, even risking losing his license to practice medicine. How had he gotten himself into this situation?

He knew. It was his one fatal flaw, a trait no medical practitioner should be burdened with. He'd allowed himself to feel for the patients, to want to go beyond the boundaries of his medical training and attempt to fix things that were unfixable.

Dr. Joseph let out a sigh and picked up his pen. Baby Boy Bland.... live birth, he checked on the form. Then it gave a choice of three: Was the infant normal, possessing physical infirmities, or mentally retarded? He stared at the paper. He decided right then and there that he'd be damned if he was going to falsify the paperwork. He checked the last two answers and in the blank for explanation he wrote: "Mongolian Idiocy with possible heart and other physical complications." He signed his name at the bottom, picked up the papers and walked them to the records department. He'd bury them here. If anyone ever found them, he'd be covered. What happened to this poor couple and their child now was in God's hands.

* * *

Jessa paced the hardwood floor in her bare feet. She bounced Russell on her shoulder, almost a bit frantically. The infant just kept fussing. She glanced at the kitchen clock. 2:10 am. She had brought the baby to the kitchen and closed the door so Raymond and Danny wouldn't hear him cry.

She was exhausted. In the week since she had been home from the hospital, she'd gotten almost no sleep. Danny was so clingy after her week-long absence. He didn't understand why she had to spend so much time with the baby. And frankly, neither did she.

Russell was always hungry. But when she would try to nurse him, he was so floppy that she couldn't get him to conform to her and latch onto her breast. His tongue. It always got in the way. He would stick it out of his mouth and push her nipple right out with it. It was so frustrating and irritating and exhausting! Why couldn't they get the hang of this? Danny had nursed beautifully and by the time he was two weeks old he had fattened up a little and was strong enough to lift his head. But not Russell. When she placed him in his crib, he didn't move. He didn't turn his head or move his legs or arms. It just didn't seem right.

Here in the dark, all alone with him, it was easy for her to allow her imagination to run wild. Was he actually lighter weight than when she'd brought him home? When she unwrapped his blanket from around him and placed him on her bed to change him, he just lay there spread-eagle. He didn't thrash his arms and legs around like Danny had. She remembered how her first born had been almost startled when she placed him down on his back. Most times, Danny would let out a wail of indignation at being unwrapped and would flail his little arms about, uncontrolled, with fists clinched. Not Russell. He just kind of flopped.

She sat down at the kitchen table and brought the baby to her breast. She did all the tricks the nurses at the hospital had shown her. She stroked his lips with her nipple, in an attempt to get him to open his mouth wide. But there was that tongue again, thrusting out and all-in-the-way.

Jessa's eyes filled with tears. She felt like something was wrong with her baby. She didn't know what exactly. But he was not like any newborn she'd ever known, including her little sisters. She knew he needed more milk than he was getting. But she didn't know what to do about it. She made up her mind to take him to

Dr. Miller's office in the morning. She had to. She needed help in figuring out how to get her baby the nourishment he needed.

Just then, Raymond walked into the kitchen, his hair all askew, his eyes drooped and sleepy. "Jessa, why are you holed up in here? Come back to bed. You're not getting any rest. Bring the baby and come back to bed."

"I can't!" she cried. "Russell won't eat. He's too out of sorts to nurse, yet he cries and I'm sure it's from hunger. Just go back to bed. I've got to keep trying. Tomorrow morning, I'm going to take him to Dr. Miller. Something's wrong, either with me or him."

Raymond bent over and lifted the fussy infant from his exhausted wife's arms. He stared down at the tiny face peeking out from a swaddle of blankets. As usual, he felt totally helpless with this child. But, he couldn't let his wife go to the doctor. Not yet, anyway. Jessa needed some rest before she heard the terrible truth. Right now she was so worn down that any more bad news might do her in.

"Jessa, Mrs. McGraff was telling me about a colored woman who has helped a lot of white folks with their newborn babies. I'll go by and see her tomorrow. She can help with Danny and maybe show you some tricks to get Russell to eat. That will help, won't it?" Raymond was on the brink of sounding desperate.

"Okay," Jessa said, exhaustion taking over. "If I go get back in the bed, will you bring him to me?"

"Sure, sweetie. You go ahead." Raymond was glad he'd gotten her to agree so easily. Jessa wasn't one to want other people around the house, especially doing work she considered "her" job.

As his wife collapsed back into her pillow, she rolled to one side. Raymond placed the infant next to her and walked around to his side of the bed. He hadn't been getting much sleep either, but right now, it was important to help Jessa get her strength back. The three snuggled into the double bed together and soon, all fell fast asleep.

* * *

The next morning, Raymond felt guilty as he drove out of his driveway. He knew the guys at Golden Life and Casualty Insurance Company were growing less and less tolerant of his daily absences from the office. He'd go in, fill out a little paper work, make a few calls to potential customers and then leave for an early lunch. He'd go straight home, help Jessa get lunch for Danny, and even send her to bed while he held and bounced the baby. Danny was growing tired of his father's new commitments, too. "Daddy, more me-ilk, peaz," he'd say. Inevitably, Raymond would be in the middle of changing Russell and would have to say, "Son, just a minute. I'll get you more milk as soon as I'm finished changing Russell."

"Busser is *not* a big boy," Danny would frown and cross his arms over his chest. "Busser smells stinky."

"You're right, son. 'Buster' as you call him, is not a big boy. He's a baby, just like you used to be. Mommy and Daddy had to change you, too, when you were little. But see how big you are now? We just all have to work together to get Russell big, too. Wanna help?"

"No," Danny said flatly. "I wan' more me-ilk." He was a true southern boy, who could take a one syllable word and stretch it into at least two.

Raymond always felt guilty leaving his family when he finally knew he couldn't be gone from the office any longer. He was lucky to have this job. He was good at it and he couldn't risk losing it. Yet he knew his family needed him, not just providing for them, but they also needed his physical presence. Jessa was still so weak and tired easily. He would just have to hire this woman to help them.

As Raymond drove on, he turned onto Raven Avenue. Then he took a quick right onto Bob White Street. Number 12, looking for house number 12. He spotted it and pulled his car over onto the curb. It was a small, shotgun-style home. Weathered, unpainted boards made up the outside. Raymond figured there was a front room, a kitchen and eating area, and possible two small bedrooms at the back. He walked up the front steps onto the sagging, covered porch and knocked. He glanced to the right toward the houses up the street. A few elderly blacks were in their yards or on their porches, watching him. He felt uncomfortable on this side of town, but he was determined to talk to Queenie Quattlebaum.

He could hear footsteps and then the doorknob turning. As the door swung open, Raymond saw a tiny, sturdy woman, probably in her early sixties, standing before him with questioning eyes.

"You Raymond Bland?" the woman asked.

"Yes, yes I am," Raymond replied. "Are you Queenie Quattlebaum?"

"I am. Please come in." She stepped aside so Raymond could walk into the predictable front room. It was neat, very tidy, and uncluttered. He took a seat in the overstuffed chair she had motioned him toward. As he sat there, his hat in his hands, dressed in his suit and tie, he noticed the woman was studying him with her piercing, brown eyes. "You like some lemonade, Mr. Bland?" she questioned? "I can also put on a pot of coffee if that suits ya."

"No, Mrs. Quattlebaum. Lemonade will be fine." Raymond watched as she walked to the next room. She seemed limber and strong enough, even though she had gray strands throughout her black hair.

"Call me Queenie," she said over her shoulder. "Everyone does, 'cept the little chil'ren 'round here. They call me 'Miz Queenie.'"

"Yes, well, Queenie it is then," Raymond said.

After she brought the lemonade in on a tray, and sat it down, she handed Raymond a glass of yellow liquid. He took a sip. Delicious.

Queenie sat down herself and once again, stared at Raymond unflinchingly. Raymond finally spoke up. "Well Queenie, I guess Doloris McGraff told her cleaning lady about me and my wife and our new baby and she told Doloris that you might be able to help us. We have a two-week-old little boy and I have to get back to work full time and my wife, Jessa is still weak. She's worn out from no sleep. Between our two-year-old and the baby, there's always something to do."

"What would you have me to do?" Queenie questioned.

"Well, if you could help around the house, take care of breakfast and lunch for Danny, my two-year-old, make sure Jessa gets something to eat and just do any chores she asks you to do, it would be a great help."

"What 'bout the baby?" the woman asked. "Das what I usually do. Help women who are having a rough start wit' they little ones. Nursing, getting 'um on a schedule, helping 'um settle into 'dis old world."

"Well, we need that kinda help, too," Raymond admitted. "The baby just has been slow to recover from a rough birth, we think. And we could really use some advice and help with him, too."

Raymond looked at Queenie and actually allowed his desperation to show through.

"Awright," she said after a minute. "I'll hep ya. It's a dollar a day, seven for a week, but I don' work on Sundays."

"Great," Raymond replied. "If you can get your things, I'll give you a ride to the house right now. You can take the bus back and forth normally, right?

"Well, Mr. Bland, I'll want to get to 'da bus stop before dark every day. I cain't see all that well in the dark. Plus, my granddaughter brings my two great-grands every night, so she can work the night shift over at County Hospital. "

"That's just fine. I'll just have to get home before dark myself." Queenie grabbed a satchel and swung it over her shoulder.

"Did you say 'great-grands'?" Raymond asked as she locked her front door.

"Das right. I'll be 71 dis fall. Got three chil'ren, seven gran's and two great gran's," Queenie said with pride.

My goodness, thought Raymond. *This woman just might have the experience to smooth things out at home.* At least that was his hope.

CHAPTER 6

Willa was stretched across her bed, tissue in hand, tears flowing, nose running, having a full blown pity party. She had finished out the day in Ms. Smith's class and had watched Mrs. Joye's role particularly carefully. The woman was in the bathroom with someone most of the time, it seemed. She was wiping kid's noses, physically lifting and maneuvering them around the classroom when they failed to "go with the program." The little bit of academics she did manage to squeeze in seemed like a waste of time to Willa. During the entire time they were in Mrs. Joye's center, the boys either stared off into space, or climbed under the table, or popped the Number Bingo Game markers in their mouths.

Willa was so discouraged. She had just finished potty training her youngest child last year. And that was the one thing she disliked about preschool, although many of her two-year-olds were better at the potty than these kids seemed to be. Toilet training was the one area she had really, truly detested about parenthood. The mess, the grossness…she barely could take it when the subject was her own child, for whom she would die….much less for these complete strangers. All she had wanted to do was work as an assistant…in a kindergarten class, the office….or perhaps the library. The nice, quiet library. She absolutely never entertained the thought of working with special needs kids...oops...kids with special needs. They were foreign to her. The way they moved, the way they looked, the way they spoke...or didn't speak. How would she ever know what they wanted or needed? It was all just too much for her. Just as she buried her head in her pillow and sobbed again, Joel walked into their bedroom.

"Aw, come on, hon. It couldn't have been that bad. They're just children after all."

"Children you can't communicate with. Children I don't understand. Joel, I'll have to change their pants and help them go to the bathroom. And these are six-year-old kids. Their poop will be like a grown man's! How gross!" she wailed. "I just don't think I can do it!"

"You act like these kids repulse you," Joel countered.

"I'm not repulsed by the *kids*...just their *poop*! Aren't you listening?" she asked, good and annoyed now.

Joel lay down on the bed beside his distraught wife. He knew she could be prone to hysteria at times. It was usually just best to let things work themselves out. But it was Friday night. Willa had told the school she would take the job. He had to help chip away at all his wife's fears, so she would be able to go to work on Monday. Besides, he believed whole-heartedly that Willa could do this. He'd never known a challenge that could beat his big-hearted wife and this one actually was more up her alley than she probably realized. She loved children. She was so compassionate. She was so...

"*Trapped!* That's what I am. I'm *trapped!* There is *no way* I can turn down this job. We need the money. We need the benefits. I've *got* to take it. So, I'll just reconcile myself that for the *next 20 years*...until we retire.... I'll just *have* to do a job I *hate!*"

Joel decided to match her dramatics. "Willamina Grizzard. You stop right now!" Joel lifted his wife into a sitting position. "You will *not* hate this job. You are *incapable* of *hating* anything you do! That's one of the things I love about you. You take tough situations, find the humor in them, turn them around and make the whole thing better for everybody!"

"I do?" Willa sniffed.

"Yes, you do. Remember when you got stuck putting the whole fall festival fund-raiser together for the church's youth department? Janet got sick and Evelyn conveniently booked her vacation that week. But you knew the young people at our church *needed* a cool hangout to bring their friends to, a place where they could be comfortable and safe and get the kind of guidance they needed at that particular time in their lives. So, you kept your eye on the goal, you booked the vendors, ordered the Porta Potties and took care of all the little details. *You* made it happen. *You* raised all that money for those kids and *ours* won't even *be* in the youth department for another five or ten years." Joel's spiritual gifts were encouragement and edification, and much to Willa's irritation, he was putting them to good use now.

"So, you think God wants me to deal with the whole potty issue again? Do you remember when I found Ray in his crib with his diaper off and poo smeared all over the wall, his bed and him? I just about didn't make it. What does God want to teach me about poop? Huh? Couldn't he just send a plague of locusts and be done with it?"

"Willa, you *know* God doesn't have it in for you! He may want to humble you in an area or two…I don't know. But I do know that He loves you and isn't punishing you. This is just the next adventure in our lives."

"What's this 'our lives' stuff? You won't be there when a kid has diarrhea and doesn't make it to the bathroom. It'll be me. All me!" The "party" wasn't coming to an end yet, Joel noticed.

"No, hon, *I* won't be there." He held her face tenderly between his hands. "But you'll look into those children's eyes, and I know you. You'll fall in love with them, despite any mess that comes with them."

"Well, it's just that I've never had any relationship with people who have Autism or Cerebral Palsy or Down Syndrome. I haven't avoided them, and I know it's weird, but I've just never known anyone personally with one of those ailments."

"I know, hon, I know," Joel continued to soothe.

* * *

Sunday evening, before Willa was to start the job, she curled up in her armchair for her weekly call with her grandmother. She knew Gram would offer a hefty dose of encouragement when she told her about her new job. "Gram, I've got to work with about a dozen special needs children. I don't know how to do this! What if I fail?"

"Willa, you have every right to be afraid. You're facing the unknown. I don't have answers for you but I sure will pray for you," her grandmother answered in a frail voice. That was something else Willa was worried about. Her beloved grandmother had congestive heart failure, high blood pressure and a variety of other ailments. Willa wanted her to be the strong, fun-loving person who had been a big part of her childhood, not the fragile, elderly lady she had become. But one thing Willa could count on was her grandmother's prayers. She knew if nothing else, tomorrow morning, she'd be "bathed" in prayer as she started her new position.

As she hung up with Willa, her grandmother paused for a moment and felt a deep sadness she hadn't felt in years. If only Willa knew how close the subject of special needs children had been for this family. Where was God going with this? Only he knew for sure.

* * *

Long yellow buses pulled up to the side of Gold Mine Elementary. It was Monday morning and as the mass of children got off, they seemed to drag a little. This was the third week in September and the newness of school had worn off for them. Now school was just a necessary chore. Willa understood how they felt. She had a lump in her stomach and felt like running to her car and going home. She could not believe this is what her life had come to.

Sue Ann Joye was there with her. She had stopped by the cafeteria and had a steaming mug of coffee in her hands.

"Now this is a bit confusing at first, but you'll get it. Unfortunately, I just have today to show you the ropes and then I'll have to start my new position tomorrow."

"What?" Willa asked alarmed. "I thought they'd let you train me for longer than one day!"

"Nope. They have been trying to fill your position since school started in the middle of August and they really are anxious to get me with the students who are mainstreamed but still need extra help in the classroom. I'll be what they call a 'resource' parapro."

"Gosh," Willa said, side-stepping a little girl pulling a rolling backpack behind her. "Okay, what do I need to know?"

"Well, first off I usually get out here at about ten till eight. That's when they start unloading regular ed buses and they use us as 'crowd control,' so to speak. Then, *most of the time,* the short buses start coming. Every once in a while one of our buses will get here in the midst of the long buses and that's a little crazy. But usually, our guys are last to arrive. However, we have two students in our class who ride regular ed buses. That's just to confuse you!" Sue Ann laughed and took a sip from her mug.

"Oh, here's Justin's bus now" she said as she started to work her way against the tide of students to get to the bus door. "He sits with his big sister, who is in fourth grade, so they've made special arrangements to let him ride the bus with her. I think it's just easier on the mom to have both her kids on one bus. Look, there he is waving to us out of the window."

Willa looked up and saw Justin's impish face with a wide smile stretched across it. Mrs. Joye smiled and waved at him through the glass. The little boy just stuck out his tongue at her and giggled. Willa noticed that next to him sat a pretty girl with long hair and blue eyes. She rolled her eyes in exasperation and held onto Justin's arm, in an attempt to pull him away from the window. Justin wasn't budging. He just shrugged off the girl.

All the other students left their seats and filed out of the bus, chattering excitedly with friends as they made their way into the building. And there sat Justin, continuing his little game. This time when he stuck his tongue out, he licked the window with it. *Ewww,* thought Willa. She could be a bit of a germaphobe. Sue Ann went to the bus door and called to him. "Justin, come on, you rascal. It's time to go to school. Ms. Smith is waiting for you." No answer. The bus driver said wearily, "I'll get him."

Willa watched as the rather heavy woman maneuvered her way between the rows of seats and came to Justin's. His sister looked up and said something to the driver and the driver stood aside and motioned for Justin to move into the aisle. The boy allowed his sister to guide him out of his seat and help him put on his backpack. But Justin's countenance had changed. Now he had a frown on his face, his mouth drooping and his chin tucked to his chest. Again, the sister spoke to him, but this time he shook his blonde head. With the driver leading the way back up the aisle, the girl used her body to prod her little brother along, all the while he was "putting on the brakes" with both feet. When he reached the door, he started crying, "No, no, no!"

"Come on, Justin. Your friends are waiting for you," Mrs. Joye was clearly taking over at this point. "Hop on down those steps and let's get going. Sadar's bus will be here in just a minute."

With the sister pushing from behind and Mrs. Joye holding his hand, they managed to get the child down the three bus steps. But the minute his feet hit the pavement, he went limp and flopped to the ground, folding in half, with his nose touching the pavement between his outstretched legs. *Ouch,* Willa thought. By this time, more big buses were turning into the parking lot and were heading their way.

"Come on, buddy," Mrs. Joye said as she quickly lifted him up under his arms and re-plopped him down at a safe distance from the incoming buses. Justin's bus driver got back in her seat, rolled her eyes and pulled away from the curb. Mrs. Joye squatted down next to Justin and said, "We'll just leave you there for now. Mrs. Grizzard is going to watch you. Remember her? She's going to be one of your teachers. She's new. Show her what movie you brought to school today."

Willa took the cue and squatted next to the boy so Sue Ann could meet the next child arriving on a regular ed bus. She looked around. There were several other parapros who were also greeting students as they arrived. Willa decided to try to talk to the boy.

"Hi, Justin. Let me see your movie. What did you bring?" The only thing he moved was his eyes. He rolled them up at her for an instant and then looked straight back at the ground again. "

"Come on, big boy, show Mrs. Grizzard what's in your back pack." She reached over and started to unzip the bag. He sat up instantly, pulling the pack away from her and said "No Wizzerd. Miff."

Well, that certainly cleared things up, Willa thought. His sister, who was lingering around, interpreted. "Mom told him not to take the DVD out of his back pack until he gets to the classroom. He's only supposed to give it to Ms. Smith."

"Oh, okay then. We want you to obey Mommy, right Justin? How 'bout you sit up here on this bench and tell me what movie it is." Willa moved to the bench and patted the spot next to her.

To her surprise, the little boy got up off the ground and joined her. "Is it Teletubbies? Dora the Explorer?" Willa guessed.

"Poopy Doo," he said, his face etched with excitement. Willa looked directly into his soft green eyes. They were flecked with the oddest white and gold spots in the irises. They were beautiful, she thought.

Again, sister had to help with the translation. "He's talking about Scooby Doo. He loves him and watches his movies all the time."

"I see," said Willa. Then she looked at the sister and said, "I'm Mrs. Grizzard. What's your name?"

"Bree Anna. I'm Justin's sister. He calls me 'Bee-Bee.' He calls our little sister 'Sissy.' Do you want me to walk him to class?" She looked at her brother skeptically.

"No, that's okay, Bree Ann. You go on to class. We'll manage," Mrs. Joye said as she walked up with Sadar.

"That girl has more on her than she should at this age," Sue Ann stated, after the sister had left. "Anyway, two down, three more to go. All the others are car riders."

About then, a small bus pulled up. Willa remembered all the jokes they'd told as kids about riding the 'short bus.' They didn't seem so funny now.

As the doors opened, students started exiting, some fast, some taking more time. Several of the students were greeted by their classroom parapro standing nearby, and then were escorted into the building and down the hall to their classrooms. The last student came to the top of the bus stairs and very slowly reached out his hand to Mrs. Joye.

"Good Morning, Jason. Come on down here, but hold onto the railing with your other hand." Mrs. Joye patiently let the boy climb down at his own pace. There was a driver and another woman on this bus. Willa guessed she was a bus monitor.

"Jason's mom said he had a hard time with his breakfast this morning," the monitor reported through the open bus door. "She wasn't real specific, but he did fine on the ride here."

"Okay, we'll watch him. He was probably gagging on it. He's ground his teeth down to nubs and it's getting harder for him to chew. Thanks, though." Mrs. Joye guided the boy, who seemed very unsteady on his feet, away from the departing bus. She sat him on the bench next to Sadar and Justin. Willa watched as

Justin snuggled up to Jason and gave him a big hug. He was smiling again, she noticed.

Another bus drove in. This time, a parapro stepped forward right away. While the driver unbuckled some students, the monitor handed a soft-sided suitcase to the parapro. "That's Drew's formula and feeding tube equipment. He's also got his backpack with several changes of clothes."

The parapro took the suitcase and waited for a boy to climb down the steps. Willa looked at the child. He was completely pasty, no color in his cheeks or on any exposed skin. His hair was very thin and growing in patches around his head. He wore a jacket, even though it was a warm, humid morning. Sue Ann leaned toward Willa and said quietly, "Drew's in Ms. Solomon's class next door to us. He's on his third course of chemotherapy. It's not looking good." Her face was solemn.

"Do we have any children like that?" Willa asked anxiously.

"No, currently we don't have any students that are labeled 'Medically Fragile.'"

This was just about too much for Willa. Feeding tube equipment? Fragile children? No one had told her that could be part of this job. Her stomach knotted again.

She didn't have much time to think about it though, because a thin, little brown-haired boy, about the size of a typical four-year-old, came bounding down the bus stairs. Mrs. Joye said, "Jeff, hold Mrs. Grizzard's hand. You remember her, don't you?"

Jeff scrunched up his face, closed his eyes and struck an air guitar pose. "Born in the USA" he belted out. Willa recognized the Bruce Springsteen song. Jeff dramatically thrust his hips forward and strummed the air. "I was born in the USA!" He pretended to sing into a microphone.

There was no time to enjoy the show because another bus arrived.

This time Willa recognized their student right away as he clamored down the stairs. It was Jon from the Thinking Chair.

He came off the bus, waved at Mrs. Joye and started walking into the school alone.

"Hi, Jon," Mrs. Joye called. Then she turned to Willa and said, "He's a little older than the other students in our class and he likes to walk to class all by himself. I usually follow at a distance and keep an eye on things while I'm walking the rest of this crew back."

She turned toward the boys just in time to see Jason retch. "Jason!" Mrs. Joye dove for his hand and started walking him towards the school door as fast as she could go. But that wasn't very fast because Jason was retching, crying and resisting her guidance all at once. Then the inevitable happened: he threw up.

"Come on, guys," Mrs. Joye said as she made a face. "Let's take Jason to the nurse and call a custodian. Then we'll get this day started."

Oh, please, God. Let's just get this day over with! Willa thought as she straggled along.

CHAPTER 7

Jessa listened to the sound of a spoon scraping the bottom of a pan in the kitchen. She was sitting with the baby in the room they called "the den." It really was little more than a wide, short, windowless hallway with four doorways leading to her and Raymond's bedroom, the boys' room, a bathroom and out into the formal living room. You had to cross the living room to reach the kitchen. A big, metal oil heater that was piped through the roof for exhaust took up a large chunk of the den. A floor radio stood in one corner. There was also an overstuffed chair, Raymond's desk, where he did the bills and a "telephone table" where you could sit and take notes while talking on the telephone. Jessa felt fortunate to have a phone. So many people didn't. But these days, she was desperate to have a way to reach the outside world.

She had been home from the hospital for a month now. Raymond had hired Queenie to help her out, but Jessa was still unsettled about having someone else in her home, besides family. She really hadn't left the house since she brought Russell home, except to walk over for a few moments to thank Mrs. McGraff for the help she gave while Jessa was in the hospital. She walked out on the front stoop every morning to pick up the fresh bottles of milk. If she timed it right, she might run into the mailman as he was coming up the walk and greet him for a few moments.

Other than that, she had sat here, in this overstuffed chair, waiting for Russell to stir in her arms so she could immediately feed him. This is what Queenie said was required to put some weight on the baby. Russell was finally suckling better, but only small amounts at a time. She could sometimes hear the milk washing back up from his stomach into his throat. Queenie said to hold him in an upright position after feeding to keep him from spitting up his meal.

Queenie also said Russell had been "touched by God." The woman made this statement the first time she saw Russell. She had proclaimed that this baby was "of a special kind," that he'd been "touched by God," and that he would never have the mind of a normal child. How could she say all this after just looking at him for a moment?

Raymond had dismissed this as superstitious talk. But Queenie had been the nanny for many children over the years. She said she'd seen his kind before. *His kind? What kind was that?* Jessa didn't want to believe this, but she *knew* something was different about this baby. He didn't coo or smile. Danny had done both by his first month. Russell didn't' wave his arms around erratically and make eye contact with her while she was changing his diaper. And at night, when she spooned around the infant in bed, she sometimes could feel his heart beat really slowly, scaring her that it might stop entirely.

Queenie had completely taken over the care of Danny. Jessa knew the old woman was doing this so she could give Russell all that he needed. But she resented it when she heard the two of them laughing in the kitchen, or saw *her* in the yard, picking wild blackberries from a thicket and giving the little boy the juiciest ones. After they filled the pail with berries, Queenie often would lift Danny onto the swing hanging from an old oak tree. The little boy laughed as she pushed him. Jessa thought Queenie took unnecessary chances by pushing him too high. She was going to speak to her about that. And Raymond's shirts were supposed to be heavily starched and ironed. Jessa thought Queenie was taking short-cuts here too.

Just then, Queenie and Danny came from the kitchen back to the den. "Let's go see how yo' mama and brotha are doing," she said. Jessa sat up straight in the chair. The small-framed woman didn't have a wrinkle on her face, even though Raymond had said she was in her 70's. She walked briskly too, swinging her arms and always going about some task or other.

"Oh, look, Danny; Russell is awake. He's ready to see you," Queenie said, trying to get the older boy to interact with his brother.

"Busser is not 'wake. He's seeping," Danny contradicted.

"Come here, Danny. Russell is awake," his mother coaxed. "See his eyes. They're open. He wants to see you."

"No, Busser's eyes are ka-wazy," Danny insisted. Jessa had to admit that Russell's eyes did have the strangest white flakes in the colored part. They were blue, but contained a faint kaleidoscope of gold and white flecks also. Jessa knew babies' eyes changed colors for several weeks, even months after birth. She just attributed her baby's eye color to that natural process.

"No, Danny, Russell's eyes are not 'crazy.' They're beautiful. See? See?" She held Russell closer to Danny's face.

"I don' like him! Take him away!" Danny asserted.

"Danny, don't you ever say that you don't like your brother! Now come here, right this minute. I want you to look at your brother. Come look at him. Now!" She was surprised by the franticness of her order.

"No!" Danny said and turned to run. Jessa lunged out of the chair after him and grabbed him tightly by the arm.

"Don't you ever tell me no, do you hear me?" Jessa screamed. Then she swatted Danny on the rear end. He ran crying to Queenie, who had stood nearby, watching all that had taken place.

"Danny, yo mama's right. You need to listen and obey her. Now go say yo sorry. Go on!" Queenie led the boy back to his mother.

Jessa sat in the chair, tears welling up in her eyes, her free hand trembling as she barely held onto the baby.

"So-wee, Mommy," Danny mumbled through his poked out lower lip.

"No, Danny, *I'm* sorry, I'm *so* sorry!" Jessa could no longer hold back the flood of tears. She grabbed her older boy with her free arm and held him tight. "Mommy loves you. I'm so sorry I tried to force you. Mommy's just so tired," she breathed into his hair.

"You take nap wif Busser. I go swing wif Queenie," Danny huffed.

Jessa looked up at Queenie for a moment and the old woman read her desperation clearly.

"Danny, I'm gonna take a turn with Russell so Mama can go to 'da swing witchya. Okay?" Queenie reached down and lifted the dangling infant. She expertly raised him to her shoulder and turned, walking off with a bounce toward the unmade bed in Jessa's room. "Now ya'll go have some fun, hear?" She turned and looked Jessa straight in the eye. Queenie's gaze wasn't judgmental. It was just matter of fact.

Jessa hesitated only a second and then grabbed Danny's hand and ran out into the sunny back yard.

* * *

Jessa sat in Dr. Miller's waiting room with her baby on her lap. For some reason, she couldn't get Raymond to sit down with her. He was in the foyer, chain smoking. He looked so tense. But that was understandable. It had been a rough 6 months since Buster… that's what they all called Russell now…was born.

Jessa was so worried that Buster was unable to turn his head when he was placed on his stomach. She tested him every day to see if he could do it. Danny had flopped his head from side to side at just a few weeks of age! Buster still didn't move his legs and arms very much but he was getting better at making eye contact with her and smiling. Still, he preferred to nuzzle into her neck, or nurse…very slowly. Jessa could tell his weight was barely different from that of Danny when he'd been one or two months old! Jessa had worked hard every day to stuff her panic down, to try and hold on to the hope that he was just a little slow, but otherwise normal. But she knew in her heart that something was wrong with her baby. She was determined to get to the bottom of it, whether Raymond wanted to hear the truth or not.

All of Queenie's comments only stirred her up. "Stop fretting, Ms. Jessa. Dis child's a blessing from God. His soul is secure wit' da Lord. His body and mind are for da here and now. But his soul…it's gonna last forever."

Jessa had run out of the room the last time Queenie said this and she overheard Raymond speak strongly to the old woman. Since then, Queenie hadn't said much about Buster. But then, things hadn't changed, so there was nothing new really to say.

"Russell Bland?" a nurse called from the office door. Jessa caught Raymond's eye and he stubbed out his cigarette, coming to join her.

"Right this way." The nurse escorted them to a baby scale. "Please place Russell here," she instructed.

Jessa lay the baby down on the scale. The nurse fussed with the weights and finally pronounced, "Twelve pounds, three ounces. He's a small little fella, huh?" Jessa nodded.

Then the nurse led the way to a private exam room with a table, two chairs and one window. A desk with books and medical instruments stood in one corner.

"Please lay the baby here on top of this paper on the table. We'll try to get a good length measurement…if he isn't too squirmy." Jessa wished so hard that Buster would fight and struggle and not cooperate. But he just lay there.

"He's a good little baby," the nurse commented as she drew a line right above Buster's head and another one right below his feet. She stretched out a tape measure. "About 23 and a half inches. Let's check his head circumference." The nurse moved the measuring tape around Buster's head. "Okay, I see." the nurse said as she scribbled more notes on her chart.

What the hell did that mean? Jessa demanded in her mind. But out loud she said, "How long before Dr. Miller can see us?"

"Very shortly. He's in a room with another patient right now and then he'll see you next," the nurse answered crisply. With that, she left the room, pulling the door closed as she went. There went Raymond, almost immediately, fumbling with the cigarettes in his pocket. "Please don't." Jessa said flatly. "It makes me and the baby cough."

Raymond pushed the pack back in his breast pocket. He ran his fingers through his hair, the way he did when he'd been thinking and had something to say.

"Jessa," he started. "Jessa, look at me." He pulled a chair across from hers and looked in her eyes. Those same blue eyes of his had caused her heart to melt the first time she'd met Raymond. He was standing along a wall at the South Atlantic Railroad's Community Hall where the Railroad was holding its annual dance.

Jessa's father was an official for South's local office here in Junction Point, so she and her brother and sisters were always invited to the dance. Raymond had been invited by a friend, and despite being a country boy, he struck an impressive figure in his Marine Corps dress blues. She'd just finished a dance with a boy she'd graduated high school with and broke away to get some punch. Raymond had met her at the refreshment table with a cup, already filled for her. He'd looked at her with his steely blue eyes and her heart had belonged to him ever since. There was nothing he couldn't fix or take care of for her. That all seemed so long ago now.

Raymond continued. "Jessa, whatever Doc Miller says, we can handle it. I'm sure he can give us some advice on how to work with Buster. We just need to help him get stronger. Please, hon, whatever he says, promise me you'll still believe in us. We're good parents. We'll work with him, whatever it takes. Okay?"

Jessa stared at him, glassy-eyed. She knew the news would not be good and he did, too. How long had he known?

Dr. Miller tapped on the door and made his way in. He was a tall man with a twinkle in his eyes. Jessa trusted him. He'd been her doctor since she was born. He was uncharacteristically serious now.

"Hello, Jessa, Raymond." The men shook hands. Then the doctor walked over to where Buster lay.

Jessa and Raymond moved to the other side of the table. Her eyes followed the doctor's every move, searching his face for some clue as to what he was finding. First, he gently pulled the blanket off the baby and began his exam. He looked in Buster's eyes, ears and nose. Buster began to whimper. Jessa held his small hand, soothing him the best she could.

Next the doctor listened to the baby's heart...for quite a long time, it seemed. He checked Buster's hands, his feet, inside his diaper and felt his abdomen.

"How's he eatin', Jessa?" the doctor wanted to know.

"Well, he's nursing all right now, but it's so hard to get any baby food in him. He can't sit up and giving him mashed bananas or baby cereal just causes him to choke," Jessa explained.

"Yeah, better hold off on spoon feeding him for now. He's got to get strong enough to sit up before you can safely feed him solids." Dr. Miller was reading a chart. He was silent for what seemed like a long time.

"Jessa, Raymond," he finally began. "I reviewed Russell's charts from the hospital. When you called with your concerns, Jessa, I wanted to make sure I had a full history. And I can tell you, in no uncertain terms, and as hard as it is for me to say it and for you to hear it, that I do agree with the diagnosis of Dr. Joseph and Dr. Hines. Russell is a Mongoloid. His appearance, his feet, hands, even his heart murmur: they all indicate Mongolism.

"Now, I know they probably told you that life expectancy for these children isn't much past a year, but I want to offer you some hope. I know a family over in Loris County that has two Mongoloids and they've got to be getting pretty close to teenagers now. I delivered Mae Long's Mongoloid girl three years ago. And I know of others who are older. The State has even started a training school for these children. So, please, know that all the medical predictions in the world won't determine what's going to happen with your child. He's blessed to have two capable, loving parents. I can prescribe some exercises, some vitamin drops and other things that will help him gain strength. It's just going to be a slow, day-by-day process."

The room went completely silent. Jessa had sunk back in her chair and Raymond stood next to the table with his arms crossed, looking down. He couldn't even look in Jessa's direction. Finally, the doctor asked, "Do you have any questions for me right now?"

Jessa looked down at the floor and took a deep breath. Then in a very small voice she said, "Dr. Miller…is…is my boy retarded, what they call an…an imbecile?" Her voice quivered.

"Yes, Jessa. I'm afraid so. I know it is so hard to hear. They do seem to be moving away from the term 'imbecile' though. The medical community would refer to him as 'Mongoloid.'"

He put his hand on her shoulder. "When you are ready, Jessa, I can gather some information for you to read. I can also make some calls about the training school. But that can wait for a number of years. Let's just get your boy stronger right now."

Jessa stood up. She clutched her sweater tight around her. Without looking up she said, "Thank you, doctor. Please send us the bill." Then she pushed by Dr. Miller, leaving the baby with Raymond.

"Raymond, try to be patient with her. You two need to support each other right now. The next few months are going to be tough. But you can do it together."

Raymond wasn't hearing the doctor anymore. He grabbed up Buster, wrapped him in his blanket as quickly as he could and ran out the door after his wife. She had already made it down the short hall, across the waiting room and out into the parking lot. She ran past their car and continued on toward a nearby, empty tobacco field.

Raymond burst out the door with the baby in his arms, running as fast as he could, wanting to take the doctor's words back, wanting to wish away this appointment like it had never happened.

"Jessa!" he yelled after her. "Jessa, wait! Come back! Jes-saaaa!" His agonized scream pierced the clear, cold November air.

He watched as his wife collapsed into the soft earth of the field, her mouth wide open in a scream of her own…a scream that pierced Raymond to his very soul. What had he done? What had he done? He walked over to her, sobbing her name, wishing he could take a beating to spare his wife this agony.

"Jes-saaaa! Forgive me. I'm so sorry! I'm so sorry. If only I had gotten you to the hospital sooner. I'm so sorry!" he moaned, collapsing next to her.

She turned, taking both hands and balling them into fists, she pounded on his chest, narrowly missing the baby. "You knew! You knew at the hospital! Why didn't you tell me? Why? You let me suffer in misery for the past six months, wondering what I was doing wrong, why this baby was nothing more than a blob! You knew what was wrong and you didn't tell me! I needed to know. I needed to know!" She collapsed weakly into him.

The three of them sat in the dirt, out of breath, unable to process completely what was happening. Then Buster whimpered, letting out a yowl. Instinctively, Jessa reached for him. She looked at his white-blonde hair, his smooth cheeks, his blue eyes and the ever-present tongue hanging out of his mouth. She looked at him long and hard. She didn't see a monster, an "imbecile." She saw her son. Raymond's son. Danny's brother. And right then and there, she stopped feeling sorry for herself. She didn't have the time or the energy to spare on pity, hers or anyone else's.

Jessa stood up with Buster in her arms, shrugging off Raymond's outstretched helping hand. No, she had been babied enough. What was it about her that made Raymond think he could not tell her the truth about their child? Did he see her as that weak? Well, she wasn't. Not anymore. She wasn't the same person as she had been. These past six months had changed her. In some way, some mysterious, unexplainable way, she had known all this time that she was being prepared…by God?…to do something big, something hard. She almost felt a sense of relief, now that she knew the name of this cursed affliction. She was ready. Ready to face life with this child, whatever it might bring.

Chapter 8

Willa's first day at Gold Mine Elementary continued after she and the crew dropped Mrs. Joye and Jason off at the nurse's office. She was glad the other woman volunteered to stay with him. Willa had a strong conviction that vomit and other bodily fluids should *not* be on the agenda for her first day. She was already teetering on the edge this morning and *that* would just about push her over. After all, she was trying to make the best of this. This job could very well be her plight for the next 25-plus years, until retirement, she reasoned dramatically. She would just have to buck up. But not today. Maybe tomorrow.

Right now, she was left to walk the three remaining boys to class. She assumed Jon had made it to class by himself. She hadn't seen him since he got off the bus.

The first thing she noticed was that Justin and Jeff were school celebrities, of sorts. Lots of older kids clustered around them, stopping them and insisting on the two of them giving high fives or hugs. She heard the other kids mentioning Bree Anna and another girl, Candy.

"Who's Candy?" Willa asked.

"She's Jeff's sister," one of the girls answered.

"*Big* sister," Jeff explained proudly.

"Bee *my* sissy," Justin countered.

So, that explained these two little "Rock Stars'" popularity! They had older siblings paving the way for them. Willa felt sorry for Sadar at first, because he seemed left out. But then she noticed several Indian students waving and saying hello to him as they walked by. So, they each had their own fan clubs, she figured.

It really was a remarkable reception, Willa thought. She hadn't known what to expect from what Caleigh had told her Friday. She'd said this was the first year Gold Mine Elementary had a full "Special Education" program for students from pre-school to 5th grade. Caleigh had been brought over this year from Lake Front Elementary to help get things off to a good start. She said a lot of the faculty, students and staff were still adjusting to having these guys on campus. Caleigh had explained that the teachers must have had a talk with their classes. The blatant stares and whispers had died down since the first of the year. She'd also said she had seen some staff members be very flexible in modifying things for her students. And.... she had seen some who were rigidly clinging to "how it has always been done."

Caleigh herself though, was committed to helping these students integrate into Gold Mine's student body, as seamlessly as possible by educating students *and* staff, one at a time, if need be. She had the county and the law on her side, she explained. Her plan, she'd told Willa, was to try a gentle approach at first. But Willa was pretty sure Caleigh was capable of pulling out all the "big guns" if need be.

Before they'd made it all the way to the classroom, they joined up with James and Jared (What was with all these "J" names, anyway? Just one more thing to get confused about!), whose parents had dropped them off in the car rider line. Jared walked quickly past them, raised his hand in a salute and said, almost robotically, "Good Morning to my friends." James, on the other hand, joined up with the slow shuffle of the rest of Willa's brood, until finally they all made it to the classroom.

There was an immediate logjam at the door. All the students were huddled around a small dry-erase board with "Lunch Choices" written across the top. Underneath were pictures of a hot dog, a pizza slice, a garden salad, a sub sandwich and a crust-free peanut butter and jelly sandwich. Ms. Smith was on hand to help the boys make their selections.

"Jon, your grandmother says you cannot order pizza or peanut butter and jelly. Do you want a hot dog?" she asked. Jon nodded. Ms. Smith made a tally mark under the hot dog picture.

"All right. Now, Justin, how about pizza today?" Justin grinned and nodded his head.

"Jared?"

"Cheeseburger."

"Cheeseburger, *please*. And that is not a choice for today. How about a hot dog?"

"Okay. With cheese."

"With cheese, *please*. And I don't think they serve cheese with hot dogs. But we'll see. Sadar, what'll you have?"

"Pizza!" Sadar smiled widely, punctuating his enthusiastic order by thrusting his pointer finger straight up in the air

"Pizza, *please*. Boys, remember your manners!" Ms. Smith said. "All right. How about James. What do you want for lunch today?"

"Hot dog."

Ms. Smith walked over to James and bent down, eye to eye with him. "Hot dog, *please*, James."

"Puh-weez," James added.

At that moment Justin snorted loudly in dismay and flopped to the ground, all in a dither about something.

"Justin, James can order what he wants for lunch, just like *you* can order what *you* want. You two don't have to have the same thing every day!" Ms. Smith said firmly. Justin didn't seem to care what she said and continued to pout, apparently about James' order.

Ignoring him, Ms. Smith explained, "Justin and James' families are close and get together all the time. They both have sisters about the same age, so they really act more like brothers than classmates. That includes bickering, teasing, wrestling and rough-housing with each other, right guys?" Ms. Smith tousled James hair.

"I'm trying to get them to function a little more independently, including choosing what they really want for lunch and not copying each other." Ms. Smith stood up from squatting in front of the lunch choices and continued.

"Maleeke is on a gluten free, casein free diet. He brings his own lunch and snacks and treats, including sugar-free suckers and cookies. A few years back there was a lot of speculation about diet and autism. So far, the research really hasn't proven a connection, but his parents and many others continue to try removing wheat and dairy products from their kids' diets. I don't blame the parents. They are trying to control what they can in an effort to help their child. For the parents of these students, there are very few things they can actually control. So, who's to say that if I had a child on the autism spectrum I wouldn't try the diet, too?"

Willa sensed that a healthy dose of empathy could really help in this job. "So Jon and Maleeke have autism?" she asked curiously.

"Oh, Willa, that is such a loaded question." Caleigh's tone was again full of patience for her newest "student." "Many times children this young don't have a specific diagnosis but are put under the autism 'umbrella.' That means they have four or five autistic-like tendencies, as determined by a psychologist. It's kind of wait-and-see at this point for Maleeke. His tests are pointing toward Asperger's syndrome, which is a high-functioning form of autism. It means his intellect is normal, even high in his case, but his social skills are very poor. He can count to 100 in Swahili but he can't look you in the eye and talk to you. Jared's the same way. He was reading out loud at 21 months, but any social interactions are usually rehearsed. He just doesn't have the ability to pick up social cues and use them for interacting with others. A lot of times he says and does things that are inappropriate."

Caleigh continued explaining as she went to her desk and punched in a few keystrokes on her laptop. "As for Jon, he is being raised by his grandparents because his mother is in prison on drug charges. She apparently took drugs while she was pregnant with him. The grandparents have the opinion that drugs got him into this situation so they are unwilling to try any meds for helping him calm down and focus. They are trying more of a high fiber, low sugar diet with plenty of fruits and veggies. I'm not sure they would approve of the hot dog for lunch, but they have definitely said no to pizza and pb&j. In addition to his behavior issues he has an intellectual impairment, which means a lower than average IQ."

Wow, Willa thought. "There is so much to learn! It really is interesting to hear about the different disabilities and how they affect these children. I hope you won't mind me 'picking your brain' on this subject. I really don't know much at all about childhood disabilities. But it is fascinating!"

"No, Willa, ask away. But just realize that this field is a complicated one. There is disagreement on what causes some disabilities, disagreement on how to best treat these kids and on-going research that turns up something new all the time. To top it off, I've only taught one year and so I'm learning all the time myself! And I've just been with these guys a few weeks longer than you have, so we'll get to know them together!" Caleigh started herding the boys towards the coat hooks and cubbies.

"Boys, let's get unpacked and in our seats. It's time for the school news and then we'll welcome Mrs. Grizzard to our class. She's going to be with us every day now!"

Willa couldn't help but cringe a little at that statement.

All morning Willa watched Caleigh with fascination. She really was enthusiastic about her work. She was firm, but loving; fun, but strict. And her patience...goodness! There seemed to be no end to her patience!

Sue Ann soon returned with Jason. The para explained that the nurse had given him a pass this time because of his sensitive gag reflex. But next time, he'd have to go home.

Willa was all too familiar with the County Wellness Policy. She'd been called to pick up her sick children many times. According to the school's handbook, a child was to be sent home after an episode of vomiting. This was the first of many exceptions to the rules that Willa would notice were given to the students in Special Needs classes.

Jack eventually straggled in late…a regular occurrence since the beginning of school according to Caleigh…and one that really griped her. What seemed most annoying to her was that Jack's father insisted on walking him to the classroom which then resulted in a long, tearful goodbye and a disruption for the whole class.

When the father had finally left and the teachers had worked to settle the little boy down, Caleigh said, "Jack has a processing disorder. That means he doesn't take in what is said and comprehend it like other children. He really only started talking about a year ago. But that should *not* affect his ability to get to school on time! He's missing precious instruction time!" She was clearly annoyed. "We need all the classroom time we can get in order to catch him up and then maybe there will be a chance he can be mainstreamed for kindergarten next year. I plan to bring that up at his parent/teacher conference next month!"

Willa got the impression that one had to tread carefully with the parents of special needs kids. They had unique circumstances and rights under state and federal law.

As she would soon learn, if you wanted to strike fear in the hearts of everyone in the administration and at the county office, all you had to do is mention legal action from a special needs family.

* * *

Willa lay in bed with her daughter that night after her first day at work, listening to her say her prayers. As the little girl asked God to bless all her dolls, Willa stroked Bella's soft, dark hair. Her eyes filled with tears. She was so thankful her three children were all healthy. How did the parents of her students *do* it, day in, day out? She was exhausted, both physically and emotionally from just spending eight hours at school with them. And Sue Ann was with them today. Tomorrow, she would be leaving Willa and Caleigh to do it all alone.

She tried to remember each child's bus number, dietary restrictions, disability characteristics and potty training requirements. And lunch time! For Willa that was the worst. After "herding" the group through the lunch line and narrowly getting them all to the table with no spilled trays, she'd looked around for where the teachers went to eat. She noticed Caleigh busy walking up behind each one, opening milk cartons, ketchup packets, cutting up food and tucking in napkins. Willa joined in. Then, after making sure everyone had what they needed, Caleigh sat down with them and pulled out her own lunch! Willa just about died! No break from them, even for lunch? When she thought about it, she knew good and well that they couldn't leave unsupervised children who gagged on their food, and were prohibited from eating what was readily available on their neighbor's tray. But she was just sure *someone* from *somewhere* would come in and relieve them! No one came.

So Willa sat down and pulled out her sandwich. Then she looked around. James had a runny nose. He'd eat a spoonful of applesauce, stick his tongue out and lick all the way under his nose and then repeat. Maleeke's "special diet" included a gray-colored hot dog and what looked like mashed okra. Jason was hunched over eating his pizza so fast that Willa was afraid he was going to choke again. His cheeks, chin and nose were all smeared with red sauce. The others chomped with their mouths wide open, burped loudly and ate with their fingers. One boy had a plastic fork in one hand, a spoon in the other and was so intense that he looked like he was eating his last meal. After seeing their table manners, Willa didn't have much appetite left. She slid her sandwich back in its baggy and put it away.

"Not hungry?" Caleigh had asked as she took a big bite from her sandwich.

"No," Willa said, glad of a chance for distraction from her surroundings. "I'm just...thinking...about how I interacted with the children this morning. It seems like I really didn't connect with any of them."

Caleigh laughed and said, "You did fine. And you'll learn as you get to know each one of them. Sometimes...and I know this sounds bad...but I think you should talk to these guys like you would a dog you're training. You wouldn't say, 'Now Spot, I want you to sit here while I unlock the door and then you are to go out and go potty and come right back. Scratch on the door to let me know you're done and then we'll go for a walk.' No, you would say, 'Spot sit. Stay. Spot, go potty.' Like that. These kids can't process lengthy directions. As a matter of fact, it is in some of their IEP goals to learn to follow 2-step directions. So really, they aren't even past one step directions right now. You need to get eye level with them, say their name first and then give one, simple instruction at a time."

There was so much Willa didn't know. She'd probably forget most of this by tomorrow and then she'd have to be told all over again. Who was she kidding? She was still at the one-step-direction-stage herself.

She prayed right along with Bella that night. She asked God for strength, for insight and to help her remember all the important stuff, like how to get these kids on the right buses home. Then she tried to think of something to be thankful for. "Thank you, God...that I'm not digging ditches. I have a nice, indoor job, working with sweet children. Help me to remember that." As an afterthought she added one more thing. "And God, please, give me a strong stomach at lunch time. I'll need nourishment to get through these days."

* * *

Willa peered through her reading glasses. Caleigh's notes were explicit. She should start with the movement-to-words song, "The Tootie Ta," then go straight into "The Days of the Week" song, which was sung to the tune of the old Adams Family T-V show theme jingle. Next, came "The Months of the Year Macarena" and then "The Shapes Song." She could do this. She had seen Caleigh do this every morning for the past two and a half weeks. Today, Caleigh had called her, very sick, asking if she felt like she could do it alone.

"I feel like crap." Caleigh had said. "But I can come in and get you started, so the boys don't get all out of sorts for you."

"No, no, Caleigh. You're sick. Stay home in bed and feel better. We'll be fine," she'd lied. "Just email me the schedule and any directions I'll need for finding the Power Points and other flip charts that they're used to. I know routine is very important to the kids, so I'll try to follow your schedule exactly."

"Well, I've called Carol Harper. She's in charge of getting subs. It's late notice, so all the good subs are probably already assigned. But I asked her to try to get you someone decent, even if she has to shuffle the subs around a bit. After all, not just anyone will want to…or be good at…working with our children. Anyway, the sub should be there shortly," Caleigh rasped

"Great, Caleigh," Willa had said. "You go rest and get better soon. We'll miss you!"

After Willa hung up, she allowed herself to panic for a moment. Thank goodness she had gotten to the classroom a few minutes early. She had about 10 minutes before students started arriving. When the teacher was out, Principal Johnson had informed her, she was to step up and take the lead teacher's role and the substitute was to take on her role.

Then she got busy putting folder games out on each desk. That would do for morning work. Next, she rummaged through a basket of CD's to see if she could find the songs that Caleigh used every morning. "The Tootie Ta" was nowhere to be found, but "The Days of the Week" and "The Months of the Year" songs were right there. She continued looking around until she remembered they had listened to a CD late in the day yesterday, using music to work on counting. She checked the player and sure enough, there was "The Tootie Ta" CD. Okay, she had five minutes till "show time, "so she made her way to the laptop and started to look for the Power Points she'd need. "The Big Count," "The Shapes Song," the September calendar, the "Walk in the Hall" song, and of course, the selection of "silly songs" that she would use throughout the day as rewards. Willa got them all in the right order and ready to play when the kids came in. She glanced at the clock and saw that it was almost time for The Goldmine Elementary Morning News. So, she synced up the white board with the closed circuit broadcast and then let out a sigh. She was ready! Or so she hoped.

CHAPTER 9

J essa worked with her hair in her dressing mirror, trying to adjust the pin curls toward her face. Finally, she sighed and placed the teal blue felt hat on her head and started fussing with the netted veil that hung just below her eyebrows.

Raymond came up over her shoulders and squeezed her tight. "You look beautiful, Jessa."

"Well, it has been a while since I've been to church. I figured I should put my best face forward. I mean, people will already be talking about how we haven't had Buster baptized, even though he's over 8-months old." Jessa had been raised Methodist and Raymond Southern Baptist.

"Oh, Jessa, I wasn't baptized till I was 12 years old. I turned out okay, didn't I?" Raymond grinned at her.

"Still, I want to get back to going to First Methodist so we can book Buster's baptism I feel funny asking Reverend Howard to baptize him when he's never even met Buster."

Jessa and Raymond generally stayed close to home on Sundays. That was the one day of the week that Queenie didn't work for them and it was all the two of them could do to get through the day with Danny and Buster. It was also Raymond's only full day off from work, so Jessa just enjoyed trying to be together as a family. Yes, enjoyed. She was trying to start enjoying life again.

She'd mourned what Buster could have been. Now she was trying to accept him for who he was and enjoy her two boys while she could. She wouldn't allow herself to even think about Buster's heart and the potential time bomb it could prove to be.

"Okay, let's get the boys in the car before they find a way to undo their dress clothes and ruin their hair," Jessa said as she pick up her handbag from a chair and headed toward their room.

Buster was lying in his playpen, propped up on two pillows. His eyes were fixed on Danny, who was standing on a stool next to the playpen, swinging his arms like a choir director and singing along with the gospel music coming from the radio in the den.

"Oh Jesus, yes Jesus. He's the answer still.
Oh Jesus, precious Jesus, He'll save you if you will,
Come to Him, Open your heart, and invite Him in.
Oh Jesus, yes Jesus. He's the answer still."

Danny's high, pure voice was right in tune. He'd heard this song on the radio many times. His little face was so earnest. And his audience was just enthralled…all three of them, for Raymond had come up behind Jessa and caught the performance, too.

These parents had not had a lot to smile about in the past few months. They'd been so devastated. But watching their older son sing so sweetly and their younger son be so captivated by his brother…It was just a moment they wanted to freeze in time, a snapshot of the happiness they both longed for so badly.

Jessa whispered, "Ray, run go get the camera."

Raymond went and got it and was back in time for the final chorus.

Danny now saw his parents in the doorway and a wide grin spread across his face. But he didn't stop singing. He kept right on going. In fact, Jessa couldn't resist joining in, as Raymond set up the shot.

"Oh Jesus, yes Jesus. He's the answer still.
Oh Jesus, precious Jesus, He'll save you if you will,
Come to Him, Open your heart, and invite Him in.

Oh Jesus, yes Jesus. He's the answer still."

When the flash went off, Jessa was looking at Danny, smiling and singing, Danny was looking back at her, also smiling. And down in the playpen, little Buster was grinning a toothy grin too. Raymond's heart almost leapt from his rib cage, with the joy he was feeling. He was beginning to see a chance that life could be good again for him and his family.

* * *

Jessa fiddled with her watchband and rubbed the skin beneath it, pressing away the deep imprints left in her flesh from the expandable band. Her wrists were thicker than she would like. She had yet to lose the weight she gained with Buster. She just seemed to be more nervous now and that in turn caused her to eat more. Jessa let the band snap back into place and it immediately pinched her again.

She winched as she looked up at the minister. Reverend Howard was going a little long again. They had been coming to First Methodist somewhat regularly since the beginning of the year. One of the young, single women, Joycelynn Owens, with the help of two of the teenage girls here, had started a Sunday School of sorts for children three-years-old to 10-years-old, and Danny seemed to enjoy it. They met in the hall where wedding receptions and other social gatherings were held. Joycelynn was working to earn her support to go to the mission field and received a small stipend for her Sunday morning efforts.

Jessa glanced over at Raymond, who was sitting down the pew from her. His head was bobbing forward, his eyes closed, his arms intertwined across his chest. He was all but snoring! Jessa reached across Buster's sleeping body, which stretched between her and her husband, and gave Raymond a sharp jab to the rib cage. Raymond sat up with a jerk, his left arm leaving its folded position and crashing down to the pew with a "thump." His wedding ring hit the wood, making the sound even sharper.

Buster's blue eyes flew open in start, then his lower lip began to quiver. Jessa tried to think quickly. The room was relatively silent, except for the minister's deep, droning voice and the occasional cough from someone in the congregation. Most of the women were already fanning themselves, even though it was only late March.

Jessa grabbed Buster up from the pew and pressed his face softly into her shoulder, whispering, "Shhhhhh." Buster wasn't going to be "shushed" though. He let out a howl, followed by more whimpering and finally full-blown crying.

Jessa had always been aware that Buster's cry sounded different than Danny's and other babies' cries. It was weaker and hoarser. More like the bleating of a lamb or goat kid. Right now, she was keenly aware of the sharp eyes staring at her and her "oddity" as they made their way past Raymond's legs and headed straight for the vestibule doors at the back of the sanctuary. Once Jessa had pushed through the doors, she stood in the entryway hall, bouncing Buster as she walked, trying to quiet him.

"We got to hold on just a little bit longer, Baby." Jessa whispered to Buster's exposed ear. "Reverend Howard is going to meet with us in just a few minutes. Then we'll go home and have lunch. Mommy has your favorite biscuit dough already in the ice box. I'll bake them right when we get home, and we can have some of Queenie's left over fried chicken, too. Your Daddy says it is almost as good cold as it is right out of the frying pan."

Jessa tried to find Buster's pacifier in her handbag. She fumbled with one hand while the bag dangled from the opposite arm, all the while trying not to drop the baby.

Just then, Dolly Mabry came out of the women's restroom. She was a tall, round woman with graying blonde hair and black-rimmed glasses perched on her nose. "Oh, Jessa, let me hold him for you," she urged, her exaggerated southern drawl lowered to a whisper, so as not to disturb the service on the other side of the swinging doors.

Jessa, unguarded and startled to find someone else truant from the sermon, turned and said, "Oh, thank you, Miss Mabry." She rolled Buster into the woman's waiting arms.

"He's getting pretty old now. Is he a year yet?" the older woman asked in a friendly voice. Dolly Mabry, who had to be in her late forties now, had never married. As her mother's eldest daughter, she had helped raise her two younger sisters and four younger brothers. She was well into her 20's when she finally moved from her parents' farmhouse and took an apartment in town. It was at about that time she started writing a column for the *Junction City Weekly Express* newspaper. It centered on the only thing Miss Mabry could reasonably be expected to have any ability to discuss long-term: children.

"Not yet," Jessa answered. "He's a little over 10 months old," she whispered absently as she peered into her bag, trying to spy the missing passie.

"I've been wanting to get a good look at him. Selma Chastain told me he has the most unusual eyes…oh my, they are startling! Blue with white and gold flecks," the woman enthused "politely," as she stared into the baby's heavily hooded eyes.

Then, the self-proclaimed "Junction City Expert on Babies" took things in a less civil direction. "Now, tell me, does he have any malformations, like clubbed feet? I've even heard their feet and hands can be webbed!" the woman said as she started to unbundle Buster.

Jessa shook her head to indicate no, her brow slightly furrowed at the intrusive question. She was both taken aback and still under the assumption this was a polite conversation worth having.

"I notice he sticks his tongue out a lot. What do you think about putting him straight on a cup and eliminating all bottles and breast feeding? That should help, don't you think, Jessa? It makes him look so queer to have his tongue hanging out all the time."

The woman rattled on. "You know, Jessa, I helped raise my brothers and sisters and now I have 17 nieces and nephews. I've got quite the experience with normal children," she emphasized the word "normal," pronouncing it more like, "nooo-mal."

"But I tell you, I have limited knowledge with children like this one. All the time and energy he demands, all the while knowing he will never be able to contribute to society. It must be so hard for you, sweetie! Thank the good Lord you have a nooo-mal child. You'll have to console yourself by putting your efforts into him."

Jessa couldn't think fast enough to say anything that would halt Dolly Mabry's wounding words. Once Dolly started dispensing what she saw as practical advice, she was a hard one to stop.

"Mothers who have crippled children or one like this one, they have the hardest time. I've seen it time and again, Jessa, when they write into me at *The Express*. Mamas have a harder time reconciling the facts. That's when the daddies have to step in. If you want, I can talk to Raymond to help him with the hard choices that have to be made.

"We all say it all the time, Jessa. We just don't know how you've done it this long. I know the colored woman helps, and we have all talked about making a regular contribution toward her expenses. We don't dare want you to try and do this by yourself. We just want to help until the time comes…"

"Hold it right there!" Jessa finally interrupted. The older woman turned her attention away from her inspection of Buster and towards his mother, who stood with both hands squeezed into fists.

"You seem so sure of what you're saying, but you don't know anything at all about me, my children, my husband! I dare you to try and talk to Raymond the way you have me. I wouldn't doubt that he'd give you a punch in the mouth…just what you deserve! I ought to do it now! My son is human, Miss Mabry. He has already 'contributed to society,' just by being himself...a human being, made in the image of God. Isn't that what Pastor Howard teaches?"

Jessa was crying now, but that only made her madder. She didn't want her tears to be misinterpreted for weakness. She reached into Miss Mabry's arms and grabbed her baby back. He just smiled up at her as she cradled him in her arms.

"You see this smile, Ms. Mabry? Do you?" Jessa allowed the other woman one last look at her baby's face. "Do you know how many times it has been this smile that has gotten me out of bed in the morning? It is this smile that has brought back my joy... this smile that makes *me* smile. That's a contribution that counts, isn't it, Miss Mabry?" Now Jessa was taking more of a pleading, hopeful, almost wishful tone.

Dolly Mabry shut her mouth, which had been gaping open during Jessa's speech. Now she straightened her back to its fullest potential, making her a head taller than Jessa. Looking down through her black-rimmed glasses, she began again to attempt to persuade Jessa that she was on her side.

"Jessa, I didn't mean to make you hysterical. And this is just what I meant by 'the mothers having a harder time with the facts.'" Miss Mabry, without knowing why, took a step backwards, away from her shorter, smaller opponent. "I just want to help you and Raymond accept the facts, Jessa, that's all." Ms. Mabry sniffed, suddenly feeling sensitive about being attacked for her "worthy" efforts.

"What are the facts, Miss Mabry? What are they that we don't understand?" Jessa asked, really wanting to know.

"Why, Jessa...." Dolly gentled her tone. "That it's just a matter of time before you and Raymond won't be able to care properly for this boy. And it's just a matter of time before he becomes a drain on your whole family. You'll *have* to send him away. To an institution. To live. He'll be taken care of there till...well, until he dies, Jessa.

It's so hard. These children never live very long." Dolly now tried to reach out to put a comforting hand on Jessa's shoulder.

It was Jessa's turn to step back this time, out of reach of Dolly Mabry's grasp. To Jessa, the Postlude, which they had begun to sing on the other side of the doors now, seemed to ring as if a good distance away. She had heard Dolly's words, but other senses were involved, too. She had seen the pity, the infuriating pity in Dolly's eyes. She had felt her words. Like they had hit her in her stomach. And in her response to a perceived blow, Jessa pushed back, nearly knocking Dolly off her feet.

Jessa backed away some more, clutching her baby tightly to her. She shook her head and turned and ran, just as the vestibule doors burst open with church members heading out to their separate homes to prepare their lunches. They had done their godly duty this morning. Now the rest of this early spring day belonged to them.

Reverend Howard was walking Raymond through the doors, with his hand on Raymond's shoulder, talking to him about their scheduled meeting. "I'll need to greet the congregants first, Raymond, so you and Jessa can wait under the big oak tree in the picnic area outside. Enjoy the day. I'll be there shortly."

Raymond turned to look for Jessa, but all he could see was Dolly Mabry and four or five other church women, all huddled together, Dolly talking fast and emphatically about some church gossip, Raymond assumed. Jessa and their baby were nowhere to be seen.

* * *

Raymond walked into the bedroom to find his wife stretched out on her side, her back to him.

"Uh, hi, Jessa. Where in the world have you been? Reverend Howard and I waited as long as we could and now we'll have to reschedule. Was Buster giving you trouble?"

"No. Buster was an angel. I wish I could say the same for Dolly Mabry. She's the devil himself, as far as I'm concerned." Jessa's voice was angry.

"What are you talking about, hon?" Raymond was still unaware of the hornets' nest he had stepped into.

"What am I talking about?" Jessa swung her legs over the side of the bed and sat up. "I'm talking about that mean-spirited, cruel, conniving woman who thinks she knows all about our life, our child." Jessa stood up and walked toward Raymond. "Raymond, I was so angry with her, I could have hurt her!" Jessa fell into her husband's arms and started sobbing.

"Jessa, start at the beginning and tell me what happened. Did you see Dolly at church this morning?"

"Yes, she was there, horns and all!"

"What did she say?"

"She examined Buster like he was under a microscope. She asked if he had webbed feet! She said she and the other ladies of the church feel sorry for me. She wants to give us money." Jessa started to lose steam as she recounted the whole sordid conversation. And she tried not to think about all that was said that she *wasn't* telling Raymond.

"Money? What for?"

"To help pay for Queenie."

"What? What business is Queenie of hers?"

"None. And that's how the whole conversation was. Everything she talked about…Raymond, it was stuff you and I haven't even talked about yet…Everything was inappropriate, obnoxious and outrageous. I am so mad that I didn't have my wits about me to tell her off, right there in the church foyer."

"Jessa, maybe she was trying to help, in her own nosey, bossy way," Raymond soothed.

"No, Raymond, don't you dare mistake her morbid curiosity for 'help.'" Jessa got fired up again. "She wants to be the know-it-all, the most informed. 'Miss Newspaper Columnist.' It makes her feel important. I wouldn't be surprised if she called a special meeting to 'share' what she's learned about us with the Women's Prayer Group. If she announces it as a 'prayer request,' then she can tell everything about us. That whole group should be disbanded. They don't pray. They gossip!"

Raymond had to nod in agreement as he remembered the clutch of women gathered around Dolly after church today. "Okay, Jessa, they may be all the things you say they are. But they don't know anything real to talk about, do they? They don't know us. They don't know the truth. *We* know the truth! And that's all that matters." He smoothed her hair and kissed her forehead.

Jessa closed her eyes and allowed him to kiss her nose, her mouth, her neck. "Hey, Jessa," he murmured. "Danny fell asleep on the drive home and I laid him on the sofa. Buster's asleep too, right? How about we take a little 'nap' of our own?"

"Okay," she agreed in a small, distracted voice. She couldn't turn off her thoughts.

She would oblige her husband even though she would have been happy just to have him lie down with her and hold her, talk things through some more.

"Jessa," Raymond loosened his tie and started working on his top button.

"Yes, Raymond?"

"Reverend Howard says we don't really have to have Buster sprinkled. He says God already has a special place prepared in heaven for people like Buster."

"What? He doesn't want to baptize Buster?" Jessa said over her shoulder. Even after all these years of marriage, she still turned her back to Raymond when she disrobed.

"No, that's not what he meant. Reverend Howard says people like Buster never reach what they call the 'age of accountability.' They never grow up intellectually. He says they always have the mind of a child, their entire lives. He said he would do it if we want him to, but he was thinking it might be too much stress for us, that we might not be in the mood to undergo such an obligation," Raymond recounted the pastor's words without much thought. He had other things on his mind.

Jessa turned, her wounded expression catching Raymond's attention. "I never thought of it as an *obligation*," she said, her voice quivering. "I thought of it as a joy." She dissolved into tears again.

Raymond walked across the room and took his beautiful wife in his arms. "Shhh, Jessa. It's okay. We can still do it. We can meet with Reverend Howard next Sunday to talk about the date and the details." He removed her slip strap from her shoulder and gently leaned down to place a kiss where the strap had been.

Jessa stared into space as he did, longing to hold onto her faith, her religion, her church. She just wanted to be normal, like Dolly said. But she knew she wasn't normal, never again would be. Her life, her family and everything else had changed forever. So here was just one more thing she would have to give up. She still believed in God. But as for the church she had been baptized in as a baby...she knew she would never be able to set foot in there again.

CHAPTER 10

It was Saturday afternoon in late October. Because of the beautiful weather, Willa had taken a table outside at the local coffee house, waiting for Suzanne Hunt to arrive. She and Suzanne had been friends for years now. They had met at church and soon figured out that their children were near in age and that their husbands both liked to fish and golf. So, a typical suburban, young-mom-friendship was born. Over the years their relationship had deepened as they watched their children on the soccer field together, took them to Library Story Time and Kindermusik classes, and even left them in a Mothers' Morning Out program, while they shopped together and got their nails done. The two had been a sounding board for each other through many of life's difficulties. Right now, Willa needed to sound off to somebody and Suzanne was "it."

Willa decided to go ahead and order her coffee while she waited. She stepped into the shop and walked up to the counter to order. Her peripheral vision caught a small commotion going on in the corner as she heard a familiar giggle. She glanced over to see a blonde-headed little boy bouncing on a couch. It was Justin, from school. Willa stood back a moment, not sure whether she wanted to have an encounter like this, outside of the confines of the classroom.

Justin was leaning his hands on the table in front of him, with his hind quarters bouncing as high as the couch springs would propel him. His mother...Willa presumed it was his mom...was on her cell phone, with a large cup of coffee, thankfully lidded, in her other hand. The woman was strikingly beautiful: blonde hair stylishly cut in a stacked bob, fingernails perfectly manicured, tanned skin and enhanced-looking breasts, which were apparent because her blouse was unbuttoned just enough to show "what nature didn't give, money could buy."

Willa didn't know why she was a bit surprised by the woman's appearance. What had she expected, a worn-out, Plain Jane with bags under her eyes? Why did she think that? She was only just beginning to examine some of her preconceived notions and was often surprised these days by her...was it prejudice? Stereotypical thinking? Ignorance? All three?

As Willa scolded herself for all of the above, Justin's eyes turned from his mother and met Willa's across the crowded shop. Before she could plan her reaction, the boy jumped off the couch, ran across the restaurant, nearly toppling a waiter with a tray and a young couple who had just joined the line. He impulsively leaped up onto Willa, wrapped his arms around her waist, his legs around her thighs and just hung on. "Wiz-ard!" he yelled, and then planted a big smooch right onto the part of her sweater that covered her boobs. "Wiz-ard!" he shouted again, looking up at her with a big smile.

Willa was so taken off guard that she thought she was going to fall down. Instead, she leaned backward and perched on the corner of a nearby table for support, with Justin still suspended from her front side. "Hi, Justin!" she said. "Oh my goodness!" Willa looked helplessly toward the corner where Justin's mom was and tried to smile good naturedly.

Justin's mom had ended her call abruptly and was coming over to help remove Justin from his death-grip on Willa. But the little boy did not disengage easily. "Justin David, let go of her and stand up right now," his mom said. Willa tried to unlock his hands from around her waist. But before the child could be overpowered by the two women, he smooched Willa's sweatery-boobs again. "I tiss," he shouted proudly.

"Yes, and what a hello it was," Willa said as she pulled on his arms.

"No, I tiss," he insisted

"All right, all right, you kissed her. Now stand up like a big boy and I'll get you a cookie from the counter," his mother shamelessly bribed. Justin let go of Willa and walked immediately up to the counter to look through the glass at the selection.

His mom turned to Willa, thrust out her hand and said, "Hi. I'm Sara Canahan, Justin's mother. You must be his new teacher?" she guessed sheepishly.

"Yes, I'm Willa Grizzard, better known to Justin as plain old 'Wizard,'" Willa replied. "He's so energetic. And *strong*," Willa said as she rubbed her back where Justin had squeezed her particularly tight.

"I know, he *is* strong! I'm so sorry he jumped on you, but he was just excited to see you. His grandparents have learned to sit down when they see him coming. He goes full throttle at them and will knock them off their feet if they aren't careful. But they know it's his way of telling them he's excited to see them. Still, we're working on it. He's got to learn more socially acceptable ways of saying 'Hello,'…like, I don't know, a nice handshake or just a simple smile? We're not there yet," Sara said flatly.

Willa smiled at Sara. "I know. Just be assured that we are also working on such things at school. So, together we'll make progress, you'll see." Willa sounded more sure of herself than she actually was.

"Well, it's nice to meet you," the mother said. "We've got to get going to Bree Anna's soccer game. She's with her dad today. Justin didn't want to go with his dad. So, now we have to drive across town to get Bree Anna and then drive back over this way to the soccer field. Her dad will probably end up coming to watch the game, but he wouldn't *dream* of bringing her a little early to warm up, so it would save me a trip. I guess it's just par for the course when you have an 'ex'."

The whole time Sara was explaining their itinerary Justin had been pulling with his full weight on her arm, causing her to bob and weave about as she talked. The boy threw back his head and giggled, as if this were a game. Willa couldn't help it. "Justin, stop pulling on your mother!" she said in a firm tone.

She and Caleigh were extra strict with the boys in school, often not joking around with them or tussling with them, just so this sort of thing didn't get started. These kids often didn't know when they had taken things too far and Willa remembered Caleigh saying they really didn't get social cues. So, once these shenanigans broke out, they were hard to stop, as Justin was proving. She also remembered Caleigh telling her that the one thing people with Down Syndrome often are is extremely *stubborn*.

"Hee hee, hee hee," he kept giggling, his little buck teeth protruding from his grin, his blonde hair standing on end as he leaned back, continuing to pull on his mother.

"Now, Justin, you heard what Mrs. Wizard said. Let go of me right this minute or you will lose TV time when you get home. And now, no cookie from here! And you will be in time out at Bee Bee's game. Is that what you want? Huh?"

"It's Grizzard," Willa said, interrupting the mounting list of penalties. She was trying to help, but this little bugger was strong...and slippery!

Realizing he was out-muscled, Justin suddenly let go of his mother, who stumbled backwards, trying to stay on her feet. Justin scooted, quick as a mouse, under a nearby table, wrapping his arms and legs around the table's pedestal, just as he'd done to Willa a few minutes earlier. The table was occupied by two men in business suits talking over a laptop computer. The men smiled, but they did not look amused.

"Now, son, be a good boy and come on out for your mom," one of them said, as they both scooted their chairs back and peered under the table at Justin. Justin just continued to hold on to the post, knowing an "enemy assault" was soon to come. He wouldn't make eye contact with anyone.

Later that day, Willa would look back on this moment and wonder what exactly had made her do what she did. But right now, instinct kicked in. Call it mother's instinct, teacher's instinct or just plain stubbornness of her own, Willa could not stand to see this little 45-pound, five-year old kid get the better of all these adults. She looked over at Sara who was just standing there chewing on a fingernail with a worried look on her brow. Willa couldn't help it. She squatted down, did a sort of duck walk under the table, grabbed Justin's folded arms and started to forcibly untwine them. "Justin, get up! Right now!" He didn't budge.

"Okay, I'll *get* you out then," she said. She managed to unhook his arms from the pedestal. Then she tried to pull his upper body toward her. He hung on to the table with his legs. Justin just leaned to the side with each pull. Willa had to let go briefly to regroup. Justin took this opportunity to untwist his legs from the table and promptly dropped his chest to the floor between his legs, as only a person with Down Syndrome or double joints can do. *Note to self,* Willa thought. *Another characteristic of many people with Down Syndrome is extreme flexibility.*

By this time, adrenaline had taken over and Willa grabbed a foot and started pulling. But her back wouldn't allow her to stay squatted even one more minute. So, as she pulled, she stood up. The back of her head had not cleared the table, so of course Willa bumped the edge of the table, sending it spilling one way and tumbling one of the businessmen to the floor. At just that time, Justin's shoe came off in Willa's hand and she stumbled backward, bumping into the line of customers that had now formed around their little scene, finally landing hard on her rump, splayed out all over the floor for everybody to see!

With perfect timing, Suzanne walked through the door of the shop to find a crowd gathered around an overturned table, a fallen man in a suit…and her good friend, sitting on the floor, peering through her hair and grimacing.

"Hello, Willa," Suzanne deadpanned, entirely nonplused by the scene before her. "Glad to see you didn't wait for me to get started."

The businessman looked up from the floor and responded, "You mean you ladies go around to coffee shops doing this sort of thing all the time?"

All Willa could do was blow her hair out of her face with an upward puff of breath and say, "We don't just limit ourselves to coffee shops. We take our show on the road all over the place!"

* * *

Willa sat back gingerly on the ice pack Joel had made for her aching tailbone. She was nursing it…and her pride.

"How's that, babe?" Joel asked his wife.

"Great. Thank you, Joel." Willa grimaced as she wiggled around to find the most comfortable position.

"Now, I still don't understand why Suzanne had to drive you home. Is our car at the coffee shop?" Joel sat on the side of the bed, facing his wife. He affectionately lifted a lock of hair off her face and pushed it behind her ear.

"She had to drive me home because I'm in pain! This *really* hurts. I wasn't sure I'd be able to slam on brakes if I had to. And yes, our car is still at that blasted coffee shop," Willa grouched.

"Okay. I'll go feed the kids and then come back to check on you. Do you need anything?" Joel was doing his best to soothe his wife's ruffled feelings.

"Just for you to sit with me for a while," Willa said as she patted Joel's side of the bed. He walked around and stretched across the bed on his side, propping himself up on his elbow.

"I get the feeling that more is wounded here than just your rump," Joel mused as he lifted Willa's hand to his lips and kissed it. "And oh, what a beautiful rump it is!" he enthused.

"It's all black and blue and tender. You wouldn't like it." Willa pouted. "Joel, I feel so stupid. How could I have gone chasing a five-year-old under tables in a restaurant?"

"You did it because that's just you, Willa. You couldn't let Justin get away with his behavior. You had to do what you had to do," Joel said with a smile. He leaned over and hugged her to him.

"I know, but it wasn't like we were in school and I was on duty. Justin's behavior today was his mother's business, not mine."

"Willa, maybe it's just being a mom…you can't just turn it on and off at will. Sometimes you just go into automatic," Joel offered.

"Yeah. Well, my poor body is really taking a beating with these students of mine. My back was already hurting from having to half-carry Jason yesterday during the fire drill at school. Even though they told us ahead of time so we could prepare our students in Special Ed, *and* even though we told them what to expect *and* we practiced in the classroom, when that alarm went off, there was mass confusion. There were those who cried, those who shut down and refused to move. There were those who tried to 'help' by pulling on their reluctant friends to get them moving.

"But Jason was the worst. Caleigh thinks he has hyper-sensitive hearing because he screamed like he was in agony. Then he flopped on the floor and held his hands over his ears. I tried to talk him into getting up but it became apparent he was just going to sit there, yelling and rocking till the alarm stopped. Well, the administration takes these drills very seriously and they wanted that building cleared ASAP. So, all I knew to do was to dead-lift that 65-pound 6-year old to his feet and then coax him to move forward. But he wasn't going to move. So, like I said, I half carried him to the playground. He calmed down pretty quickly after we were outside. I just pray we don't ever have a *real* fire," Willa sighed.

"Caleigh says we have to have a tornado drill on Monday. That's going to be even worse because with a tornado drill, we have to *stay* in the halls with the alarm blaring and practice taking cover." Willa sounded weary. "*That's* going to be a blast."

"Babe, I know it's hard," Joel said. "I just hope I can get some more hours at work soon. Then maybe you won't have to work there anymore."

"You know, Joel, I'm not wishing that at all. I just have to blow off steam sometimes. I really like my teacher. I like my students. It's just all so new to me. Everything is a learning experience. I just feel so out of my element. But I really find all of their different peculiarities to be fascinating. And I can't help loving them all. I just wish I knew more about all of this...all their conditions and how to best help them. Then maybe I could be more of a help to Caleigh."

"I think you've done great learning what you have already," Joel encouraged.

"Joel, you are my rock. You encourage me, even when I'm being impossible. I love you so much." Willa put her hand on Joel's cheek and drew his face to hers for a kiss.

"Well, you know, there is a way you can repay me," Joel smiled devilishly.

"Oh, yeah? And what would that be?"

"You and your bruised tushy could come here for a little somethin', somethin'." Still the devilish grin.

"Well, what are we going to do about the kids?"

"I'll lock the door just in case, but you know when they are out playing in the yard it is impossible to get them to come in."

"Okay," Willa smiled.

"Okay?"

"Yes, okay!"

Joel leaped off the bed and raced to the door. After peering down the hallway, he shut and locked it. Then, running back to his side of the bed he leaped on, again on his side, looking up at Willa and getting that all-too-familiar hazy-eyed look that meant he was ready to get down to business.

"Joel?"

"Hmmm?" He was guiding her down towards him.

"I think you're really going to like this."

"Why's that?" he murmured.

"'Cause this time, there's no jockeying about who's gonna be on top. It's definitely gotta be me Ouch!" she exclaimed as she rolled off her ice pack toward her very pleased husband.

* * *

The Monday following Willa's coffee shop encounter started off as a regular day, except for the fact that they did have a school-wide tornado drill. And, as expected, Jason was in hysterics the entire time. Caleigh had Willa just concentrate on Jason while she handled all the other children herself. Luckily, two speech teachers came over to assist where they could.

Try as she might, Willa simply could not soothe the boy. So, she ended up sitting on the hall floor with her back against the wall, holding him on her lap, her bruised tailbone griping at her the whole time. Then, when the "take cover" command came, Willa did her best to roll Jason over and she ended up just crouching over him, rubbing his back as he sobbed. The whole drill lasted less than 10 minutes, but with the siren blaring it seemed like a whole lot longer.

By the time the two women had herded their students back to the classroom, Willa had a throbbing headache and felt like she could use a break. But that's the thing about working as a teacher or an assistant in a special ed classroom: There are no breaks. The children have to be supervised at all times and they are all so needy. They need help getting their jackets off in the morning; they need help making lunch selections. They need help going to the bathroom and they need help when they don't make it in time. And all that assisting happens before any academics are covered. It was usually one of the women trying to instruct or work with small groups while the other was solving some minor crisis in the back of the classroom. But this morning, it would take both of them on bathroom duty.

The classroom was separated from the special ed classroom next door by a small storage hallway, connecting two bathrooms, each with a toilet, sink and shelves. The shelves contained a change of clothes per child, clean, spare underwear, wet wipes, plastic grocery bags for soiled items, gloves, even plastic aprons to cover the teacher's clothing.

After the drill, Jeff was sitting on one potty crying because he was constipated and couldn't go. Actually it was more like wailing than crying. Willa sat on a small chair in front of Jeff and coaxed him to "Push past the pain," feeling somewhat like a labor coach. Meanwhile, Jared managed to slip into the other bathroom because he had the opposite problem. He had already gone poo poo in his pants. The six-year old was physically large for his age, but emotionally, he was still just a toddler. When he got to the bathroom, the first thing he did was try to pull off his jeans and underwear. But he had forgotten to take his tennis shoes off first, so everything got stuck around his ankles. He tried to take short steps to the toilet, but ended up falling down, smearing the mess from his bottom to the floor.

Jared reached his hand around to his backside to "check things out," and came back with a handful of poo. Now what? Instinctively, he leaned over and wiped his hand onto the wall. Becoming more and more panicky with each new mess he created, the child finally managed to pull off his shoes, followed by the jeans and dirty underwear. He stood up, found his bag of clean clothes and got out fresh underwear. Without thinking to clean himself he put on the new pair and turned his attention to the wall. Hmmm. What to do? He spotted the wet wipes and emptied the whole box at once, scrubbing the foul mess and then plopping the un-flushable wipes into the potty.

About this time, Jeff finished his "deed" and was trying to clean his bottom, with Willa giving him directions from the chair. Out of the corner of her eye she noticed a small pool of water seeping from under the other bathroom door. Walking with great fear and trepidation toward the water, she leaned in and cautiously pushed the door open. She couldn't help it. She screamed.

"Ahhhhhh! Jared, what have you done?"

Standing before her, the boy smiled sheepishly, wearing only his poop-smeared socks and holding a plunger over the overflowing toilet bowl. "Hee hee," he laughed. "I pooped!"

"You sure did," Willa replied as she composed herself. Turning around, she saw all Jared's and Jeff's classmates gathering in the storage hall looking concerned for their very vocal friends. Caleigh was right behind them, suiting up like a "hazmat" clean- up crew.

"Boys, let's give our friends some privacy, please." Ms. Smith said. "Go back to centers and continue working. Mrs. Grizzard, call the custodians. They'll have to clean the bathrooms because we are going to have our hands full cleaning the two boys!"

Chapter 11

Jessa's walk to Conner's Market usually took her about 20 minutes. She had left Danny with Queenie, who had just finished the washing and had agreed to push her pesky "helper" in the backyard swing as a reward for his hard work. Jessa looked down at her drowsy second son, who was in his carriage, fighting hard to stay awake and watch the autumn-colored trees pass in and out of view overhead. The carriage's large rubber wheels tended to bounce the spring-supported chassis in a rocking motion, and the tires squeaked just loudly enough to make a nice rhythm but not so loud as to keep a sleepy baby awake.

It was a glorious, crisp, early October day and Jessa was enjoying this outing, which was one of only a few she made each week. It was to the market once or twice a week, then over to check on Mrs. McGraff, to visit with her and have a slice of one of her scrumptious cakes. Now that Jessa didn't go to church, that was about all, unless she had to go to the post office, the doctor or occasionally, the library. Sometimes, when she needed to, she'd drive Raymond into work and then take the car downtown to shop or over to Cartersville to see her elderly aunts. She hadn't done that in a long time. Her two younger sisters had moved with her parents when the railroad transferred her father to California almost a decade ago. That was right after Jessa and Raymond got married. Her brother was serving in the Air Force, stationed in France. So there really weren't that many people for her to go and see. With outings being such a rarity, it was no wonder she just about knocked Queenie down when she saw the postman put letters in the box. *She* was the one who checked the mail! It was *her* job...her chance to get out of the house even for the few minutes it took her to get to the curb and back. Her personal correspondence was her main source of staying in touch with the outside world.

Jessa was reconciled to her fate. She was the wife, the mother, the woman. And she wasn't complaining.....much. It just seemed that everything at home took so much longer than it used to. Like getting everybody up, fed, bathed and dressed in the mornings. Sometimes it was nearly 10:00 a.m. before Jessa could accomplish this task. By the time she and Queenie got all the bedrooms picked up and started the laundry in the backyard, it was time to get lunch for everyone.

Jessa's days were long and monotonous and they differed only in the way in which the inevitable crisis for Danny or Buster would erupt. For instance, did Danny get his favorite spoon to eat with—the one with the shepherd boy on the handle? If not, Jessa could count on him folding his little arms across his chest and with a frown, saying, "I will not eat wifout Shepherd Boy!" Jessa couldn't help but admire how Danny had started talking in complete sentences these days. Even if it was to argue with her.

Then of course Jessa would say, "Oh Danny, can't you eat your grits and ham without Shepherd Boy today?"

"No!" Still the crest-fallen countenance.

"Danny, Shepherd Boy's still dirty from dinner last night. You don't want to eat with a dirty spoon do you? See how Mommy is feeding Buster? You eat up too with the "big boy" spoon Mommy gave you so we can all go play outside in a bit."

"No, Mommy! *You* give Shepherd Boy a *baff!*"

Now Jessa 's admiration of her little rascal's growing intellect was definitely waning. In the days before Buster was born, Jessa would have put her foot down and insisted on obedience from Danny. But she knew this type of banter could go on indefinitely and she just didn't have the energy to argue.

So Jessa usually ended up getting up, digging the spoon out from the bottom of the stack of wet, slimy dishes in the sink and then washing it, drying it and handing it to Danny. He would then beam a smile up at his mother, just to let her know he was completely satisfied with himself. "Thank you," he said when Jessa gave him the look that meant he had better remember his manners. Next, he would plunge Shepherd Boy right into his grits and into his mouth, without another word. Buster, on the other hand, was not at all happy about having *his* breakfast interrupted, so the whole scene would set him off. Jessa felt like she ended up losing, no matter what she did.

By the time Jessa arrived at Conner's Market this particular morning, she looked down to see that Buster was definitely asleep now. So, she stepped up on the front stoop of the market and tried to back into the store, pulling the baby buggy in with her. But she'd forgotten the door pushed out to open and so, she worked the buggy back down the stoop. Jessa then reached up and pulled the door open, propped it ajar with her foot, and again tried to get the buggy up the step. Buster scrunched up his sleeping face in a frown, showing his displeasure with the bumping and thumping and commotion he and his carriage were being subjected to. Jessa gave another big tug on the carriage handlebar and felt it lift up onto the stoop. Grateful for small favors, Jessa pursed her lips and blew a wandering, blonde curl from her forehead. No wonder she usually made this trip to Conner's alone!

Stepping inside, the store was dark compared to the bright sun and blue, fall sky outside. The hanging door bells tinkled as Jessa pulled the door shut behind her. The smells of a variety of grains and spices, mixed with those of sawdust, shellac and the faint aroma of vinegar from the pickle barrel. Jessa's eyes began to adjust as she scanned the store, trying to make sure she didn't crash the stroller into any canned food displays that Dwight Conner may have put on special and set up in the aisles. She heard Dwight Jr., or D.W. as his family called him, before she saw him. He came trouncing out of the stockroom, riding a broomstick pony and wearing little red, leather cowboy boots with black trim and a red cowboy hat.

"Well, howdy, D.W.!" Jessa smiled at the boy who was about a year or so older than Danny. She looked forward to when Danny would be able to amuse himself for at least a little while with a broom pony.

"Hold it right there," D.W. said, pulling a toy pistol from his pocket. He pointed it at Jessa and said, "Ma'am, whatcha got in there?"

"Oh, this is precious cargo, D.W. It's a little fellow named Buster and I'm trying to help him escape from a horrible gang of bandits, who stole him from his Mama," Jessa played along.

"Lemme see," the boy lowered his sidearm and rode his "mount" over to get a look inside the carriage.

"See, he's sleeping now that he's in safe hands," Jessa allowed the little boy to pull down the blanket just a little so he could get a good look.

"Why's he sticking his tongue out?" the boy said, dropping his "sheriff's" voice.

"He's trying to show the bandits they didn't get the best of him."

"Why's his eyes so fat and bulgey?"

"Just are. Can't say why. That's a question for God. It's just how he made him." Jessa explained patiently.

"Oh." With that, the boy turned around and clopped off, leaving scuff marks from his boot heels on the hard wood floor.

Just then his father came out of the stockroom and stopped the boy by grabbing his shoulders. The grocer bent down to look him in the eye and said, "D.W., if you don't quit harassing my customers, you are going to have to stay at home with your mother."

"Noooo, Daddy, nooo! I like it here!"

"Well then, quit asking all those embarrassing questions, boy. Don't you know when to leave well enough alone?" he spoke in a whispered voice. Then Mr. Conner stood up but not before swatting his retreating son's bottom.

"I'm sorry about that, Mrs. Bland. The boy just hasn't learned not to ask personal questions yet. We're working on him though." He smiled apologetically at his customer.

"Oh, Mr. Conner, his questions are harmless enough. He just sees something and asks whatever comes into his mind, that's all. He's just like my boy at home." Jessa smiled back. "By the way, how's your fabric selection right now?" she asked, changing the subject.

"Got some heavier materials and some new colors in earlier this week. Take a look. You know where the sewing stuff is, right?" he motioned toward one side of the store.

Just then, the bell over the front door jingled and a man in a suit walked in. He removed his hat and walked up to the counter.

"Hi, Dwight. How're things going?" he said tiredly, as he slid a dollar across the counter. "Give me some tobacco and some rolling papers."

"Sure, George. Got it right here," the store owner hustled over to a cabinet near the cash register.

Jessa fingered a heavy wool fabric that would be perfect for a winter coat for Danny. Maybe Buster would be able to sit up without help soon, so he might need a coat too, instead of the blankets she had kept on him last winter.

"How's business, George?" Mr. Conner asked.

"Oh, you know, Dwight, this dang Depression just won't let up on us. I just hope Roosevelt's New Deal will help people out. I don't know how much more this country can take. You know, I read in the New York Times that a record number of women and children are in the bread lines up there. Now ain't that somethin'? Women and children having to stand in line for food with criminals, the feeble-minded and imbeciles. I tell you, George, this country would be doing us all a favor if they would just round up all the idiots and Mongoloids and the demented and either confine 'em so they will quit breeding, or go ahead and gas 'em all and be done with it. That may be the only thing the Nazis have right. The least they can do is fix 'em so they can't have children. Have you read about that? Eu…Eugenics I think it's called. Anyway, they're nothing but a bunch of leeches, draining society and taking food right out of the mouths of your children and mine. I hear they've built a fancy place for 'em up in Chesterfield County. My cousin, the state senator, he says they're asking the legislature for funds to put a swimming pool in for 'em! Can you believe it? Waste of money. I don't know what's going to happen to this country, Dwight, if we don't prioritize better."

Mr. Conner had been trying to stop the tirade that had just spewed from the other man's mouth, but he had been unable to interject even a word. Now, his eyes locked briefly with Jessa's, who was standing in the aisle, clutching her baby in her arms now. The customer turned around and followed Mr. Conner's gaze.

"Oh, hi, ma'am! How are you?" His tone suddenly sounded downright cheerful. "I didn't know you were back there. You know, while you're here, you really should look at the new pots and pans I brought for Dwight here to stock his shelves with. Stainless steel, all of 'em! Why there is no better cooking pot than a stainless steel one. Nice and heavy so they don't dent and pit from the heat. Food cooks more evenly. I'll be glad to get them out of my trunk and show you. Just wait right here." With that, the man grabbed his purchases and his change and ran out of the front door.

Mr. Conner just looked down at his shoes. Finally, he said, "Mrs. Bland, I'm sorry. George is just worried about feeding his family, like we all are. It makes him say things he shouldn't and I hope you….."

By the time Mr. Conner heard the jingle of the door bells, he lifted his eyes to see Jessa half out of the front door, still holding the baby in her arms, and the buggy giving her a hard time at the threshold. He raced to assist her, but by the time he got there, she had managed to yank the buggy from the grips of the door and was already furiously pushing the stroller toward home.

Just then, George came back up the front stoop carrying a box, presumably loaded with pots and pans…of the stainless steel variety, of course.

"Hey, lady, you haven't seen my pots yet!" he yelled after her. When she didn't acknowledge him at all, he muttered, "Dumb broad!"

Mr. Conner frowned down at him and said, "Shut up, George. Just shut up!"

* * *

The second winter of Buster's life was an especially tough time for Jessa. She had grown more and more isolated. After the encounter with the man at Conner's Market, she had decided that the world was just too mean for her to be involved. She would concentrate on her family and that would have to be enough. She wrote to her parents and her brother. She cooked and cleaned and sewed for Raymond, Danny and Buster. And she drew strength from the one person she could count on; Queenie.

In fact, Jessa's relationship with Queenie had slowly changed from employer/employee to one that felt more like a mentorship… Queenie, the older, wiser mentor to Jessa, the hurt, angry and depressed younger woman. Jessa had grown to depend on Queenie. She loved her matter-of-fact, upbeat way of handling things. Queenie was very dear to both children and they related to her more like a grandmother. A grandmother who laughed, fussed, and if need be, swatted a backside.

Jessa looked forward to Queenie arriving each morning with tales from her "other life." She would talk about her daughter, her grandchildren, her neighbors, her church friends. And together, Queenie and Jessa listened to the radio ministry of Velpo W. Montgomery on the Radio Bible Network.

"I just love Brotha Montgomery," Queenie would enthuse. "I feel like he's talking right to me over dat radio. He brings da' Bible stories to life," she would say.

"I know just what you mean, Queenie. Do you want me to read the story of David and Mephibosheth out loud again? I just want to reread it while Reverend Montgomery's message is still fresh on my mind."

"You go 'head, Ms. Jessa. I forgot my specs and I gotta peel these taters for dinner," Queenie replied. Jessa knew Queenie was illiterate, so she was glad she could read the passage for both of them.

As Jessa read, Queenie would interject a comment or a gasp or a sigh, depending on what the text called for. The two women truly had a bond over the Bible. And they also could be caught robustly singing along with the hymns on the radio, Danny dancing around them and Buster clutching his mama's skirt and trying to stand.

Those were the good times. But truthfully, they were all too brief and far between. The rest of the day could be exhausting for both women. Jessa had been anxious for her second son to develop more quickly *physically*. She thought he would never roll off his propping pillow and start to crawl, but when he finally did, things came very rapidly. In a matter of weeks, Buster went from belly scooting to outright crawling. Very soon afterward, he began to reach up and grab hold of something...anything...and pull himself up. He'd fall back down on his padded bottom quite often, but he was undeterred. He would still pull on anything he could reach...and that was the problem. He would pull on the dining room table cloth, noisily spilling the silver tea set Jessa kept on it. He would grab hold of a broom leaning in the corner, then pull himself up, only to find he was unsteady. Then falling face forward onto the corner of a table, Buster would yowl in pain and bring his mother and nanny running as fast as they could. Jessa kept hoping she would get somewhat used to the facial bruises and the ear-piercing cries. But she didn't. Instead, she just felt guiltier. She remembered Danny doing some of this, but when it was just the two of them, she was able to be there to prevent many falls. It broke her heart that she couldn't do the same for Buster.

There were many days in February when they could not even leave the house. First there was a rare, deep, southern snow fall, followed by temperatures dipping into the teens for over week. Jessa found it hard to muster the energy to bundle up her boys in four layers of clothing, boots and mittens, only to have them crying to go in from the cold after only a few minutes in the back yard. So, there were days…many of them…when they just stayed in the house. More specifically, they stayed in the kitchen, which they closed off from the back of the house, and used a large kerosene heater for warmth. Between it and the wood stove, the kitchen stayed quite warm. Raymond learned to come in the front door, close it quickly, walk through the chilled front room, where he could see his breath oftentimes, then slip through the kitchen door, quickly shutting it behind him. By not using the outside kitchen door, the room never lost a huge amount of heat and didn't have a chill come into it that had to be endured until the heat sources could ward it off. So toasty was the kitchen that the boys could sit around in their undershirts.

But Jessa found the cramped, indoor living to be claustrophobic. She was always worried that Danny or Buster would burn themselves on the stove or topple over the kerosene heater and cause a fire. She got tired of reading the same books to them, of playing the same "Eye Spy" game. Even their meals were mundane. Corn bread and some sort of meat, if Raymond got to stop at the meat market. She would open a jar of corn or beans that she had canned last fall. Lunch might be soup. Breakfast was grits and biscuits.

Jessa knew that she and Raymond had it better than many did during this damn Depression. But she found it harder and harder to be grateful. After all, they had a 21 month old who still couldn't walk. And Jessa didn't know what to do about it.

During one of those cold February mornings, Raymond had left to go get Queenie. Jessa had stuck her cold nose under her blanket and was preparing to turn over and go back to sleep. But, she could hear Buster "yelling" for her from his crib.

"Maaaa," he called in his hoarse voice. He sounded like a goat, she thought.

"Maaaaaaa," he persisted.

After his fourth call, she could hear Danny's padded feet hit the floor and shuffle over to his brother's crib. "Mommy, Buster's ready to get up," he said, yawning sleepily.

Danny was after her too, she thought. What would they do if she just lay there? Queenie would be here soon enough. Maybe *she* could get the boys up and feed them. So, Jessa snuggled down deep into her mattress and shut her eyes tight. After not hearing anything from the boys, other than a giggle or two, Jessa started to doze.

She woke with a start to the distant sound of a crash. Her bare feet hit the wood floor before she was even fully alert. She ran from her bedroom, not bothering with a robe, then across the den that separated her room from the boys. Nothing. She turned a bit frantically and opened the door that closed the back part of the house off from the front room. Cold air greeted her and crept quickly under her gown and up her legs. Jessa scarcely felt it. Where were they? As she bound across the front room, and pushed open the kitchen door, she heard Queenie coming in the front door. Raymond always dropped her off and went straight to the office without coming back inside.

Jessa quickly scanned the kitchen. Raymond's coffee cup and dirty breakfast plate sat on the counter to the right. She looked to the left and felt a chill go up her spine that no weather front could match. Danny and Buster were next to the overturned kerosene heater, in a huge puddle of fuel. Their pajamas were soaked in it. Danny was holding a stick of wood with fire on the end of it and the wood stove door stood wide open, embers glowing in its gut.

Queenie came up behind Jessa and said in a stern voice, "Danny, don' you drop that stick, boy. Whatever you do, you keep hold of it, you hear?"

Jessa sobbed, "Danny, come here to Mommy."

"No, boy, don' come. Just stay put right where you at. Queenie is coming to get the stick." The old lady pushed past Jessa and, without letting her feet touch the kerosene puddle, firmly took the stick from Danny's hand. She threw it into the stove, slammed the door and carefully lifted Danny out of the kerosene. Turning, Queenie handed him to Jessa. Going back over to the puddle, she knelt down right at the edge and coaxed Buster to come to her. Holding her arms open wide, she said, "Buster, you come to Queenie!"

The little boy's fat, pudgy cheeks scrunched up into a crinkly smile. He leaned forward and crawled toward Queenie. Holding up his little arms when he got to her, the old woman took the opportunity to slip his night gown over his head and immediately dropped it to the floor. As she held him up, she ripped the plastic pants and soaked diaper off him as well and lifted the naked baby with her strong arms.

Queenie's eyes met Jessa's panicked ones as she urged, "Go ahead and take off Danny's gown and pants, too, Ms. Jessa." Jessa did as she was told. Both women carried their precious cargo out the kitchen door, across the front room and into the heated back of the house.

When they closed the door and looked at one another, Jessa lost control. She started sobbing and moaning, making a guttural noise deep from her stomach. What had she done? How could she be so lazy and stupid? How could she put her children at risk by leaving them unattended, even for a few moments? Queenie admonished her to "Get control of yo'self, Ms. Jessa. The boys are watching you to see if everything is okay." Jessa took a deep breath and let it out. The boys needed baths.

* * *

Later, as the women were pulling Buster and Danny out of the tub and toweling them off, Jessa was still in a state of stunned disbelief and embarrassment. Her bloodshot blue eyes met Queenie's calm, liquid-brown ones.

"I can't do this anymore," she said. "I am a horrible mother and I can't be trusted with these boys. I'm telling Raymond tonight."

"Now hold it right there, Ms. Jessa. You a good mother. You love yo' children a lot. You take good care of 'em.

"No, I don't! They go for days without leaving this house and today, I almost lost them both. I don't deserve to be a mother."

"Ms. Jessa," Queenie was standing, holding Buster's toweled body. "You having yo'self a pity party. And that's okay. You got it tougher than some. But you got it better than a whole lot of other folks. These boys are yo' crowning glory! Now don't talk like that ever again. The good Lord wants a thankful heart, not a complainin' one. Let's get up and go get 'em breakfast.

Jessa turned to lift Danny out of the tub, wrapped him in a towel and followed silently behind Queenie's determined gait. She'd have to pull it together. After all, if she didn't take care of these boys, who would?

CHAPTER 12

T he outer office of the Goldmine Elementary School was decorated with framed student artwork. The receptionist was busy with a non-English speaking family, who were trying to register their son for school. Ms. Cook was bustling back and forth between Mr. Johnson's office and her own. Willa sat on a couch just outside the principal's office, trying to relax and reason that she had been called there for some innocuous conversation with her boss.

She thought back over her three months as a Special Education Parapro and couldn't believe all she had learned and how far she'd come. Now she didn't hesitate to wolf down her lunch as she tried to instruct the two or three children who sat around her in proper dining etiquette. "Sadar, use a fork and start eating your chicken nuggets. Lunch will be over soon. Maleeke, you need to leave the napkins alone and stop pulling them out of the holder. You have 12 of them already and *definitely* stop stuffing that one up your nose!"

Willa had come to realize that these kids were, overall, better behaved in the lunch room than most of the regular ed. kids. Most of her students were serious eaters, looking forward to lunch all day. After they finally managed to wait in line, get their tray, drink and silverware, order what they wanted and make it to their assigned table, they were focused entirely on the food before them. The rest of the kindergarteners were playing with their food, talking loudly, picking on each other and getting up and down from the table to harass another student. Willa's students were quiet when "the music" was on, which played on a loop to allow each lunch period to have 15 of their 30 minutes in relative silence, so students could focus on eating their lunch.

But the problem for Willa was that the loop never changed. The same dozen, tired songs played over and over so that she could time their lunch schedule around the songs. Mozart's "Spring" played as they walked in, followed by the Beatle's song, "Yesterday" (the elevator version, of course). Next came two other classical pieces, an instrumental version of an old Carpenter's song, the 1970s movie theme for "Love Story," several instrumental versions of old Motown hits, finally culminating in a Liberace' piano piece that worked into a crescendo and ended abruptly after that. It was the Liberace song that, for some reason, got three or four of Willa's student's furiously shaking their heads in time with the music. It didn't take long for the whole class to copy their friends and join in with relish, shaking their heads as the music rose and fell. Caleigh and Willa tried desperately to intervene when the song started, using any distraction they could think of.

Usually, they would instruct the boys to, "start cleaning up." It was always their joint goal to prevent their students from losing dignity among their peers.

Lunch was followed by what Willa had come to feel was the worst time of the day.....dumping lunch trays and using the hall bathroom. The lunch trash cans were marked with different colored plastic bags. All students were expected to move through the line, efficiently pouring leftover milk into the blue container, placing the cartons into the red one, the leftover food in the black one and finally making it to the dishwasher's window, where they were to stack their trays and place silverware into a separate basket. Willa's class's trouble with the process started at the table with cleanup. But Caleigh was firm that everyone had to pick up after themselves, carry their own trays, to the best of their ability, and learn to sort like all the other students. This was no small task. The children were stubborn about leaving the leisure of lunch time, so it wasn't uncommon for one of them to stage their own "sit down" at the table, causing one teacher to be totally consumed with issuing warnings, telling the consequences or offering a bribe, if need be.

Willa learned by watching Caleigh that she didn't have to hold them accountable for every little thing, as long as they were moving in the right direction. Some things got overlooked, just so they could keep the class moving.

A few of the students were very capable of cleaning up and getting through the line. Their struggle was what to do while they were waiting for the others. They impulsively ran up on the stage, which was at one end of the cafeteria. Willa wondered whose bright idea it was to put it there. Or they would play behind the drapes to the side of the stage. They might wander off or get into a knock-down/drag out fight over who was line leader and therefore got to stand in a certain spot. Willa and Caleigh would try to keep one eye peeled on this group while helping the slower students precariously balance their trays on the walk to the trash cans. If there was a long line at the cans, it was almost certain one of the students would tire out and drop their milk, spill food or even send their whole tray crashing to the floor. The custodians, who were lined up at the dishwasher window would slowly, tiredly walk to the mop closet and come over to clean up the mess. In the meantime, Willa would try to straddle the spill to keep others from sliding in it.

Jason, who was inevitably the last in line, had his own issue; he was fixated on the dishwashing machine inside the window. He would make his way up to the window and then plant himself, jaw slack in fascination, and watch as the lunch ladies slid the trays and plastic silverware baskets into the open end of the machine. The conveyor belt pulled the items deep inside the washer, sending sprays of steaming water all over them.

Jason just stood and watched, even as the next class in line was backing up behind him. The other children would grumble loudly, "Hey, move out of the way!" but Jason didn't care. He had an uncanny sense of his own balance and was very strong. So when he planted himself, Willa could try to urge, prod, pull or stretch him along and all she did was get one foot off the ground. He managed to stand there on the other foot, grunting his complaint at being bothered and it wasn't until Caleigh came to lend a hand that there was enough strength between them to unearth him, with Jason squalling in protest all the way to the line of his classmates.

All of this was a daily occurrence and provided a great spectacle for the other teachers, students, staff and visiting parents. What made Willa angrier than anything else was when some adult, either a parent or even a teacher would treat her like a "saint." They would look at her in a pitying way. Some of them didn't stop with a look. There was one Kindergarten parapro who would regularly come up to Willa and whisper, "Poor you. I have no idea how you can deal with all that. It would drive me crazy!" The first few times this happened, Willa was too shocked that someone who was in the teaching profession would make such an ignorant remark. So she responded with a weak smile and silence. But she vowed next time she would be ready with a reply.

Once they were through the cleanup line, the real fun began. Caleigh would have dismissed the boys to the bathroom, especially if they were running late for Specials. By the time the two of them had dislodged Jason from the window, there would be quite a ruckus coming from the bathroom. The teachers just never knew what they would find upon entry. Not paying a bit of attention to the fact that it was a boys' restroom, the two women would burst upon the scene, sending any regular ed. students scurrying out in shock. Some of them would be caught in the act of trying to get the boys from special ed. to do things they knew they shouldn't... like crawling on the floor under doors they'd locked from the inside, or bullying the boys by blocking the stalls so no one could use them. There was usually two or three of Willa's boys playing in the large round spray sink, shirts soaked to the elbows. The next few minutes were spent scraping children off the floor, helping them wash their hands, buttoning pants (that were just a *little* wet with urine!) and wiping faces. They could end up unstopping sinks, wiping bottoms, cleaning stalls or who-knows-what, all the while trying to maintain the students' privacy and dignity as much as possible. The goal, after all, was to help these children eventually be able to visit a public restroom independently.

Inevitably, Justin would park himself in one of the stalls to have his daily bowel movement. It was just "his time" of day. He would strip from the waist down, shoes, socks and all, while Caleigh and Willa were distracted with the others. Then he would sit, legs folded crisscross applesauce style, on the pot. It took him some time to relax and he was usually a good five or more minutes behind everyone else. When bathroom time was finally over and they were once again plodding down the hall toward Specials, Willa couldn't help but feel she needed a good, hot bath.

But this morning, Assistant Principal Patty Long had stuck her head in Caleigh's classroom and asked Willa to come to Mr. Johnson's office as soon as the morning was underway and Caleigh could spare her. Caleigh had no idea what was going on, so the two of them speculated about it all morning. Was she being moved to another class? Was she being reprimanded? How about praised? Who knew?

So here Willa sat, with just 25 minutes until lunch time, waiting to see the principal. If she could just time this right, maybe she'd miss today's "lunch performance" altogether. No, she thought, that would be too unfair to Caleigh.

Finally, Ms. Cook said, with irritating efficiency, "Willa, you can go on in."

Inside the office, Willa was met with Mr. Johnson's chair back. He was on his computer and did not acknowledge her entry.

When he finally turned around, Willa tried smiling. "Hi, Paul. Am I in trouble?"

"Sit down, Willa. Let me buzz Mrs. Long to sit in with us." Uh oh. He needed a witness. Willa felt a bead of sweat roll down her spine and onto her underwear waist band. What was going on?

Mrs. Long came into the office with a fake kind of chirpiness. "Hey, Paul. I just told Cathy to order lunch from Ippilito's. I was craving Italian." She swished across the room to a chair on Mr. Johnson's side of the desk.

"Thanks, Patty. Willa, thanks for coming. We wanted to do a brief evaluation of your work so far. Is that okay with you?"

"Okay, sure," Willa replied with hesitation. Was it a human resources requirement that they get her to agree to undergo what was beginning to feel a bit like a court sentencing?

Patty started out. "Willa, when we hired you 90 days ago, you had no experience with Special Needs children, did you?"

Willa shook her head "no."

"Well, now you do! How do you like it?"

"I feel very close to the children and am learning a lot from Caleigh. No two days are ever the same. I think I have picked up quite a bit. I feel like in many ways, working with these children is really no different than working with regular ed students. They all need patience, firm guidance, discipline and love."

"Well, yes, Willa. That's true. But this student population *is* very different from other students as well."

"Sure. Our guys have obstacles to overcome. But again, patience, guidance, discipline and love go a long way to leveling the field," Willa asserted.

"Willa, I guess what I am asking is, do you realize just how fragile these children can be? I mean we feel that perhaps this is an area where you can grow professionally. The students you work with are not 'just like all the others.' They have very real disabilities and you have to make allowances for that."

"I guess I don't really understand what you mean and how it pertains to me," Willa said flatly.

At this, Principal Johnson leaned across his desk. "Willa, we in education have a mandate to serve all students, regardless of their handicaps. So, we are trying to do our best here at Goldmine Elementary to do just that for all our student sub-populations. But in the meantime, we want you to realize that Special Education is a hotbed of controversy and we have to walk a fine line between serving these children and overstepping our boundaries. Do you understand what I am saying?"

"Not exactly. Have I done something wrong in working with these children?"

"Willa, we are concerned about all that goes on in the lunchroom with your class. We have heard comments about you being pretty rough with some of the students. Does Caleigh tell you to do that? Because you know we are really not supposed to put our hands on any student. That's a good way to get slapped with a lawsuit," Principal Johnson explained.

"Well how would you suggest I clean their bottoms without putting my hands on them, Mr. Johnson?" Willa was getting just a wee bit hot. "Or how about wiping their noses? Buttoning their pants? How do I do those things without touching them? And no, Caleigh and I don't talk about touching the children. We just do what has to be done. I am sorry about how crazy things get in the cafeteria, but it is a very difficult set of circumstances for our boys to grasp and we have to guide them through the process every day."

"Yes, Willa, we understand. But we just want you to avoid putting your hands on the students in such a public place as the lunchroom. Others don't understand that you mean well."

Mean well? What she meant was for the students to learn to follow directions the first time. "I see. Well, I'll try to work on that," Willa conceded. "Is that the only problem?"

"There is one other thing," Mrs. Long interjected. "Did you run into Jason and his mother at the Starbucks Café just a few weeks ago?"

Uh-oh again. "Yes, but it was more like a couple of months ago," Willa again gave in.

"Well, a member of the county's Special Ed department happened to be there at the same time and was alarmed at your behavior. It really is concerning when we get a report like this from the county office, Willa," Mrs. Long said.

"I was trying to help his mother get him out from under a table," Willa protested.

Mr. Johnson interrupted. "Yes, Willa, we heard all about it. We were told that two businessmen were caught up in your actions as well. Do you realize how you opened the county up for a potential lawsuit?"

Again the lawsuit thing. "I guess I never really thought about that. I just try to do what seems right at the time."

"Well, that's the problem. What seems right to you may not be right when it comes to county policy. And county policy says you should avoid touching students whenever possible. It seems like you pull and push on them at the drop of a hat."

"Now, wait a minute!" Willa defended. "I use what I call a 'helping hand' on the back or shoulders to help guide them in the right direction. I don't 'manhandle' them, if that is what you mean. But these kids are stubborn and don't want to do what they don't want to do. Asking them politely or giving them to the count of three doesn't work. I do know that."

"All we are saying is that you need to be conscious of how you handle one of our more fragile student populations."

"Fragile! Ha!" Willa laughed. "Do you know what my back is like when I get home? These are big, strong boys who want to do things their way. It's our job to teach them to cooperate so they can eventually fit into society more seamlessly."

"No, it's our job to make sure they stay safe and well cared for until we put them on the bus for home."

Babysitting? Is that what she'd been hired to do? "I feel like we do more than just that."

"And that's our point, Willa. We want you to stop trying to do more and just simply watch over these children and keep them clean, well-fed, and safe. Okay?" Mrs. Long's perkiness had given way to bluntness.

"All right. I see." Willa was so off-kilter from all that was said that she didn't have anything else to say. As they wound up the meeting, Willa stood to go and Mrs. Long called to her one last time.

"Willa? If I were you, I'd look into getting some extra insurance to protect your assets in case you are ever sued personally by one of these parents. It's not mandatory, but it would just be a good idea for you. You can contact the State Teacher's Union about it, okay?"

"Okay," Willa said, not buying for a moment the other woman's concerned tone for her. "I'll look into it."

Willa left the office feeling bruised and beaten up. She was outraged that two people who sat behind their desks and judged her could make her feel so bad. She shuffled toward the lunchroom, looking for Caleigh to see where she needed to jump in.

She found her class stopped in the hall in front of the cafeteria. Jeff was sitting on the floor right in the middle of the line. Willa glanced at Caleigh.

"He's upset that he can't order lunch today. He brought his lunch and I didn't order him a cafeteria lunch today. I was trying to prepare him for that fact and he staged a "sit down.""

"I see." Willa rolled her eyes. "Well, from what I've just been told, we are to coax him into standing up and proceeding without laying a finger on him. So do you want me to do that or continue with the group into the cafeteria?"

"Oh, dear," Caleigh responded to Willa's upset face. "I'll take care of Jeff if you can get everybody else through the lunch line."

"Okay," Willa replied.

So Willa stood in front of the line and said, "Boys, let's go to lunch." That was all it took to get the big eaters moving. The rest of the students followed. Going through the lunch line was always a frenzied affair. So Willa tried to react preemptively and stood in front of each boy as they reached in to make their selections. "That's it Justin. Just one French fry for you. Jason, just one hamburger for you!"

She continued on till the whole group was at the table, settling in from the chaos of the lunch line. Caleigh and Jeff eventually joined them too. "I promised him computer time this afternoon if he would get up." Caleigh whispered the explanation. Again, Willa rolled her eyes.

Caleigh sat next to her and said gently, "Tell me more about what the admin's had to say."

Willa, on the brink of tears, relayed the scene from the office. "They reprimanded me for doing the job no one else wants. For doing the best I can." She let out a little sob.

"Ms. Smith, why is Mrs. Grizzard crying?" Jon wanted to know. He looked at her with deep sympathy in his eyes. "Is she hurt?"

"Well, Jon. She is hurt. But it's her feelings inside that hurt. Not her outside."

"Oh," Jon replied, nodding his head wisely, like he could relate to Willa's hurts.

Willa dried her eyes and looked at Caleigh. "What am I doing wrong? Tell me the truth! I thought I was doing so well!"

Caleigh said, "You are doing well. You're doing a great job, especially since you have never done this sort of thing before. It's just a fact of life in Special Ed. You are going to get reprimanded. There's twice as much paperwork, twice as much oversight and twice as many reprimands."

"Gosh, then why even put up with all of this? If you can't hope to please your bosses and get professional recognition, then why stick with this?" Willa dabbed at her eyes with her napkin.

Caleigh moved her food around on her plate with her fork. Then she looked up and said, "I had to realize a long time ago that getting the recognition I felt I 'deserved' could not be my professional goal. I had to realize that I am doing this for the kids. I just have to keep my head down and work with these children to the best of my ability. So when I get reprimanded, and I do occasionally get called out for something, I have to realize that they don't understand what I'm all about with my class. They are worried about lawsuits and stuff. I just have to pick myself up and dust myself off and continue on with my work. It's not easy but that's just how it is."

"You can't be that selfless," Willa asserted. "We all need positive feedback to thrive."

"I get that feedback. From the parents of my students. Most of them love me for taking their child for the day and teaching them simple skills that will help them at home and out in the real world. I also get positive feedback from my fellow Special Ed teachers. And I get it from these kids themselves. Every time one of them remembers to hang up their coat when they come to class, or they recognize a new letter or number, I know that I am doing what I'm supposed to do. It fulfills me." Caleigh smiled and said, "Willa, you and I know we are as careful as we can be with these boys. But from now on, we will have to be especially careful with our gang when we are out of the privacy of our classroom."

Willa nodded, as she felt a little better. She would have to process all that had happened today. She was suddenly aware of all the eyes on them and she knew she, for sure, was going to start being more careful with the students outside the classroom.

CHAPTER 13

Raymond had started to enjoy a whiskey or two after work. He usually got home after Jessa had the boys in bed and the drink helped relax him. He reached into the cabinet where he kept his bottle, up high out of the reach of the kids...and Jessa. Raymond knew she never approved of alcohol in the house. It seemed after the whole Prohibition experiment went wrong that liquor brought out extreme feelings in folks. Either they thought it was the Devil's elixir or it was nectar from heaven. There was rarely an in-between sentiment. Raymond knew where he stood on the issue....and he knew where Jessa stood.

He opened the ice cooler. Jessa kept a bowl with a few chips of ice she chiseled from the block they had delivered every few days. The drip pan needed emptying, he noticed. Raymond poured the melted ice from the tray and re-inserted it under the ice block. Then he grabbed a few ice chips for his glass. Pouring the honey-colored liquid over the ice, he then added just a splash of water from the spigot. Perfect.

Jessa came into the kitchen from the back of the house. She stopped short upon noticing Raymond's glass, but said nothing and quickly got to warming Raymond's supper. While he waited, he smoked a cigarette.

"Raymond, thank you for coming home early. Danny is listening to the radio and he's clean and fed," she started with her instructions. "You can read him a story and he'll be ready for bed. Make sure he pottys first and don't forget to brush his teeth. He'll want Lambie and Blankie in the bed with him. I'll be home with Buster at about 9:00. Do you think you'll be okay?"

"For crying out loud, Jessa, of course I'll be okay and so will Danny," Raymond slung back the last swig of his cocktail. "Just go, have fun and don't do anything too 'spooky,'" he joked. Jessa looked nice. Mighty nice. She had on lipstick, a saucy hat and one of her spring dresses that he didn't get to see her in very often. "Or you could put the boys to bed and stay right here with me. You wanna?" he asked hopefully.

"Raymond, you know me and Queenie have been planning to go to hear Brother Montgomery tonight since we heard he was coming last winter. I gotta go! It's Buster's only chance to have a normal life."

Raymond's eyes followed his wife's hips swishing back and forth as she bustled around the kitchen to prepare his meal. Her dress plunged at the neck line just a little lower than her normal ones and his eyes traced her figure. Getting up, and almost toppling his chair backwards, he crossed the kitchen and came up behind Jessa. Circling his wife's waist with his arms and burying his face deep in the hair at the nape of her neck he moaned, "Oh, Jessa, stay with me! You and Queenie go another night."

"Raymond!" she playfully pushed him away and started working on his plate again. "You'll mess me up. And I gotta go! I hear Buster and Danny fussing. I'll be back."

"I know, at 9:00," he said resentfully.

Jessa placed the plate before her hungry husband, hoping it would satisfy him, and pranced out of the kitchen, across the living room and into the den. They kept the doors open now that the weather was warmer and the house felt more like a home and less like a series of rooms separated by closed doors. She found the boys struggling together, Buster standing behind Danny, holding onto a handful of Danny's blonde hair and Danny protesting and trying to untwine his brother's hands.

"Buster, let go of Danny's hair!" Jessa fussed, a little more strongly than she felt. She knew that Buster was just using Danny to pull up on and balance himself. Besides, nothing could ruin tonight for her. It was the final night of Velpo Montgomery's tent revival and there was another traveling evangelist who would be there for a special healing service. That's the part that truly thrilled Jessa's heart. She, Queenie and Buster would go to the service and she would present Buster for healing.

Kneeling before Danny, she smoothed his hair and lightly kissed his check, more to sooth his upset feelings than to address any sort of real injury.

"Danny, Buster didn't mean to pull your hair. You know he just grabs hold of the nearest thing to steady himself. He hasn't been walking very long. Do you forgive him?"

"No!" pouted Danny dramatically. He had had his hair pulled and now he was about to be left. "I don' forgive him! He is the meanest brother ever!"

"Oh, Danny, Buster doesn't mean anything by it. He's not being mean; he's just figuring out the world. You did things like that to me when you were learning to walk," Jessa remembered, although Danny had been a good 10 or 15 pounds lighter and at least a full year younger.

Jessa suspected Danny's tears might be more about her and Buster going out without him than any physical suffering he may have endured at the hands of his brother.

"Danny, I tell you what. Daddy is eating supper right now in the kitchen. As soon as he's finished, you two can have a special night together, playing and reading and all kinds of stuff."

"I want to go with you and Queenie," Danny conspicuously left out his assailer.'

"Not tonight, Danny," Jessa, who was still kneeling between her two sons, looked into Danny's blue eyes. "You know, Daddy has been counting on being with you tonight. It would disappoint him so much if you didn't stay to play with him."

Danny looked less than convinced. "What are we gonna do? Daddy will just read the paper and listen to the radio."

"No. I heard it straight from him. He is really counting on building a blanket fort tonight. So he's really going to need your help with that. What do you say?"

Danny couldn't resist his mother's charms any longer. He grinned and grabbed her hand, pulling her up from the floor. He didn't stop there. He dragged her through the door of the den, across the living area and into the kitchen. No Daddy. Jessa went back to pick up Buster and returning to the kitchen noticed the screen door was unlatched from the inside. He was trying to escape!

"Come on, Danny!" Jessa grabbed her boy's hand and pushed her way through the screen door. No Raymond. She could smell the smoke coming from Raymond's cigarette. She looked to her left and noticed the side door to the garage was open. A thin trail of smoke came curling out of the opening, carried along by big band music floating from the car radio. Jessa, still carrying Buster, dropped Danny's hand stepped down off the stoop, trying to get to her husband before Danny could. When she burst into the garage she saw Raymond sitting behind the steering wheel of the Buick. He had his eyes closed, one arm folded behind his head and a fresh drink in the other hand. Saboteur!

Jessa quickly walked up to the car, reached through the open window, grabbed Raymond's drink out of his hand and before he knew she was there, dashed the liquid on the compacted dirt floor between the two paved strips that the car was parked on.

Raymond sat up with a start, dropping the cigarette from between his lips. "Jessa, cut it out!" Raymond was more startled than mad. "What did you go do that for? It's a waste of perfectly good bourbon!"

"I'll tell you what's a waste: me trying to go anywhere and leave you with your children! You've known about this for weeks and you said I could go. You said you would watch Danny and play with him. Now all you want to do is smoke and get drunk. Just forget it. I'll just stay home."

Raymond had recovered his wits by now and came up behind Jessa's retreating back. He gently put his hands on her shoulders to stop her. "Jessa, I'm sorry! I won't drink any more tonight, I promise. I want you to get to go. I know how important this is to you."

"Not to *me* Raymond! To us! This is important to our whole family. To Buster! God can heal him! Don't you want that?"

Raymond had turned his wife around to face him. He dropped his forehead to touch hers, still holding her shoulders. "Jessa, you know I want that! I'd die to make that happen! It's just I don't have as much faith as you do. I don't believe this is going to work. I don't want you to have to go through any more pain or disappointment. That's all."

Jessa pulled her face back from Raymond's. "Don't say that! You've got to believe! Queenie has gone to this Healer's services before and she has seen people who she knew were crippled walk! She's seen sick friends healed! We just have to have faith! *Both* of us!"

"Okay, Jessa, okay. I have faith. I have faith that God can do anything he wants to do. I just hope he wants to heal Buster."

Jessa pulled away, still not satisfied with Raymond's response. She turned to walk inside, Danny trailing along behind her. "If I am going to go, I have to leave right now to go get Queenie. Come inside now, Raymond. Danny has big plans for your night together."

Raymond ran his fingers through his hair and let out a sigh. He just didn't have a good feeling about all of this. Still, he opened the garage door, got in the car and gingerly backed it out. Leaving it running, he closed the garage side door, entered the house through the kitchen and found Danny running in with a stack of blankets.

"Oh, I see! A blanket fort it is then, Danny!"

Jessa could hear her oldest son squeal in delight as she pulled the front door shut and carried Buster to the waiting car.

* * *

It was late when Jessa pulled the car into the garage. She shut off the motor, then walked to pull the garage door down. Next she lifted her slumbering son from the back seat of the Buick and entered the house through the kitchen. Everything was dark and Jessa chose to keep it that way, stopping to allow her eyes to adjust. Where was that flashlight? She opened a cabinet with one hand and cradled Buster with the other. There it was. That would help her make it to the back of the house without falling.

She shone a path of light ahead of her and quietly made the way to her bedroom. Raymond was asleep, snoring lightly from his side of the bed. She didn't dare shine the light in his direction and in fact decided to shut it off all together so that she didn't disturb him. As she crossed from the doorway to her dressing table she suddenly became entangled in something long and soft. Tripping slightly, she landed with one hand on the dressing table. "Thump." A bottle of hand lotion tumbled from the table and perfume bottles clanked together. Buster let out a howl in protest. The blanket fort! She'd walked right into it. Jessa shushed Buster, bouncing him in her arms slightly, but she could tell Raymond was stirring.

"Jessa? Is that you?"

"Yeah," she whispered. "I just tripped over the fort."

"You okay?"

"Yeah."

Something about his wife's voice made him snap on his bedside lamp. He could see her stepping out of a swath of blankets and walking toward him. When the dim light hit her face, Raymond could see that Jessa had been crying.

"Jessa, what's the matter?" Jessa gently lay Buster on the foot of the bed and fell across it to Raymond's chest.

"Oh, Raymond, I can't believe all that went on tonight."

Raymond sat up as best as he could without disturbing Jessa or Buster. "Tell me all about it, hon."

And she did.

"I picked up Queenie at a little after 7:00. Then we drove across town to the empty lot between Hanson's Hardware and the lumber yard. Only it wasn't empty. There was a huge tent set up and people everywhere! Hundreds of them. It was the last night of the Revival and everyone was jockeying for a seat.

"Queenie hung back with the other coloreds and I went to find a chair so I could sit down with Buster. I had a hard time walking in the sawdust that covered the floor and I wanted Queenie with me so she could help with Buster but she wouldn't come into the seating aisles. So I just sat down alone.

"Raymond, they had the best choir! About 75 people, some from churches around here and some from churches from other towns. They sang like angels! There was a piano and an organ. It was like I was going to see a show!

"I could have left after the singing and felt like I had had a little glimpse of heaven, but then Reverend Velpo Montgomery started preaching. He was filled with the Holy Spirit, Raymond and spoke the most wonderful message about Jesus casting out demons from a man and putting them into pigs! It was so uplifting and gave me a sense of hope! Again, I felt satisfied for myself, but that wasn't why I'd come. I'd come to have Buster healed."

Raymond looked skeptically at the sleeping child on the foot of his bed. He looked exactly the same as he always had.

"So then it was time for the visiting Healer to come to the stage. His name was Leroy Duncan. He was so old, Raymond, I thought he might need to be healed himself before the service was over! He was large, and had wrinkles that almost closed his eyes completely. Anyway, he jumped up on that stage like a 20-year old man! That got the crowd going. Everyone was saying, 'Amen brother!' And 'Praise the Lord!' Stuff like that.

"So Reverend Duncan spoke awhile about having faith like a mustard seed and about a woman in the Bible who had touched Jesus' hem, just expecting to be healed, and she was! Finally, he issued the invitation. He asked anyone who needed healing to step forward. Raymond, I'm not kidding you. I almost couldn't get up! My legs were like mush, partly from emotions and partly from holding Buster so long. That's when I felt a strong hand under my arm, helping me to my feet. Queenie! She took Buster from me and the three of us walked to the front.

"We were behind a few other people. An old woman had fainting spells and Reverend Duncan and Reverend Velpo and some other men with the Revival laid their hands on her. She seemed to feel she was healed! The music was so strong and the men were so earnest. I had a feeling that God himself was right there with us!

"Then, it was a farmer from Hartsville who had caught his hand in his mower while he was trying to clean it. His arm was still attached but it was all twisted and maimed. The Reverends spent a long time with him, praying, crying out to God for mercy and healing. When they finally laid hands on him, the farmer cried out too and it seemed like his arm was loosening up! I just about fell out myself. I wanted it to be my turn so badly. But there was an albino child and another farmer with a head injury before us.

"Finally, Raymond, it was our turn. When Reverend Duncan looked at me he asked, 'Who is it in need of healing?' I could scarcely speak. I said, 'My child.' And he said, 'What ails him?' and I said, 'He's a mongoloid, sir.' So Reverend Duncan stared at me and Buster and Queenie for a long time. Finally he said, 'Ma'am, in my experience, the Lord doesn't often reverse these things. He's given this child to you for a reason.' And I said,

'Please, sir, we've come here tonight just so my son can be healed. Will you please try? Please!'

"He looked at me with the wisest eyes and stepped back and talked to the others. Raymond, I just about turned around and ran out. I couldn't stand the possibility that they wouldn't even try! But then Reverend Duncan came to me and said, 'The Lord's Will be done.'

So both Reverends took off their jackets and knelt down beside us, mumbling prayers, some I could understand and some I couldn't. Then they asked for a special hymn and a woman came out and sang, 'Great is Thy Faithfulness.' Reverend Duncan asked for the crowd to pray out loud and I prayed out loud too. So did Queenie. I asked God to please take this child's mind and heal it. I told Him how badly I wanted my son to be normal. I told Him that I had learned my lesson and that I wouldn't take His goodness for granted any more. I told God that I believed He could do anything and would He please, please, please give me back a normal son!"

Jessa was crying again, but she went on.

"Then Reverend Duncan stood up, lifted his Bible up high and said, 'We are making an offering to you tonight, Lord. We are offering up songs of praise and prayers of grateful hearts. May you find it pleasing and acceptable." Then he and all the men gathered around us and they took Buster from Queenie. Me and Queenie kept clinging to each other and praying. Then Reverend Duncan lifted Buster up to Heaven and cried out to God for healing. Buster seemed almost in shock. He didn't make a sound. The music stopped and everything got silent for a moment. Next thing I knew, things went black."

Jessa was sitting upright now, tears streaming down her face, her voice rising as she described what happened next. "Raymond, I found myself lying in a field...a sunny field of wildflowers. They were all around me, bright as the sun that shone down on them. I noticed that my head was being cradled, not just lying on hard ground. When I lifted my eyes I tried to look on the face of The One who had me. All I could see was sunshine, not so bright as to hurt my eyes, but calm and cheerful and loving light. I knew who it was! I wanted to talk but I heard a voice that said, 'Jessica, do I love you?' I nodded my head yes. 'Do I care for you, Jessica?' Again, yes. 'I have given you a special gift. A son who will always have the mind of a child. Do you know what a blessing this can be?' I started to cry out that I didn't, but I didn't have to speak. He knew my response. He also knew that in my heart, I was arguing. 'It's too hard!' I thought. 'It's not fair to him! To Danny, to Raymond, to *me*!' I cried and sobbed. He just held me.

"When I finally exhausted myself with crying and was lying there quietly again, he said, 'Jessica, I can heal your son's mind. But if I do, I will lose his soul. He will never be one to humble himself and come to me for salvation. Would you want that?' I shook my head as hard as I could. Then he said, "I know you wouldn't want that. I know that would be too much for you to bear. And I love your child too much to lose him. So, I have allowed him to be like this, with the mind of a child, to save his soul. Do you understand?' I nodded my head slowly, finally absorbing what He was saying, to the best of my ability. Buster would not be healed. He would not be changed. He would always be the way he is."

Jessa hung her head and wept quietly. Raymond was sitting upright too, tears streaming down his face as well. He was crying as much for Jessa's lost hope as he was for the lost chance that some God would care enough for him to undo his mess. "Oh Jessa! I'm so sorry! I would change it if I could..."

"No! We don't want Buster to be changed! He's safe just like he is. Don't you see? He *needs* the mind of a child. Otherwise, his soul is at risk. God told me those exact words himself. Not out loud, but in my spirit, he spoke directly to me. So, no more praying for God to change Buster. I told Queenie after the service that I would never ask God to heal Buster again. I would accept him just as he is."

Chapter 14

Willa kept her head low at work for the rest of the school year. She had told Caleigh all about the meeting with the principals and Caleigh had been outraged.

"You and I both know what it takes to keep this class running and to help these children learn. If you don't have experience with the stubbornness of the Down's kids or the unpredictability of the Autistic kids, you just don't understand what is needed to motivate, educate and discipline these kids. Willa, I know you would never hurt a child or do anything abusive. You're just doing what needs to be done. You're firm, not mean. You laugh with these kids, you love on these kids, and when needed, you get tough on these kids. We just have to be more careful about what we do when we are out of this classroom."

Willa felt better after her talk with Caleigh, but she still had a slight sense of paranoia. Were people watching her all the time or what? She knew in her heart that the answer was, "yes."

In the spring, the school district held a teacher education day and Willa was sent for Crisis Diversion and Management...or C.D.M. training. She and her peers were put through 10 hours of training on how to intervene in a classroom crisis to prevent the student from becoming violent. Willa followed along in the workbook as the instructor taught the group about the different stages of Student Crisis Escalation and techniques of how to intervene at each stage to prevent things from escalating. There were techniques to defuse student anger, techniques to learn to read body language, and techniques to help the student reduce his tension and return to his "normal" frame of mind after an outburst. But the big message: You only touch or restrain a child when the student is a physical threat to themselves or others.

Caleigh had taken this exact class last summer, so Willa knew she knew the drill. Still, in everyday classroom life, both women found themselves in frequent physical contact, if not struggles with the children.

During the afternoon session of Willa's C.D.M. training, the group took to the center of the classroom to work on physical restraint holds. Willa learned she was to take a thrashing, angry, small child who was, say, banging their head against the wall and place them backwards on her hip. In other words, the child was to be facing away from her body, with hands wrapped under elbows in a sort of "straight jacket" hold. Then the teacher was to lean away from the thrashing legs and head butts of the out-of-control child.

The teachers practiced contorting each other and themselves in these positions and Willa thought she had gotten the hang of it. Then they practiced what to do with a larger child and how to transport an out-of-control child to the office or out of a public hallway. They learned self-defense moves like how to get a child to release his bite on you or how to get out of a choke hold or a hair pulling. Each technique was practiced between the teachers as they took turns being the offending child.

Next they discussed in depth the risks involved in a physical restraint. The child could suffer from asphyxiation or bruises or broken bones. All during the class, the instructor urged the teachers to exhaust all the other possible solutions they had studied before restraining a student, and again, only when the child posed a physical threat. Finally, the instructor re-emphasized that these techniques were to *protect* the child, not *punish* them and there should never be any physical pain to the student.

As the group was breaking up for the day, Willa and her partner talked quietly while walking out together.

"I don't know about you, but with my older students, the strength they can display is enormous," said the partner. "I mean, I can restrain *you* doing these moves, but you're all soft and gentle. One of the big ol' boys in my class will take me down if I try to put my hands on him. And where in all this is the safety message of how to protect *us*? I mean we spent the day learning all about how not to hurt or inflict any pain and even minimize embarrassment for the *student*. But what about *us*? I mean I have been spit on, slugged in the stomach, bit, scratched and who knows what else. How do I protect *me*?"

Willa thought about what she had said and had to agree. There had really been very little about how to specifically protect yourself. After all the training, Willa left feeling it was basically a course that helped the district cover itself in case of a lawsuit by saying, "We trained this person on what to do in a crisis and he/she didn't follow the rules."

One other thing bothered Willa. She had been shown a technique by Caleigh, Sue Ann Joye and even another parapro who had worked specifically with Down Syndrome children in the past. It involved lifting a non-compliant child by putting your fingertips under the armpits. The idea was that the underarm pressure would be uncomfortable enough for the student that they would have to put their feet down and then they could be led to their next activity.

Willa had done this several times. Every day, a student with D.S. would shut down to the outside world when she or Caleigh asked them to do something they didn't want to do. It could be that it was bathroom time and they didn't want to stop working on a puzzle. Or it could be time to go to Art and one of the kids didn't want to get off the computer. It didn't matter what the request was, it was ignored. They would just sit, crisscross applesauce and stare sullenly at the floor. Willa learned from experience that she would run out of patience waiting on them to "come around" long before the student would come out of their stubbornness. Some of this was because of the strict schedule they had to keep in order for the students to get to participate with the general ed students in Specials, lunch, library time and hall bathroom visits. But there was also Willa's belief that these kids should be held to the same standards as other students, when possible. And there would be discipline for a regular ed student who did not do what their teacher requested. So Willa felt her students should be required to follow directions. They would just ignore all verbal attempts to get them moving in the right direction.

Willa found some of her evolving methods of dealing with her students had to do with the rules and regulations of the school system. Some had to do with the specific dynamic between these particular students and their teachers. But Willa had to admit, some of what she did was definitely because of her personality and personal beliefs. It was this later reason that would continue to plague Willa in her newfound career.

Something else Willa noticed about herself is that she had become more attuned to people with special needs in the general population. As she continued to immerse herself in the world of the disabled, with County Training Days and gleaning all she could from Caleigh, Willa just felt her antennae were more "tuned in" to people with special needs. For instance, a neighborhood boy who had been coming for years to her house to play with her son; now, Willa had heard the same monotone he spoke with, in some of the kids in her school's autism class. The way he fixated on one thing...in his case dinosaurs...was also familiar. Little Stuart would follow Willa around her house, when he was supposed to be playing with her son, instead quizzing her on the beasts.

"Mrs. Grizzard, did you know I want to be a paleo-biologist when I grow up?" he would lisp.

"No, Stuart. How fascinating," she'd replied the first dozen times he told her this. She'd learned, though, to keep folding laundry or whatever, and just let him go.

"Yeah. I do. Do you know that pterodactyls aren't dinosaurs at all? And they aren't really supposed to be called pterodactyls, but Pterosaurs."

"Wow, Stuart, you sure know a lot about Pterodactyls…I mean Pterosaurs. Now run along and go pretend you're a pterodactyl and lay your eggs on Daniel's bed. You can use all those stuffed, small footballs he has from Happy Meals. Just don't try crawling up the banister and leaping down to fly like a pterodactyl, like last time. You almost broke your arm!"

"Mrs. Grizzard, do you know they are called Pterosaurs. Not Pterodactyls. You said Pterodactyls," he would drone.

"I know, Stuart, I'm sorry. Pterosaurs," she'd say, trying hard to keep her patience. Then she would usher him toward the stairs, hoping that was the end of her "lesson."

"And they died out toward the end of the Cretaceous period," he'd call over his shoulder as he reluctantly went to join her son in his room for play with rubber dinosaurs. "Probably due to a meteor."

Yeesh!

Willa also found herself noticing different people in the grocery store, and generally treating them with more patience and kindness. At the store Willa often shopped in, they hired special needs employees. Most of them found work as "baggers," which Willa supported…in theory. But she was the first one to be out of patience and in a hurry by the time she reached the checkout line. Still, she tried to be supportive.

One elderly gentleman almost always seemed to be the bagger on the isle Willa chose. When she was in a hurry, she'd even try to inconspicuously change to another checkout register, because she just couldn't be bothered. But lots of times, he'd move to the new aisle too, as baggers rotated in and out of the store.

The man was probably in his sixties, Willa guessed. And she also figured he'd had a stroke because one arm was drawn up, the hand clutched in a permanent fist. That made one arm completely un-usable, which when bagging groceries, could be a considerable handicap. He also drug the foot on the same side of his body as the twisted arm. Yup. A stroke was probably to blame, Willa surmised.

One rainy, cold day in late March, Willa once again got "her" bagger, as she came to checkout. He tried to give helpful advice as he went through the effort of bagging and loading $200 worth of groceries. Willa always worried about the eggs making it. But today Charles (she had learned his name and that he was unmarried and a big Georgia Bulldogs fan) wanted to talk about the sodas.

"You know you got diet soda?"

Willa nodded her head yes, not wanting to engage in too much talk because Charles ended up slowing down or stopping altogether as he conversed.

"Well, I like to ask all of my customers if they are aware they picked up diet drinks off the shelf." Like almost everything with Charles, talking took some effort on his part. "I had a lady a couple of weeks ago who came back in here so mad she had gotten diet when she wanted regular. So now, I consider it part of my job to ask all the customers if they realized they got diet drinks."

"Yes, well, I gotta have my diet cola," Willa answered as she tried to run her card through the debit card machine. No luck. It wasn't taking it.

"Try running it again," the cashier suggested. Maybe turn it around the other way and run it."

Willa tried and was relieved to hear the beeps of acceptance from the machine.

"Yeah, I know how it goes when you get diet soda and you don't want it. I've had to through a whole six-pack out because I opened one can and tasted it only for it to turn out to be diet. Bleah!" Charles' bagging had now come to a complete halt. The cashier, a great multi-tasker in Willa's opinion, started putting a few things in bags while waiting on the register to print the receipt.

"It's never fun to get diet soda when you just want plain, ol' regular," Charles continued.

Willa smiled a pressed lip smile as she too started reaching for a bag to fill with her groceries.

"Oh, no ma'am," Charles quickly positioned his body between her and the bags. "I've got this. We here at the Pig and Prime want to wait hand and foot on our customers. Let me get those groceries for you."

Gladly, thought Willa.

"So, have you ever gotten the wrong drinks and not noticed 'till you got home?" Charles asked as he slowly started filling a plastic bag with produce.

Finally, the two made their way through the parking lot, Charles insisting on one-hand-pushing the towering buggy of groceries. A cold rain started falling, making everything a little more slippery.

"I'm right over here," Willa pointed, as she pushed her key fob to open the back of the minivan. The door lifted up, giving the pair at least a small amount of shelter while loading the car.

"I've got the groceries, ma'am. Why don't you go get in the car, where it's warm and dry," Charles suggested.

"Oh, no, I'm not leaving you out here with this pile of bags to load. Here, let me help you." Willa managed to get a few bags into the trunk before Charles put up a real stand.

"Ma'am, you really have to let me do this. It's my job," he said, trying to take one of the bags Willa had away from her.

"No, Charles. The rain is picking up. Let me help out," Willa said firmly, pulling back on the bag.

For a moment, the two engaged in a struggle before the inevitable happened: The bag split. Two half gallons of ice cream fell to the ground, one of them rolling a bit under the back bumper.

But that wasn't the one that worried Willa. The other half gallon of ice cream fell on Charles foot, spiking him between his toes.

"Oh, oh, oh!" he moaned. "My toes, my toes. And it's my good foot, too!" he wailed.

Willa was mortified. First, she tried taking the bags off Charles good arm and then she started apologizing, doing everything but falling to her knees on the wet pavement. How could she hurt a disabled man? Why had she been so impatient and tried to load the car faster? She was a horrible person!

"Charles, you stay here. Let me go get a manager. You can file a Workman's Comp claim or something if you have to go the doctor. I'm so sorry! I'll be right back."

Charles was hopping around and moaning but when he heard her mention getting a manager, he quickly collected himself and insisted he was all right.

The two continued loading her groceries in the cold, steady rain.

* * *

When Willa told Joel about her mishap that night, he laughed on and off and tried to soothe his wife's frantic feelings.

"Willa, accidents happen and I'm sure Charles knows you didn't mean to hurt his 'good foot,'" Joel said with another chuckle.

"It is not funny, Joel. That man is barely able to do his job as it is and now I've probably messed that up for him, too!"

"Hon, was Charles walking when you left him?"

"Yes. I kept trying to get him to let me tell a manager about what happened. But he wouldn't let me. He just hobbled back to the store with the buggy as I drove away. What a klutz I am! How could I hurt a man who only has one good leg to begin with?"

"Willa, what would you have done if this happened with another bagger?"

Willa thought for a moment. "The same thing I guess. Why?"

"Well, I think you're being pretty closed-minded to think Charles needed special treatment. He's a man, doing his job. He didn't want to file a claim because like it or not, managers can consider that a nuisance in many ways. He just wanted to work through the bruised toes without making a big deal out of it. Just like any other guy. I think you're feeling guilty because of the way you think about him. You don't think he can do his job. You see his handicap and it makes you feel he needs help. He doesn't. Let him do his job! If you'd spiked a half gallon of ice cream off the foot of any other bagger, they would have yowled about it, but then they would have gotten on with the day, just like Charles did."

Willa didn't like how Joel was portraying her. But, as she thought things through, she had to admit she needed an attitude adjustment. She needed to start noticing people's Abilities, not just their DIS-abilities.

Her most dramatic encounter with people with disabilities in the everyday world happened a few weeks later, on a beautiful Spring Sunday at Goshen Community Church. Willa and her family arrived at church by 8:30 a.m. for the first service. Willa volunteered on the Host Team for the Preschool department, helping to check babies into their classrooms and soothe nervous moms' misgivings about leaving their little ones. Joel volunteered on the Parking Lot Team, directing the 2,000 cars of church attenders in for the first service, then back out afterward, when another team took over to handle about the same number of cars for the 11:00 service. Their three kids attended various, age-appropriate programs in different parts of the large, modern building. This was what some people referred to as a suburban "mega church," but to Willa, this huge, amped-up, God-serving, Jesus-preaching church, while not perfect, was absolutely refreshing.

The church she had grown up in had been painfully small, with no more than 200 people at a time ever attending any service. Usually it was closer to 100. She could remember sitting in her middle school Sunday School class with three, "immature," 6th grade boys. She was in 7th grade and could barely believe the humiliation of being lumped in with those three lugs.

The church itself was very conservative, both culturally and biblically speaking. Women wore dresses only and weren't allowed to speak in any service. The Bible was God's Word and every word of it was true, she was taught. Still, Willa was thankful for her Christian upbringing, because it had taught her a lot about the Bible. Her own parents' resisted the legalism within the church, and therefore, she had avoided being scarred by the petty arguments of some members, like whether songs with a beat should actually be allowed.

Now, Willa still believed that the Bible was God's Word and that every word in it was true. But, over the years, after attending a variety of other style churches and studying the book on her own, she had grown to love God and cherish what he had chosen to say to humanity in the 66 individual books that make up the Bible. Plus, she had broadened her perspective on what church actually was. In her mind, it wasn't a building, but a gathering of like-minded Christians, who wanted to praise God and learn about Him. It was however, also a hospital for the hurting, a safe place to explore questions of a spiritual nature and somewhere to exercise the "gifts" with which each member had been endowed. And in the case of Goshen Community Church, it was especially a place aimed at "outsiders" and not an incubator for "insiders," like those petty but well-intentioned folks of Willa's childhood.

On this particular morning, the Grizzard family all met in the balcony, as usual, to sit in the same area, as usual. This time, it was on the front row of the balcony, which gave them a great view out over the crowd below and of the stage, to the lower, front of them.

People were just starting to file in as the band members set up their equipment on stage for the second time that morning. Willa glanced through the brochure she'd been handed as she walked in and read announcements that flashed on the jumbo-sized screens on both sides of the auditorium. The atmosphere was one of excitement and anticipation. Bella snuggled up under Willa's arm, seeking protection from an over-enthusiastic air-conditioning vent, which seemed to be aimed right at them. But nothing could chill the family's overall feeling of joy at coming together with lots of others from their town to worship God. The Grizzard family members had all had many different spiritual experiences in this place, whether it was receiving Christ as their Savior, being baptized or just having "awakenings" or "convictions" or "revelations." They were all sure that there was something here to look forward to today.

It was at about that time that Willa noticed a child's raised voice. She couldn't understand any words that he said, but was just aware of the "noise." Willa's critical nature immediately kicked in, and so, she began an argument with God Himself.

"God, why does someone bring a small child into the sanctuary? We have so many great venues for children in this church. Someone should go tell that family to put the kid in the nursery, so the rest of us can enjoy the service."

Willa chided herself for her criticism of others and tried to refocus. But, there was the child's voice again, rising up over all the other racket a crowd makes as it is preparing to settle down for a service.

"God, you know I love children. After all, I have three of my own (all of which stayed in the nursery, by the way, until they were able to sit quietly through the service!), I work with them all week and I just got finished volunteering with them a few minutes ago. Now it's *my* turn to worship you, so can you please just shut him up?! You are God after all, so this would be such a *small* prayer for you to grant."

Willa?

"What?" Willa never heard God's voice audibly, but often found him communing with her spirit in a way that felt like conversation. "Oh, pardon me, God? I'm just irritated. What would thou like to saith to me?"

Willa, settle down.

"Settle down? I can't, God! I want to, I really do, but I'm not sure how you can settle down yourself with all that noise he's making."

Who's making, Willa?

"That…that boy," she thought, as she peered over the edge of the balcony to see just who had made it their mission to upset her before worship today. Her eyes settled on a woman, about her own age, sitting in the middle of the row to the far left side of the auditorium's bottom level. Willa, who sat in the top right of the balcony, could not be any further away from the lady and still be in the same room.

"There, God. There. That's the lady. She has the nerve to sit in the middle of the row, where she couldn't possibly be any more distracting if she has to take the boy out. "

Look closer Willa.

"What? Oh. She has one arm in a sling. And she does seem to be alone, except for her 'noisemaker.' So?"

The band began playing and the lead singer invited everyone to stand and greet those around them. The band's sound could be most closely described as "Christian Rock," so things got pretty loud as they started into their first song. Good, Willa thought. Maybe the child will watch all that's going on onstage and will be quiet after that.

Willa?

The "voice" was strangely audible over the sound of the guitars and drums. "Yes?"

Are you looking?

"At them? No, Lord, you know I am not looking at them. I'm trying to forget them. You *know* I want to worship you this morning, Lord. It's been a rough week and I really need to worship you with all my being. So let's…shut…uh, be quiet so I can start!"

Willa, my sweet, sweet love. You are my child, my baby daughter, crying and whining for me while you are seated on my very lap.

"I am, Lord?"

Yes. You are being as distracting to my purposes as that boy is being to you. Don't you want to see what I am up to? Don't you care?

"Well, yes, of course Lord! I care very much! What do you want me to do?"

Look.

"At them? Oh, okay. I see her with the boy. They're both standing with the rest of the crowd. Actually, there is one difference. *He's* standing on a pew. Rather he's got one foot on the pew and the rest of his body wrapped around her. Doesn't he know her arm is in a sling? Doesn't he care?"

No, Willa, he doesn't. He's too young to care. He has the mind of a child. Children don't know the agony their parents go through for them.

"That's true, God. I know my children don't."

Mine don't either, smiled the Lord.

"Okay, well, I'm looking at them. I really can't stand looking at them Lord! I want to go give that boy a good spanking!"

Have you noticed how big he is?

"Well, yes. Now that you mention it, he isn't a toddler, like I expected. He's a six- or seven-year old boy. That makes all of this even worse!"

Just watch, Willa. Keep watching.

Willa tried to concentrate on the song she was mouthing, while keeping an eye on the boy and his mom. He really was relentless. He would put his hands on both sides of her face, and try to force her to look him in the eye, which was possible, since he was standing on the pew next to her. When the songs turned more quiet and worshipful, he continued talking during the momentary breaks the band took to transition to the next song. Talking was too nice of a term.

He was making noises. Just low, guttural.....

Willa stopped singing. Suddenly she was struck with the fact that this was a child with special needs! He couldn't help himself! Once she determined this, her "antennae" went up and she observed other facts. He would make sudden outbursts and got loudest when the crowd was singing loudly. He was trying to sing!

Willa's heart was pierced. She was sitting in judgment of a mother who probably rarely got a chance to attend church, much less sit for uninterrupted worship, like Willa did each Sunday! This precious mother was trying her best and her arm was messed up. From the way the child flailed around, he very likely could be the reason for the bum arm. Oh, how convicted she felt! She was such a judger! And she was supposed to leave judging up to God Almighty Himself! She..she…she…she just couldn't stand herself! She was so sinful, so full of pride! How could she come to worship her beautiful, precious Lord when she was so covered in muck!

Oh, no! The music had stopped, people were settling in for the sermon and the lady was tripping over all those legs between her and the center aisle. She was carrying the large boy! She was leaving! Willa couldn't stand it! She whispered something jumbled to a startled Joel about having "go help that woman!" and started crossing legs of her own.

"Excuse me, excuse me. So sorry!" she muttered as she made her way down the aisle and over to the side entry of the balcony. She raced down the steps, carefully trying to prevent the doors she passed through from slamming. Once out in the huge rotunda area, Willa looked both ways, frantically hoping to see the woman and her child. She did not! Oh, wait, there they were, getting a drink of water. Willa made a mad dash to reach the lady before she could leave the building.

"Wait! Wait! Ma'am? Please wait!" Willa whisper-shouted in the echoing hall.

The lady paused, took the boy's hand and turned to face Willa. She looked much younger than she had from the balcony. And the boy looked much more angelic than he'd first appeared. What should she say?

"Hi. Hi." Willa kept repeating everything it seemed. It must be that she was out of breath and the lack of oxygen was starting to affect her brain.

"Hi, ma'am. I'm Willa Grizzard. I know this sounds crazy, but I...I...I...I just wondered if you need help with your boy? You see, I'm a special education parapro for the county school system and I'd be glad to sit out here with your son while you go back in and listen to the message...I've probably heard it before...or at least something like it and I would really like to...well, to help you," Willa blurted all in one breathless sentence.

The woman stared straight into Willa, causing her to be even more discombobulated. "I see. That's so nice of you, really. But I have people waiting on me. I was only planning on staying for the singing."

"*Really*, it's no trouble. I really *want* to do this. *Please* let me help you," Willa pleaded.

"Thank you so much. It's really kind of you to offer, but I've got to go. He really needs to eat something," the lady said, gesturing toward the boy with her good arm.

"Okay. If you're really sure," Willa didn't know how much to push, being a crazy, unknown woman to this lady.

"Thank you again," the lady said and turned, grabbed the boy's hand and walked toward the exit.

Willa started walking back to the balcony's side entrance when suddenly she thought to ask the lady and boy to join her family at a local restaurant for lunch. She turned on her heels, expecting to see the pair only a few steps away. But they were gone. Completely. The outside door wasn't moving, the water fountain alcove was empty. Nothing.

Willa started to run outside to look, but she suddenly came to a realization that sent chills down her spine. These "people" could be angels, sent by God, to test Willa's sense of hospitality, to convict her of the lack thereof! And she'd almost failed the test! She'd been so immersed in what she needed and wanted that she almost griped her way right past a blessing. It was all she could do to make it to a nearby bench without collapsing to her knees to beg for forgiveness. She sat down and buried her face into her hands. With tears coming from her eyes, Willa tried to re-ignite the conversation with God.

"Lord, I'm soooo, soooo sorry! Forgive me for my lack of love! You say in your Word that people will know Christians when they see them by their love, yet I had absolutely no love in my heart today as I sat and tried to go through the motions of worship… singing a song, raising my hands, praying, listening to a sermon. What a joke! You also promise that angels will visit us from time to time on this earth, when we are completely unaware of it. I don't know whether those were angels you sent to teach me a lesson, or if they were people you used to teach me a lesson, but I promise, Lord, I've learned my lesson! I will love people. I will love them, even when it is inconvenient or un-fun or whatever. I'm just so sorry I didn't actually get to help that woman. Maybe I was too late and the opportunity to do Your Will had passed. I wish I could do it all over again, Lord and I'd show you I've changed. I'd show you!"

God had one last reply to Willa's spirit that day. As she sat hugging herself on the bench, she felt him say, *You already have Willa. You already have! Now it's time for your true test. And as you know, I will always be with you, even when you don't feel I am there.*

Chapter 15

December 23, 1939 dawned cold and dreary in Junction Point. These kinds of days often made Jessa feel like she was on the brink of that "blackness" she'd experienced last winter. Since the healing service this past spring, Jessa had reconciled herself to the fact that Buster was going to be the way he was forever. In a way, her one hope was gone…that he'd be healed. But when she remembered God's words to her about what could be…if Buster were to be healed…well, she shuddered. That truly would have been too much for her to stand. And God knew that. So she'd have to trust Him.

The weather notwithstanding, Jessa had last minute errands to run before she'd be ready for Christmas at her house. Tomorrow was Sunday and all the stores would be closed, so she'd gotten up extra early this morning to get everything done.

First stop: Gibson's Furniture Store on Main Street. Jessa walked up to the front of the store, trying to decide whether to take the revolving door or the regular one. A blast of sharp, cold wind propelled her right into the revolving one. Inside, she was greeted by Christmas Carrols playing in the background and the smell of upholstery and shellac, mixed with the surprising aroma of spicy apple cider.

Jessa removed her gloves and walked over to the side counter, where a large pot of warm cider stood. Looking around and seeing no one else, she grabbed a cup and ladled some of the elixir into it. She took a couple of long sips and as the cider started to work its magic on her, she turned around to see the salesman who had helped her last week…and the week before….as she'd gone through the long process of considering which beds to buy for the boys. Anytime she and Raymond spent any amount of money over about $5 they had to work and scrimp and save. Their budget was tight and didn't allow for spur-of-the-moment purchases.

"Well, Mrs. Bland, you sure do like to push things to the last minute," he said good-humoredly.

"You gonna get those boys some beds today?"

"Well, Mr. Smith, they've outgrown their cribs and I really have to do something. I think we've finally managed to save up enough to get them the beds." She'd chosen matching twin beds with oak head and foot boards and iron frames. Sturdy, almost boy-proof, she reasoned.

Mrs. Bland, if you are ready to place an order, we can deliver and assemble them for you late this afternoon," the salesman said, seeming pleased with himself.

"Oh, that's going to be a bit of a problem. These are young boys after all! How am I going to explain that Santa came early? Danny's too smart for that. He'll ask questions. Is Mr. Gibson making any deliveries tomorrow, by any chance?"

The salesman rubbed his jaw and thought for a moment. Then speaking out of the side of his mouth, like he was telling a secret, he said, "I tell you what Mrs. Bland. I happen to know that Jeanine Hart is clearing out her dining room today. Her poor husband is probably breaking his back to get her old set moved out into the garage. Anyway, she's cooking Christmas dinner for her entire family and needs her new set. She is insisting on taking delivery tomorrow afternoon. Mr. Gibson has two of his colored boys making that run. I'm sure if I tell Mr. Gibson about your sons and Santa and all, he'll agree to have them make one more stop at your place. It'll be kind of late though. Maybe 4 or 5:00.

"That's okay. We will be visiting my aunts tomorrow until about that time. Then Raymond or I will meet the truck while the other stays with the boys at the neighbor's house. Will that work?"

"I think it will, Mrs. Bland. Let me write this up with specific instructions to the driver and we will try to get everything in order. Merry Christmas, Mrs. Bland!"

"Thank you!" Jessa said excitedly. "And Merry Christmas to you, Mr. Smith."

* * *

Jessa smoothed the sheets across her sleeping boys' chests. She'd fixed up a pallet on her bedroom floor for them to spend Christmas Eve. It really hadn't been too difficult to keep them out of their room after the beds were delivered earlier this afternoon. It had worked out that Mrs. McGraff was able to let the delivery men in and showed them where to set up, while the Bland family was at Jessa's aunts' house. By the time the family returned home, they'd been able to corral the boys in the kitchen for a light supper of scrambled eggs, biscuits and milk. Then, they were so excited to see the pallet in their parents' room that both boys barely noticed their own room was off limits.

Jessa tip-toed out of her bedroom, pulling the door closed behind her. There! She and Raymond still had quite a bit of work to do to be ready for Christmas morning. One thing the couple did to make things special was to open up and heat the front room. They even had logs for a fire in the fireplace, in addition to turning up the oil furnace in the back of the house and using one of the kitchen's kerosene heaters as well. The room was really very cozy.

Raymond was waiting by the fireplace, a bottle of sparkling wine in his hand. Jessa slipped up beside him and circled his waist with her arms. "They're asleep," she reported in a whisper.

"Good," he murmured back. "Want some?" He held up a glass. Jessa nodded. As the two sipped their wine and talked, Jessa worked on getting the boys' stockings stuffed. Each one would get a few wrapped trinkets, an apple, an orange and some candy canes. In addition to the new beds, Jessa had bought each boy a broom stick pony and cowboy hat. It really was a big Christmas, by Bland standards.

After working for more than an hour to get everything just right for the morning, both parents collapsed back on the sofa, laughing at the scene they could picture happening here in just a few short hours.

"If we get to sleep till 6:00 we will be lucky," Raymond remarked.

"That's okay. I'll need an early start to get the turkey in the oven."

Raymond groaned. "My idea of a great Christmas morning is sleeping till about 9:00. But that won't happen with those two boys around."

"Nope. So just prepare yourself," Jessa said good-naturedly.

"Well, with you planning on being so busy in the morning and all, I guess I better give you your present tonight," Raymond smiled.

"Okay. You know you didn't have to get me anything," Jessa said coyly.

"Don't even pretend you didn't have a list as long as the boys'. I am on a first name basis with Mr. Claus and he told me just what you wanted," he handed her a large, flat box with "Evans," the name of the department store on Main Street, on it.

Jessa let out a little squeal and accepted the package. She carefully slipped her nail under the tape on the back of the box. Then she gave the tape on the end of the box the same careful treatment. The Depression had taught her to use and reuse almost everything.

"Oh, we'll have none of that," Raymond said as he grabbed a handful of wrapping paper and ripped.

"Raymond! The package was almost too beautiful to open! Now look what you've done!"

"I've helped spare you from feeling like you have to save *everything*. I want you to get to the good stuff and that's *inside* the box."

"Oh, okay," she said as she ripped the paper, too. Lifting the lid off, she found carefully folded gold tissue paper inside. Spreading it apart, Jessa gasped and pulled out a red dress. She stood up and held it up to her.

"Oh, Raymond! It's beautiful! How does it look?"

"Like a dream, babe, like a dream. You'll have to model it for me."

"Okay," she said as she swirled around the room, still holding up the dress. It had a high neck, with pleats from the neck to the waist, a belt covered in matching cloth and a full, pleated skirt.

"But not till you open your gift." She looked at him teasingly.

"A gift? For me? Noooo. I don't believe it." Raymond played along.

"Oh, yes, Mr. Bland. You see, I have connections with Mrs. Claus and she knew just what *you* wanted." She walked to the front closet and reached up to the top shelf. Pulling down a small, square box, she dropped it into Raymond's upturned palm.

"Thanks, dear; you really shouldn't have…" Raymond truly meant this sentiment.

"Raymond, you work so hard and are so good to us. You deserve a Christmas gift, like the rest of us," Jessa smiled at her handsome husband.

He blushed ever so slightly, and then took his time opening the wrapping.

"Oh, no, you don't!" Now it was Jessa's turn to jump in and help with the gift un-wrapping.

Raymond opened the small box and pulled out a pair of cuff links, studded with small, round diamonds. He looked really surprised.

"Jessa, you shouldn't have! But they are really sharp looking. I can't wait to wear them the next time the bosses come down from the home office. They'll really help enhance my image."

"I'm so glad you like them, dear," Jessa replied as she snuggled up to his side. She looked up into his face and kissed him, then burrowed her head against his chest. "I love my gift, too. Oh, yes!" she said leaping up. "You wanted to see me model it."

Raymond pulled his wife back down. "I tell you what, Jessa. I want to see that dress on you, right after we go and inspect the new beds in the other room. I think they might need breaking in, don't you?"

"I think you might be right, Mr. Bland.

"Well, come on then! What are you waiting for?" Raymond asked as he grabbed his wife's hand and pulled her to her feet. Then the two of them scampered off to the boys' room, leaving a trail of wrapping paper behind them.

* * *

Buster ran out of the bathroom, completely naked and dripping wet. He had over-powered Queenie again and was headed right for the oil furnace...the hot oil furnace.

Jessa managed to intercept him before he burned himself again. Last time he had fallen and his cheek had landed on the flat metal hearth at the front of the furnace. It burned his cheek, but not badly and Jessa tried to remind Buster that hot meant pain. Unlike Danny, however, Buster didn't learn from his mistakes. He just repeated the same frustrating, irritating or dangerous behavior, over and over again. But when it was something you didn't want him to do, like push his elderly nanny over so he could get out of the tub and run naked, he learned exactly what he needed to do to accomplish that task. It was enough to make Jessa crazy.

As a matter of fact, things had gotten harder for Jessa over the past year or so. Once Buster turned three, he had mastered walking and moved right on to running. He ran through the house, out the back door, all around the back yard and even ventured into the front yard. Jessa knew it was only a matter of time before he would make his way into the neighbors' yards and right out into the street.

There was another problem. Not only had Buster gotten stronger and more stubborn, but Queenie had grown more frail. Danny would watch in horror as his brother would push Queenie off balance, causing her to fall right over. And when that happened, Buster would have enough time to make his escape.

Jessa and Raymond would spank Buster's fat, bare bottom a time or two and tell him "no." But the very next time Buster got the chance to gain his freedom he'd do the same thing. Jessa worried that Queenie was going to be seriously hurt during one of these episodes. But so far, the tough old lady had come through with no permanent injuries.

This time, Jessa took her second son into the bedroom and after the requisite spanking, she tried to think of a way to explain to him that he was hurting his beloved Queenie.

"Buster pushed Queenie and hurt her," Jessa said, trying to make her voice seem like she was wounded as well. "Mommy is very angry when Buster hurts Queenie. Not nice!" She frowned and turned a cold shoulder to the boy, trying to drive home her point.

Buster yawned and wiped the tears from his eyes with his fists. The little booger was sleepy! Now Jessa was really at her wits' end. How did she get him to empathize with another's pain? If she couldn't figure out how to make him see the pain he was causing and have that realization bring him pain, then there seemed very little hope that he could learn right from wrong.

Buster was acting out in other ways, too. He was very rough on Danny, slapping, hitting and pulling his hair when he wanted something. Jessa knew that part of the problem was that Buster couldn't talk…not at all, except for a few special grunts that pretty much only she could understand.

Jessa determined to take Buster to Dr. Miller for a checkup. Maybe he could tell her how much Buster understood and what to do to get through to him. It broke her heart not to be able to communicate with her now three-and-a-half-year-old son. He swatted his bowl of oatmeal away when he didn't want any more. He grabbed and yanked what he wanted from his brother. He cried pitifully in frustration over almost everything. It wore on Jessa. And Raymond.

When Raymond was home, he would hole up in the kitchen, away from the back part of the house where the "action" was happening. But he was still able to hear the commotion....Jessa making a request, then loud thumping, as she tried to physically force the issue, followed by yelling and guttural sounds. Oftentimes, Raymond would hear a slap, followed by Danny crying, Buster yelling, some pushing back and forth, and finally, a full-blown tantrum. When this happened, Raymond often couldn't take it. He would either walk out the kitchen door, or storm back to add his own, raw emotion to the brouhaha. Sometimes he would be so angry with the whole situation that his fury frightened him. Again, his reaction was to walk out of the room, the house and maybe even into the car for a drive. He just couldn't take it. He didn't know what to do. He hesitated to spank Buster, which is what Raymond felt he would deserve...*if* he were normal. But Buster couldn't help it. He wasn't normal. He was damaged. And this is what happened when a child was damaged. Raymond found it almost too much to bear to think of life being like this all the time now.

For Jessa, her fury came as she watched her husband's retreating back. Oftentimes, she would be in the floor, comforting Danny, struggling to keep Buster from banging his head on the wall during a tantrum. Clothes, toys and books would be strewn all around and she would be on the verge of tears herself. And yet her husband could walk away. Again, something that made Jessa so close to crazy it was scary.

* * *

Jessa walked into the darkened room, hushed by several dark-skinned women, who stood around the edge of the room, whispering. On the bed, lay another woman, her ebony complexion standing out against the whiteness of the sheets. The women in the room had expressions that were anything but welcoming, but Jessa didn't care. She was going to say good-bye to Queenie and nothing was going to stop her.

Queenie had gradually gotten what Jessa called, "less spry" but was really weaker than that term implied. Jessa had quit having her do any laundry, reasoning that the heavy wet sheets and garments were too much for the small, elderly lady. Instead, Jessa had kept her working in the kitchen, fixing meals and minding after the boys. If Jessa had been honest though, she would have had to admit Queenie wasn't much good at those tasks either. Many times, Jessa would come in from handling laundry to find Queenie dozing in an arm chair while Buster worked on unlocking the front door. He was getting pretty close to mastering it, too.

But it was when Queenie started falling that Jessa got really alarmed. First it was in the bathroom, cleaning up after the boys' baths. She'd slipped and skinned her knee. It could happen to anybody, Jessa reasoned. But then it happened going out the back door to keep an eye on Buster. She had tumbled to the grass at the bottom of the back stoop. Neither fall had seriously injured Queenie.

But when she fell in the kitchen, just a few weeks later, with pots boiling on the stove and Buster underfoot, Jessa knew things had to change.

She talked to Raymond about it. "I think we need to cut Queenie back to five days a week. She needs an extra day of rest. Don't you think?" she had worriedly asked him.

"Jessa, Queenie needs seven days of rest. She's too old to be of much use to you and I know you need the help. We need to tell her that we no longer need her services. I'll do it if you can't."

"No! No, we are not treating Queenie as a servant, as an employee we can cast away. She's been here the past five years, since Buster was born, doing the hardest chores, day in and day out. I shouldn't have given her such hard tasks to do. What was I thinking! I wore her out."

"Jessa, you were asking Queenie to do what we hired her to do...to help you with the tough work of keeping up with this family, of helping to keep up with Buster, especially. He is such a handful that it really does take two people to watch him."

Raymond wasn't telling Jessa anything she didn't know first-hand. "I know what we hired her to do and she has done it for years now. Since Danny has gone off to school, it's been easier to watch after just Buster. I don't need Queenie to be so sharp now."

"Jessa, who are you kidding? If anything, Danny helped keep an eye on his brother. He is so good, he's really no trouble at all. But Buster....It's like we have two of him. We need some help with him and bottom line, as harsh as it sounds, Queenie can't do the job anymore."

"Oh, Raymond," Jessa started to cry.

Raymond came over to his wife and hugged her, trying to soothe her. "Jessa, I love her, too. She's been good to our family. What if I continue to pay her $5 a week and we try to find someone else to help you? I can probably just afford the second woman with the raise I got last month. What do you think? Then she can stay at home and rest and she won't be going hungry."

"Raymond, if you'll continue to take care of Queenie like that and bring her here for visits every week, then I guess we can do it that way. I just hope she'll accept the help. She's got her pride."

"Then you will just have to figure out a way to explain the $5 so that she'll take it. You know her best, Jessa. Tell her it's her 'retirement.'"

"There's no way that would work! No, I'm going to have to give her some work to do. What if I have her stay home and bake bread, cakes, and do some laundry for us? I think that'll work!"

So, that's what Jessa told Queenie. She explained she was going to have to cut her down to five days and it wasn't convenient for Raymond to continue driving to pick her up every day, so she would be giving her a basket of hand-washable laundry and she would expect fresh-made breads and cakes. Raymond would stop by once a week to pick her up and bring her to the house to deliver the laundry and baked goods. Then she would stay and "help out" the rest of the day.

Queenie bought it. And for several months it had been working. But yesterday, Raymond had stopped to pick up Queenie and was met by her daughter, Elvira, at the door.

"I'm sorry, Mr. Bland. Mama can't work fo' ya'll today. She fell last weekend and she been bed-ridden ever since. We don't 'spect her to make it much longer." The daughter's eyes had filled with tears.

Raymond told Jessa as soon as he got home and Jessa had wanted to go see Queenie that night. But Raymond had assured her that the daughter felt she had a few more days.

So Jessa came today. And as she knelt beside the bed, Queenie turned her bloodshot eyes toward Jessa.

"Hey, Queenie; hey, old girl."

"Hey, you," she mumbled.

"Queenie, Danny drew you a picture. It's of you and him." She held the drawing up before the old woman. "See, Danny even let Buster color right here in the corner." She pointed at a scribble. "And Danny didn't even get mad at Buster for coloring on his paper."

Queenie smiled weakly and then her eyes closed and her face grimaced. Jessa pulled her arm with the drawing back.

"Mama's hurting. Dr. Jackson gave me sumpin' fo' da pain, but it ain't time fo' her to have it yet." Elvira had entered the room behind Jessa.

Jessa was unfamiliar with the colored Dr. Jackson. But she knew she didn't want Queenie to hurt. "Let's go ahead and give it to her now. She doesn't need to hurt. What exactly does the doctor say?"

"Well, he says Mama broke a hip in the fall and she hit her head real bad." Jessa could tell from the big bandage around Queenie's head that the head injury had been serious.

"Elvira, I don't mean to pry," Jessa had pulled Elvira to a corner and was herself whispering now. The others moved around the bed side to tend to Queenie. "...but why isn't Queenie in the hospital? She might have internal bleeding or worse." Jessa said a little panicky.

"Is it money? Because me and Mr. Bland will pay for her to go to the hospital."

"No, no, Mrs. Bland. Mama won't go. She won't go to no hospital. She says she ain't never been in one and she ain't gonna start now at 82 years of age.

"Well, I'll just talk to her, tell her she's gotta go," Jessa tried again.

"No, Mrs. Bland. That ain't what Mama wants. Let's 'bide by her wishes."

Jessa acquiesced. "All right. But I want to help with her, stay with her."

Mrs. Bland, Mama's sisters and aunties are taking care of her. They won't leave her."

Again, Jessa gave in, but walked back to the bedside broken-hearted. "Queenie, Queenie, you hear me? I want you to know something." Tears ran shamelessly down Jessa's face. "I want you to know. You are my best friend. I didn't ever learn all that much about you. You didn't talk about yourself much. But you sure listened to me talk about myself. You were always there for me. You are the one person on this earth who knows what I am going through every single day with Buster. You're my best friend. I need you! Don't go!" Jessa clung to the side of the bed as she kneeled, sobbing and praying for her friend.

Queenie never opened her eyes again while Jessa was there. But once, she did reach over and pat Jessa's hand. That would have to be enough. That would have to be good bye.

CHAPTER 16

In Willa's opinion, May was second only to December when it came to busyness and costliness. There were team play offs, dance recitals, final exams, school choral performances, class parties and field trips. There were teachers' gifts, fines for lost school library books, balances due for yearbooks and flowers for the bus driver. Willa had nothing against any of these events or causes, it was just a lot in one month.

She managed to get off from work for a day so she could chaperone Daniel's 5th grade field trip to Chattanooga. It meant she had to pay $95 dollars to go along, but it was worth getting to watch Daniel as he had one, last romp with his elementary friends. Some would be going to his middle school with him in the fall, but many had been districted to attend a different school, so he'd have to say good bye to them in a few, short weeks.

Willa enjoyed hanging back and giving the 10-year-olds their space as they explored the Chattanooga Aquarium. She watched from a distance, which would never have been possible with her students. With Daniel and his friends, she could say, "Meet me at the water fountain in 10 minutes," and they'd actually show up... pretty much on time. Her students didn't have much of a concept of time. And they could not be relied upon to meet deadlines or follow directions that stretched much out into the future. *Would any of them grow to be able to meet these every day constraints, or would they be dependent on their loved ones forever?* Willa wondered?

The month of May whizzed by as Willa went from one school activity to another. She also was making mental preparations to separate from the young charges in her class. Maleeke was going to be moving to Nevada with his parents as soon as school was out and so Willa reasoned she'd most likely never see him again. And several of the boys were moving to different classes next fall, for one reason or another. Willa had never thought about how emotional the end of the school year could be for a teacher. Yes, she was ready for a break and some time with her own kids that the summer would offer, but she really had no experience in working so closely with children and then having to say, goodbye to them.

Caleigh, being a relatively new teacher herself, was having her own issues with letting go. She didn't want her students to be with another teacher. *She* was their teacher. So both women kept a tissue handy as they held their class's end of the year party. Parents sat around the room in miniature chairs, sipping punch and watching the PowerPoint Caleigh had put together, with pictures of the school year mixed with tear-producing music.

As the party came to a close and parents and students started trickling out of the classroom, Willa couldn't help but think about how far many of them had come. Jeff was really doing well reading his flash card words. He still often acted more babyish than a boy of six should act though, and his slight build allowed his mother to continue to carry him around on her hip. He could "shut down" if things weren't going his way, so for these reasons, he would be back in Caleigh's class again next year.

Jared was throwing fewer tantrums and was academically ready to be in a kindergarten class next year. If he could just keep his behavior under control, he'd do fine. And from what Caleigh said, his mother was looking into medication to help him with that.

One thing that worried Willa and Caleigh was that Jack was also moving into the same "inclusion" class as Jared. Jack had matured some and was doing better verbalizing his thoughts and feelings. The two boys were good friends, often playing together outside class. But they knew how to set each other off. There had been many times when the two had to be pulled apart as they came to blows in class. Willa and Caleigh would intervene and put an end to it right there. In a regular education classroom, the protocol would be different. There was zero tolerance for physical violence and one or both boys would probably end up in the principal's office for that type of behavior.

Jon, while older than most others in this class, still had far too many behavior issues to move on this fall. He'd be returning to Caleigh and Willa's class for another year. Sadar, while academically on a first grade level, was far too shy and socially awkward to be in a regular ed class full time. So he would be in Caleigh's class, but she would try to schedule him for several periods in a typical peer class, so he could continue honing those emerging social skills. His parents were thrilled, thinking it meant he was getting stronger academically, but Caleigh knew that it was only a matter of time before Sadar hit a plateau with his school work. She was concerned that he learn to get along with his typical peers and learn life skills that would carry him far in life.

Three of the slower Down's kids would definitely be back in Caleigh's class. James, Justin and Jason's progress had been hardly noticeable in some areas. But Willa and Caleigh were thrilled that Justin had done very well with his potty training, James had stopped running away on the playground, and Jason had started to show periods of social interaction with the other students. Progress would always come slowly and with much effort for these three. But it did come nonetheless, if one was willing to look very closely and count even the smallest gain.

As Willa leaned over wiping table tops with disinfectant, she felt a strong hug around her legs from behind. She turned and found Maleeke wrapped around her like a python. She untwined his arms momentarily so she could stoop down and look him in the eye.

"Maleeke, I will miss you very much," Willa said as she tried to hold back tears. She thought of all the times she'd had to hold his thrashing body in the safety hold, how many times he had soiled his pants and sworn to her that he hadn't, how many times he had insisted on getting every alphabet puzzle off the shelves, taken them all apart, and then reordered them into some sort of mathematical pattern that made sense only to his brain. He even had taught Willa to count in Swahili. This one was going to be a heartbreaker.

With his mother standing in the doorway, Maleeke handed Willa a piece of messily folded paper. She opened it up to find his version of the alphabet printed over and over.

"For me?" she asked. He nodded.

"Thank you, Maleeke. I'll keep it always." She reached out to hug him but he drew away sharply…his way of saying his "hugging window" had closed for the day.

"Okay. Well, you be a big help to Mommy and Daddy as you fly on the plane to your new home. Remember what we talked about. The airplane has people to help you, so you don't need to be afraid. And you can wear your earphones so you don't hear all the announcements from the cockpit. I know how you hate announcements. And I will miss having lunch with you every day, watching you eat your casein/gluten-free hotdogs. Gray was just never my choice for food color. Anyway, you be good."

Willa stood up and looked at his mother, who had tears running down her face.

"Mrs. Grizzard, I can never thank you for all the good you have done my boy. He loves you, even though he can't show it and I just hope we get teachers half as good as you and Ms. Smith in Nevada."

"I hope you get a great school with great teachers. Maleeke will thrive in the right environment."

Later, as Willa drove home, she thought to herself about how much she had grown in the few short months she had been at Goldmine Elementary. She'd learned so much about her students…about herself. But even admitting all that, she couldn't have imagined how all she'd been through this year was preparing her for some very rough roads just ahead for her.

* * *

The summer started off just fine for Willa. She and the kids went to the local pool a lot. They visited a nearby water park and enjoyed late suppers on the back deck. Willa decided she *really* loved her position at Goldmine Elementary now. What other job could she have that would give her the entire summer off? And the way payroll was structured, she got paid the same rate all year long, so even while she was enjoying the summer with her family, she received a pay check.

It was while Willa was cleaning up after one of those late summer meals that the phone rang. Willa had just finished with the dishes and had wanted to go back outside to watch the kids catch fireflies. She almost ignored the ringing phone but glanced at the Caller ID and saw it was her parents calling.

"Hello? Mom?"

"Hi, dear. It's me and your Dad is on the other phone." This was weird.

"Is everything okay, Mom? Is something wrong?" Willa could almost sense trouble traveling through the phone lines.

"Yes, dear, there is something we are calling to tell you. It's bad news, hon. It's Gram. She…she passed away this morning. Died in her sleep, the doctors say. We didn't know until we went over to take her some dinner at about 5:00 this evening.

"Ohhh," Willa could feel the sound catch in her throat. Joel, who was drying off the last pot and putting it away, walked over to his wife, feeling from her reaction that something was wrong.

"Mom, Dad, I'm so sorry," she started to tear up, despite wanting to remain strong for her father, who had just lost his mother. Willa stayed on the phone for another few minutes, the three family members just helping each other process the sudden loss.

Willa hung up the phone and instantly felt very alone. She and her grandmother had been extremely close. Growing up, she had stayed for long visits with her grandparents, learning to cook and sew at her grandmother's side. Now, the two had talked on the phone at least once a week, with Willa depending on her grandmother for advice and encouragement. Last summer, even though Gram had been getting increasingly frail, Willa brought her from South Carolina to stay with them for two weeks. The children had enjoyed getting to know their great-grandmother. By the end of the visit, they had even started to accept moving at her slower pace…taking time to read together or crochet, color in coloring books, watch old movies or just talk together for long periods of time. Now what would they all do without Gram?

Willa's parents had not begun to think of funeral arrangements yet. They were still calling Willa's two sisters and Gram's few remaining relatives. Willa thought about calling them back to see if she could help with that task, but right now, she could hold back no longer. She collapsed into Joel's arms and sobbed. Gram was gone.

* * *

Willa's car was speeding along at about 70 miles per hour, up I-85, north of Atlanta toward Greenville. She was behind the steering wheel, but thanks to cruise control and her mind-full of thoughts, the car was really operating on auto pilot.

She should be thankful. How many women could say they got to enjoy their grandmothers until they were into their forties? She had so many good memories with Gram. Her children had *known their great grandmother*. How priceless! And yet, she was so sad and already missed Gram more than she could bear.

The Georgia summer heat was fierce and Willa's car air conditioning blasted full throttle in her face. She had her Capri pants rolled up to her thighs so the air vents could help dry the sweat beads that ran from the backs of her knees. Her discomfort with the temperature mirrored that of her spirit's. She let her mind wander over recent years.

Gram had always been a spark of light in their family. She enthusiastically enjoyed every moment of life. She was truly the stereotypical sweet, little, old lady. She savored each morsel of food on her plate. She made an art of making friends with strangers. She listened intently to every conversation she was in…and even some she wasn't! She worshiped God with a full heart and made it to church services as often as she was able to go. She handed out small devotional booklets to drive-thru window clerks, waitresses, checkout cashiers, and anyone else who would take one. She left them in public bathrooms and in doctors' waiting rooms. She really considered it her ministry to use these booklets to help spread God's love to the lost souls around her.

Gram had her downsides too, of course. Mainly, she could be manipulative through the deftly honed use of guilt. If you came to see her for one hour, she wanted two. If you cooked dinner for her, she wanted you to stay, eat it with her, wash the dishes and take her out for dessert, that sort of thing. And she was somewhat of a hoarder, probably because of the hard times she saw during The Great Depression. Her kitchen counters were littered with old fast-food containers she was sure she would use again. Her pantry was loaded with paper goods and cleaning products, because she couldn't resist a sale. She'd only been in her last home for 10 years, but the inside looked like she'd been there for decades more.

Willa's parents had decided, with the reluctant agreement of her grandparents, to move the elderly couple to a new house, just a few miles from their own. The new home was a patio home, with two bedrooms, two full baths, an eat-in kitchen, a living room/

dining room combination and a small sunroom….just right for the two, who were in their late seventies.

The small yard was landscaped in a haphazard, almost accidental fashion, but was well-kept, thanks to Willa's father. Gram had loved growing flowers and had all sorts of them planted around her home. Willa's father had dug up several old Camilla bushes, of the sasanqua variety, from their old home and brought them to the new house.

In addition to the Camilla bushes, her father had dug up some antique tea roses, and several heirloom shrubs to plant around the new place. Her grandmother had loved that, once again, not sensing that it was enough that everyone was helping with the monumental moving process, much less custom landscaping the yard. She shamelessly insisted that her son dig up the plants, including her prized beefsteak begonias and carefully fit them into the moving van. Willa's dad had just gritted his teeth and done it and Gram had managed to keep most of them alive to this day.

Everyone thought the move would be hard on her grandmother, and in many ways it was. She was wistful and overwhelmed with emotion about leaving a home they'd been in for forty years. But Gram had embraced the move with unexpected excitement and relish, surprising even herself.

Willa's grandfather managed to adapt to the new place, but his health went slowly downhill after the move. First, he gradually lost his ability to drive as his eyesight and reflexes diminished. He eventually became bedridden, and finally died after living in the new home for almost eight years.

Willa turned the air conditioning blower down to just a strong breeze. She was finally cooling off. She reached into a paper sack filled with Super Bubble Bubble Gum. It was her favorite. The hard, pink chunk of gum filled her mouth with its sweet flavor and the giant bubbles she blew kept her entertained. Super Bubble was the only bubble gum she would chew, and after she had sucked all the flavor out of a piece, she would spit it out into its wrapper and immediately grab another piece and start chewing again. It helped the time pass. It wasn't unusual for Willa to go through 50 pieces on a road trip, flying along in her van, smacking and noisily chomping her gum.

Willa hated traveling alone, but the kids stayed home so that Willa could concentrate on helping her parents over the next few days. Then on Friday, Joel and the kids would drive the four hours to Columbia, arriving in time for the Saturday funeral.

Willa's heart was heavy as she drove. But it was comforting to allow her mind to conjure up old memories. Like the time she'd gone searching for golf balls that her grandfather had chipped into an overgrown field out behind the old house. She'd been about 10-years-old and was in the middle of one of her two-week stays that she had with her grandparents every summer. She had run out into the field, thinking she would please her grandfather with the recovered balls, even though Gram had told her to stay clean because they would leave for Wednesday Night Prayer Meeting in a few minutes. Willa couldn't imagine getting dirty in the field, but when she emerged from the brambles, with a grocery sack full of balls, she'd managed to pick up a few extra things. Her long, blonde hair was matted full of cockleburs....small, spiny, round seed pods that had been hanging loosely from the bushes in the field.

Her grandmother had been aghast and her grandfather had to stifle a chuckle. When Willa saw what she looked like in a mirror, she cried. Her grandmother had patiently worked through her whole head of hair, pulling each pod out by hand, with Willa crying and yelping in pain with each pull. When the job was finished, her usually smooth, blonde hair was frizzy, broken off and dirty-looking. Willa had wanted to stay home, but Gram had helped her get her hair into a pony tail and the three had made it to Prayer Meeting with a few minutes to spare.

Willa remembered spending the week of Spring Break with her grandparents one Easter. She'd been about six and remembered fretting and worrying that the Easter Bunny wouldn't find her.

Easter morning dawned, and sure enough, there was no Easter basket to be found. Gram suggested that Willa look around and as she did, her grandparents steered her closer and closer to the back door. Finally, Willa saw a plastic, yellow basket on the back stoop. She squealed in delight and threw open the door. Not only did the basket contain candy and treats, but it also held a real, live, yellow duckling. Willa loved the duck and called him, "Dubby" for some reason. He followed her around the rest of the week and Gram had even allowed Dubby to sleep in the Easter basket next to her bed.

At the end of the week, her parents arrived to pick her up and quickly let it be known that ducks were country animals and wouldn't be allowed in their suburban neighborhood back home. So, Gram had made an arrangement with the lady next door to keep Dubby with her flock of chickens and ducks and allow Willa to visit with him whenever she was at her grandparents. Willa cried a little when she had to leave Dubby, but it helped that he would be just right next door to her grandparents.

Willa could remember being even younger and lying in bed at night, giggling with her grandmother for what seemed like hours. Her grandfather would call out from the next room, "Hey, you two, be quiet! Lights out! It's time for bed." Gram would turn the lights out and lie silently in the bed, putting her finger to Willa's laughing lips, shushing her. Finally, they would hear her grandfather start to snore and they would resume their chatting and giggling.

Willa's memories stretched from almost the time when she was a baby, her parents' first born. Her grandparents had fawned all over "Little Willamina," lavishing her with small gifts and taking her along on trips to the mountains and beach. But what made the biggest impression on Willa's heart was the time her grandmother would spend with Willa, reading, scratching her back, fixing tomato sandwiches and just talking about "stuff." The two had been exceptionally close when she was a pre-teen. One minute she would be cooking in the kitchen with her grandmother (something she was never allowed to do at home) and the next she would be spending hours up in a bare-limbed fig tree, pretending the branches were gear shifts in a make-believe airplane. Her long, leisurely visits with her grandparents were some of the best memories Willa had.

It was hard to believe she was now speeding toward the funeral of the keeper of those memories.

* * *

Willa fanned her face. No matter how high the air conditioning blasted in this old church, it still felt steamy when it was filled with bodies. Willa had greeted people as they came for the viewing last night. She'd done the same today before the funeral. She was exhausted, but now she had to go to the graveside for another service. Joel and the kids were standing by, wanting to help, but not knowing exactly what to do. Willa couldn't blame them. She didn't know exactly what to do either. It was ironic that at one of the lowest points in her life, she had to be at her most gracious.

Her parents filed out of the church first, followed by Willa and her sisters, Cora and Lara. The sisters' families came next and they all stood out at the front of the church, waiting for the limousines. Funny how Dad was directing people, as usual. He was dividing the crowd up between the two limos. Her sisters were whispering and laughing. The kids were playing with each other. If she didn't know better, Willa would have thought this was a typical Sunday with the family choosing where to go eat after church.

But no. This was the day she had to put her grandmother in the ground. She knew her sisters loved her grandmother, but she and Gram had been so close, and being the oldest grandchild, she felt responsible. Her father was very upset and she didn't want to bother him. There were no brothers or sisters for him to lean on. So Mama was taking care of Dad and Willa was trying to do everything else...decide how much makeup Gram should wear, where to put each flower arrangement, where to put cousin Judy, who seemed to dissolve into tears at the mere mention of Gram's name. Willa just did it all.

The family poured into the limousines and shut out the rest of the world. Willa and her family rode with her mom and dad.

"It was a beautiful service," Joel offered.

"Yes, yes it was," Mama offered back.

"They kept saying the wrong name," Willa said. "We need to mention that to the pastor when we get to the grave site. No one knew her as "Jessica."

"True," said Joel.

"Mommy, where is Gramma Jessa now? Is she dead?"

"No, she's not, Bella. That's a good question." Willa started to choke up.

"Gramma Jessa is in Heaven with Jesus. She's more alive now than she was when she was here on earth with us. She's happier and has no tears or pain. As followers of Christ, we will see her again."

"Then why are you so sad, Mommy?" Bella asked gently.

"Well, just because I miss her so much. I know I'll see her in heaven again but I miss her being here with us right now. I'm just selfish that way I guess, Bella."

"I'm selfish that way too," Bella concluded as she snuggled under her mother's arm and the limos pulled into the cemetery.

Back at Willa's parents' house, Joel was preparing to leave with his two boys and head back to Goshen. Willa and Bella were staying behind so Willa could help with going through her grandmother's things. The clutter had added up over the ten years in the new house, so she didn't want her parents to have to face the daunting task alone. In fact, her mother could watch Bella for her and Willa and her Dad would go through the stuff.

As Joel was putting the last suitcase in the car trunk, Willa came up behind him and hugged him. Joel turned to see his wife's downcast face and tenderly lifted her chin so he could see into her eyes.

"Babe, it's going to be all right. The hardest part is behind you. Now you've got the rest of the summer to help your parents out. Just stay as long as you need to. I'll farm the boys out to different friends during the weekdays and we'll get by. Just take your time.

"Okay, Joel. You're the best husband a girl could have. Thank you."

The two kissed and the boys, looking out of the car's back window, made gagging sounds.

"All right, you two gangsters. We'll stop the mushy stuff. We gotta go anyway," Joel said.

Willa reluctantly loosened her grip on Joel and walked him to the driver's side door. With another short kiss, Joel and the boys were in the car, on their way home. And Willa was left standing on her parents' driveway, tears running down her face.

Chapter 17

D anny sat under the fig tree in the back yard, his arms folded across his chest and his eyes red and puffy from crying. He'd done it again. Buster had done it again. He and his friends had been playing fort in the back yard and Buster had insisted on coming outside too. Mama always let Buster do what he wanted and then Danny was supposed to watch him.

Well, this time, Danny was *not* going to play with Buster. Johnny and Freddy were here and he wanted to play with them...alone!

That had worked all of about two minutes. Then Buster started calling in his hoarse voice, "Dan-nee! Dan-nee!"

That's when the teasing started. "Hey Danny, listen to how he says your name. Like a baby. Is wittle Buster a tiny wittle baby?" Johnny jumped down from his lookout in the fig tree and came close to Buster's face and repeating his words. "Are you a baby? Huh, Buster?"

Not knowing the meaning of Johnny's chant, Buster just clasped his hands in excitement and nodded, "Yes." The other boy, egged on by Buster's response, exploded with taunting laughter. "Yeah? You *are* a baby? That explains a lot. Why you smell like pee and you always have that dumb look on your face. He's a goof ball, isn't he fellas?"

Danny laughed uneasily. All he had wanted to do was play fort. How had things gotten so out of control so quickly?

"Okay, fellas, let's just ignore Buster and play."

"This is more fun," Johnny retorted. But he put his rifle at the base of the tree and started to climb back up.

When Buster caught a glimpse of an unattended gun, he couldn't resist. He grabbed Johnny's gun and lined his eye up with the barrel in preparation to shoot. When Johnny saw what happened, he jumped out of the tree again, this time landing on top of Buster, hitting him from behind and knocking the younger boy to the ground.

"Hey! Give me back my gun!"

Buster stubbornly clutched the gun and curled up in a ball over the weapon.

"No!" he said.

Without another word, Johnny started pummeling Buster's back with punches. "Give it back, give it back!" Johnny shouted with each punch.

At about this time, Jessa came running out of the back door.

"What's going on here?" she shouted, as the boy continued yelling for his gun.

Jessa reached down, pulled Johnny up and tried taking the gun away from Buster, who was crying now. "Let go, Buster, let go!"

The boy finally loosened his grip on the gun and Jessa handed it to Johnny and said, "Johnny, Freddy, it's time to go home. You cannot play like this at our house."

Jessa's eyes then flashed toward Danny. "And you, young man. Just wait until your father comes home. You'll be spanked, for sure! Boys, you can expect a phone call to your homes about this."

As the boys started to leave, Johnny didn't go quietly, shouting over his shoulder, "My dad always tells me to fight for what is mine! He won't be mad!"

Jessa just stood there, helplessly trying to get Buster to stop crying. She had no reply.

Then, she did what Danny hated worst of all. She started making him feel guilty. He'd rather have the spanking.

"Danny, what were you thinking? How could you stand back and watch as your brother was being punched? Why didn't you stop that boy? Why didn't you protect your brother?"

Danny just turned his head away from his mother and brother and didn't answer. He had no answer. Not one that would help him win in this situation. How could he tell his mother that he had wanted to punch Buster too?

* * *

Raymond's Buick sped down the two-lane road. Jessa was in the back seat with Buster, who had his head in his mother's lap and was dozing. The three were headed to Duke Hospital at the Duke School of Medicine in Durham, North Carolina. Danny was staying with Mrs. McGraff.

They were going to have Buster examined by specialists, hoping they would have good news about things like his heart problem. Buster had always tired pretty quickly, but in some ways Jessa considered that to be a saving grace. It was the only way she ever caught him when he took off running. But more than anything, Jessa wanted Buster to be as healthy as possible.

After a five-hour car ride, the three arrived at their motel room ready for a rest. At least the two parents were ready to rest. Buster had slept in the car and had no intention of lying down again. So, Jessa decided to put him in his bathing suit and try taking him to the motel pool while Raymond caught some shut-eye. Jessa knew this was an ambitious undertaking but she wanted to give it a try. There would rarely ever be a chance like this again.

The two walked across the parking lot holding hands, Buster excited to see what was to come. He loved a bath, Jessa reasoned, so he should love the pool too. As Jessa opened the gate to the pool area, she noticed a couple lying in chaise lounge chairs while two children about Buster's and Danny's ages frolicked on the stairs leading into the water. The boys both had colorful floating rings around them and for a moment Jessa wished they had bought one for Buster. Then she thought, no, it would be too hard to hide from Danny what they had done if there was evidence like that lying around.

Buster squeezed his mother's hand hard, partly out of excitement and partly out of shyness that there were new people looking at him. Staring at him was more like it. Jessa tried to push down her annoyance and said in a loud voice, "Hello. What a nice day for a swim!" The man of the couple nodded and waved his hand briefly, but went right back to the newspaper he was reading. The woman also waved, but didn't smile and almost immediately started whispering to her husband.

Jessa turned her back to them and said to Buster, "Want to go in?" which was a silly question because Buster was already leaning into the pool with his hands feeling along the first step, his butt up in the air.

"Whoa, wait a minute Buster," Jessa said as she pulled him back from the edge. The two children had stopped splashing and were staring at Buster, slack-jawed.

"Hi," croaked Buster in his throaty voice.

"Hi," the older boy said. "What's wrong with him?"

"Oh, he's just never seen a pool before," Jessa answered, ignoring the real meaning of the question. She was about to introduce Buster when the woman came running from her chair and started calling to her boys, "Jason, Andrew, out of the pool!"

"Mooommm, whyyyy?" the older one bellowed.

"Don't ask me why; just do what I say. Out of the pool." She repeated. Then she turned to the man and said, "Charles, let's go."

The man walked sheepishly by Jessa and Buster, folded one of his boys in a towel and followed the woman and the other boy out of the pool area.

"I should have been prepared," Jessa told herself. "We're not in Junction Point where at least people have gotten used to seeing Buster." They really hadn't, it was just Jessa never took him anywhere to expose him to such scrutiny.

Buster watched the family walking away but not as long as Jessa did. He slipped back to the water's edge, this time not near the steps. He went to put his hands in and since there was nothing to stop him, he tumbled right in, face first.

The splash sent a chill down Jessa's spine. She yelled before she even turned around.

"Help! Somebody help me!"

Jessa didn't know how to swim very well, so she turned around and looked at the family, pleadingly. They were staring back at her but not making any move to help.

Without thinking any longer, Jessa turned around, kicked off her shoes, ran to the steps and quickly made her way down them. The skirt to her dress filled with air and floated up around her. She couldn't see Buster! He had dropped to the bottom like a rock. How could she get him? She reached her arms out, flailing them underwater, trying to feel anything in the shallow water. An arm! Or leg. She didn't care. She just grabbed on and pulled. Buster came up sputtering at first and then cough-crying. Jessa quickly worked her way back up the steps and into a lounge chair, grabbing the motel towel she'd brought along.

The whole incident took less than 60 seconds, but it seemed like a lot of time passed. Jessa just hugged her boy to her chest, sobbing right along with him. Feeling the presence of stares again, she looked back at the family and saw they were still there, watching all of this and never moving to lend a hand. Buster's life wasn't worth saving, even getting wet for, she thought angrily. Once again she realized, if this child was going to be kept safe it was going to be solely and completely up to her.

* * *

The visit to Duke Hospital had gone okay, in Jessa's opinion, but the doctors there could not tell her much more than she already knew. He had Mongolism, his heart was weak and everything for Buster would come very slowly, and with a lot of hard work from the parents. The doctors prescribed exercises and educational activities to try and help Buster reach his full potential, which their educated guess would be about that of the average two-year-old. Jessa had left the hospital feeling disappointed and overwhelmed.

How would she ever have time to do all that the doctors prescribed? What about Danny and Raymond? Didn't they deserve a little of her time too? Without Queenie, Jessa found it difficult to do much more every day than put three meals on the table and keep up with the laundry. So, it was back to business as usual.

Buster had made some strides with his words. He could say, "Hi," and "Bye," "Mama," "Dad-dee," "Dan-nee," "Bath," "Dog," "Biscuit," "more," "nope," and "Co Cola." Jessa believed it was huge progress that he could express his wants. It had helped to cut down on Buster's tantrums.

Now what to do about his stubbornness? When Buster made up his mind that he didn't want to do something he would plant himself on his bottom, fold his arms across his chest and poke his lower lip out. He could sit like this for 30 minutes or more when he wanted to. Jessa knew. She had tried him.

Just yesterday she had called the boys inside from the backyard to wash up for supper. Danny had reluctantly come in, mumbling something about just capturing the bad guys and not being hungry anyway. But he came in, prepared to wash his hands and come to the supper table, nonetheless.

Buster, on the other hand, continued playing in the dirt just like he hadn't heard his mother. Exasperated, Jessa wiped her hands on her apron and decided to go out and get Buster. She didn't want Raymond to come home and see Buster disobeying, because that would almost certainly mean a spanking and Jessa didn't want to disrupt the dinner hour any more than it already was being disrupted. When Jessa reached Buster he continued to stir the dirt with a stick.

"Buster, it's time to come in. It's getting dark now and Daddy will be home soon. So, come on, let's go inside." She held out her hand to him, which he ignored.

"Okay, if that's the way you're going to be, there will be no dessert after dinner. No apple cobbler. You can't have any." Nothing. No response.

"Buster, listen. Your brother is already at the table waiting on us. Now come on!" With this she walked over to him, got him by one arm and tried to pull him to his feet. He just went limp. Gelatin had more consistency.

"Buster, get up! Get up right now!" Jessa let go of his arm and went around behind Buster, trying to circle him from the back with her arms and lift him that way. Now he went stiff. He completely held his form as she lifted him from the ground, so that he was sitting cross-legged in mid-air. At seven-years of age, Buster weighed at least half of what his mother did. She couldn't carry him more than a few feet at a time. But by this point, Jessa was just as determined as Buster. He was going inside, even if she did have to carry him.

When she reached the screen door, she struggled to hold it open and lift Buster. Danny, who had finished washing his hands for supper, ran up and held the door open for his mother. Then he said, "Buster, let's go make soap bubbles in the sink. I bet I can make more than you." And just like that, the boy put his legs down. He started smiling and nodded and ran off with his brother to wash his grubby hands. Jessa smiled a weary "thank you" at Danny, who was looking over his shoulder at her. They'd make a mess in the bathroom, but that was okay. Cleaning up after them wasn't nearly as exhausting as trying to win a battle of wills with Buster.

* * *

The day of Danny's 10th birthday dawned chilly and bright, a typical start to a spring day in the south. By noon, things would warm up considerably and when the party started at 2:00 pm it would be in the 70's…very pleasant for an outdoor birthday party.

Jessa worked hard all morning, baking and frosting the cake. It was chocolate devil's food with swirls of fudge frosting. Danny's favorite! She'd made lemonade and cookies. There were finger sandwiches and an ambrosia salad Jessa had on ice. They also had some beautiful, whole pecans Raymond had harvested from their own yard. Jessa had buttered and salted them, preparing to pop them in the oven to roast at the last minute.

Raymond usually worked Saturday mornings, but he had taken this morning off to help with the party. He moved the picnic table into the right position under the pecan tree and had borrowed Mrs. McGraff's card table and chairs. This, coupled with their own card table and chairs, plus a few extra lawn chairs scattered strategically around the yard, would hopefully make for enough seating for the six boys who would be attending the party, along with their parents, whom Jessa would invite to stay.

Then there were the games to prepare. Raymond had tacked a paper donkey to the tree. He had the tails and pins ready, along with a blindfold. He also set up some boxes as obstacles in the egg-and-spoon race game. And he brought his record player outside for the musical chairs game. Then Raymond had two errands to run right at the last minute before the party started. He needed to pick up extra ice from the ice company and a few pastries from the bakery.

Inside, Jessa was preparing the "birthday boy." For his present, she had gotten him a miniature, genuine U.S Navy uniform, starched it crisply and ironed it flat. It was all white, except for the navy blue piping along the collar and the navy tie. It came with a white sailor's hat, which Jessa cocked at an angle over Danny's slicked back hair. When she had finished with him, she walked him up to her vanity mirror and knelt down beside him, enjoying his reflection.

"Danny, I can't believe I gave birth to you right here in this bed 10 years ago, today. You look so handsome and all grown up!"

Danny smiled at himself in the mirror. He was so excited he wasn't sure he could wait till 2:00. His very own party! He'd never had one, other than a family party. He couldn't wait until Johnny and Freddy and the gang got here. He couldn't wait until they played the games. He couldn't wait until they ate the food... and he especially couldn't wait until he got to open his presents!

Danny tried to help the time pass by going out and examining the backyard. The transformation made him grin from ear to ear. His parents had really gone all out to make this a great birthday for him. He would have to thank them again.

Just then he heard the back door slam. It was his mom. "Honey, can you help me put this table cloth on the picnic table? I've also got two small ones for the card tables. "

The two of them stretched out the cloths across the tables, only to have the breeze blow them off again.

"Tell you what, Danny, I'll run go get your cake. It can hold the big cloth down and the lemonade pitcher and sandwich platter can hold the other two. Daddy will be back from his errands soon and then your guests should arrive. All right?"

Danny nodded excitedly. "Okay, Mother."

He practically floated behind his mother back into the house. In his state of near-delirium, he didn't notice his mother coming to an abrupt halt as they reached the kitchen. He bumped into her from behind and heard her gasp, "Oh, no!"

Danny peered around his mother only to see Buster sitting in the middle of the kitchen table. At first that was all that registered with Danny. But soon he realized that his brother was sitting, barefoot and shirtless, legs circling a three-layer, devil's food-with-fudge-frosting cake. *His* cake!

His mother moved quickly and grabbed the cake stand and cake and whisked it to the countertop, out of reach. Next she turned to Buster and saw that he had frosting in his hair, all over his face, on his hands and on his chest. He smiled at her and licked the palm of his hand.

Jessa grabbed a kitchen towel and screamed, "NO, Buster, NO!" and started wiping his hands.

Raymond ran into the kitchen from outside, his arms full of parcels. "What did he do?" He asked almost automatically.

"Look! Look at what he's done!" Jessa was still screaming. "He's ruined the cake and the guests are due to arrive in 15 minutes! I worked all morning on this cake! Now it's a mess. Why did I even try to do this? I should know we can't have people over!"

"Jessa, calm down," Raymond ordered. "I'll take Buster and bath him, you fix the cake the best you can. Raymond picked up Buster, trying to hold him away from himself so the chocolate frosting didn't end up on him. As he bustled out of the kitchen, Jessa turned from the cake and her eyes stopped on Danny.

He was huddled in the corner, tears welling up in his eyes. "Oh, Danny, Mother's so sorry about your cake. I can fix it. It looks like all Buster did was eat the frosting and I've got extra I can smooth around it. It'll be okay, I promise."

Danny nodded and wiped a tear away. He swallowed deeply and then turned a smiling face toward his mother.

"Okay, good boy. Now you go to the back yard and wait to see if any guests show up there. Let me know as soon as they do. I'll fix the cake and keep an ear out for the doorbell, all right?"

"Okay, he said and tried to smile bravely again. Turning and walking back outside, Danny looked over the beautiful party setting. He tried to get that giddy feeling back again, but it was gone. Now Danny was nervous as the words his mother spoke rang in his ears: "We can't have people over." It was true! He would be embarrassed, it was almost certain, by something Buster did. It happened every time his friends came over to play.

Just as Danny started feeling really sorry for himself, he was distracted by Bobby and his parents coming around the side of the house.

"Hi-Ho, Birthday Boy!" Mr. Miller said. "We're just following the trail of balloons."

"Happy Birthday, Danny!" Mrs. Miller said.

Bobby hung back a moment and his parents nudged him and his present forward. "Happy birthday, Danny," Bobby said as he handed Danny a wrapped package.

"Thank you," Danny said shyly, suddenly feeling self-conscious. As he walked over to put the present on a table, the back door slammed. It was his mother.

"Hi everyone, welcome!" Danny marveled that this gracious woman was the same one screaming at the top of her lungs just a few minutes ago.

Things started happening really fast now. Johnny and his mother arrived and soon Gil and Freddy Jameson came together, having walked the few blocks to Danny's house without a parent. Charlie and Christopher came right behind them, with their parents in tow. It was time for the party to begin.

Danny didn't even remember the sound of the back door slamming this time. But he could clearly remember every single thing that happened after that, like it was all in slow motion. After the door slammed, Danny turned his head to see who it was. All he could do then was say, "Mother, Buster," and point. There was Buster, running, naked, from his father, who was in hot pursuit. Buster was laughing his head off at the "game" as he dodged among the guests, pulling one of the table clothes and bumping the picnic table as he went. Jessa and Danny joined in the race to catch Buster, cornering him long enough for his father to catch up, throw a towel over the boy and carry him back toward the house, apologizing. Jessa apologized to the guests too, and then tried to breeze over the incident by suggesting everyone make a plate of food for themselves.

Danny didn't apologize. He knew it wouldn't make any difference at this point. He turned, knowing what he would see before he saw it. There stood Johnny, with all the gang gathered around him, his head thrown back, laughing and holding his stomach. The other boys looked at Johnny, then Danny, then back at Johnny and joined in with the laughing. Danny had no choice. He started to laugh too, just as hard as the others were laughing. Then Johnny started. "Hey Danny, what a show! Is this how all your parties are? I mean, what a retard! Running out here all naked and stuff."

"Yeah, that was real funny, huh?" Danny managed.

"Funny? It was weird, just like that weird brother of yours."

"Johnny!" The boy's mother grabbed him by the shoulder and marched him off to the side. She scolded Johnny in hushed tones while the other adults tried to change the subject. But as far as Danny was concerned, the subject couldn't be changed. It was the same subject as it always was: Buster.

* * *

That night, Danny put on his pajamas and got ready for bed just like any other night. But it wasn't any other night. It was the night of "The Day Buster Ruined My Birthday Party." And Danny wasn't forgetting it this time, like he had all the other times Buster had ruined things for him. He was mad and Buster was gonna know it!

His brother sat in the floor of the den, trying to build a tower with blocks. He could get up to about four and then they would fall over. Buster started calling for Danny.

"Dan-nee. Dan-nee. Come!"

He said it over and over again until Danny couldn't stand it any longer. He walked into the den and said, "What do you want, retard?"

"Danny!" His father had heard him and Danny didn't care. "Don't you ever call your brother that again! You're getting this from Johnny, aren't you? Now go sit on your bed and think about what you just did."

Danny stomped to his bedroom and flopped onto his bed. Lying there on his side, he could see almost straight out into the den and to his parents' bedroom door on the other side. His father was sitting at his desk, working. His brother was in the floor, playing. Then Danny noticed his new toys sitting on a corner chair. A sling shot, a new car, some soldiers, a yo-yo, a game, and his favorite, the new gun and holster set from Johnny.

For the next few minutes, Danny lay there on his bed, watching his brother struggle to stack the blocks. Each time the pile fell over, Danny secretly rejoiced. "Good!" he thought. He *wanted* the stack to fall, he *willed* it to fall.

Buster tried again and again and finally lost interest. As he was looking around the room for his next pursuit, his eyes landed on the pile of new toys. Danny watched as his brother got up off the floor and headed for his birthday presents. Without thinking, Danny leapt off the bed and ran, full force, at Buster. Just as the younger boy was reaching his hand toward the toys, Danny pushed him as hard as he could. Buster fell backwards, thumped his head on the ground and lay, sprawled out and stunned for a minute. Then he let loose a squall, loud and long.

Danny didn't care. He didn't care that his parents came running. He didn't care that they both were mad at him, he didn't care that his dad made him lie across the bed and get four lashes with a belt. He had pushed Buster down for the first time in his life, and it felt *good*. He didn't care what the consequences were. His brother was the worst brother a boy could have, and he was finished being nice about it. It was time he started showing how he truly felt about Buster. He hated him.

CHAPTER 18

Willa placed a stack of books in a box marked "sell" and went back to dust the shelf of the bookcase before emptying the next shelf. She and her father had been working at her grandmother's house all morning. Willa's sisters both had full time jobs and had to return to their own homes immediately after the funeral. They would come back over the summer to help with the sale or whatever. But the nitty-gritty work in between those visits would have to be done by Willa and her parents.

Willa had been able to close her eyes in the kitchen and pretty much sweep everything from the counters into a garbage bag. "Gram sure liked her plastic take-out containers," Willa chuckled to herself. She found this annoying habit endearing, now that Gram was gone.

She'd made slower progress going through the kitchen cabinets. They were filled with dishes Willa had eaten from as a child, Depression glassware and forks and spoons with sentimental value. There was the silver baby's spoon with the handle that curved under, so that a mom had something extra to hold onto while feeding a frisky baby. There was the child's spoon with a shepherd boy on the handle and a large, sterling silver spoon stamped with "U.S. Marine Corps." None of them valuable, but hard to part with, all the same.

It had taken her about three-hours, but now the small kitchen was clear and items were sorted in boxes marked, "Keep," "Sell," "Donate," and "Garbage." She and her father had discussed holding a garage sale in a few weeks, but the thought right now almost overwhelmed them. "One step at a time," Willa kept telling herself. She was trying to shelter her father as much as possible so soon after Gram's passing. He seemed especially sensitive and tender right now and she wanted to ease his grief as much as she could.

Mom had explained privately to Willa that losing one's mother was one of life's most finite, displacing things that could happen. Mom had said when her own mother died she'd felt very ungrounded, almost like she was floating at sea without an anchor. She'd said that's how mothers were. Even when you are grown, just knowing your mother shares the same Earth is consoling, in an almost undetectable way. A mother serves as a jumping-off place, a marker of where "home" is supposed to be. And when a mother passes, well, life is just sort of set adrift for her children.

"Willa, hon, do you think you're ready to go home and grab some lunch? I'm getting kind of hungry," her father said.

"Sure, Dad. I'll be right there. I'm just about finished with this bookcase. I found Gram's Bible. I want to go through it when I have time," Willa was excited to see what passages Gram had marked and what notes she'd written in the margins. As she held it by its spine and prepared to gingerly place it in a "Keep" box something slide out from the pages to the floor. Willa stooped and picked it up. It was a black and white photograph. In it were two small children, sitting on the back stoop of a house. There were day lilies blooming around the children and a huge old begonia plant sitting beside them in a pot. Willa recognized it as her grandparents' old home. Behind the children, off to the side was a woman in an old fashioned, full apron, her face as black as coal. She wore a kerchief on her head. The children were boys, dressed for summer in play suits, typical for the era the picture was from. Looking closer Willa noticed the younger boy, with white blonde hair had the unmistakable look of one of her students. He had Down Syndrome! Who were these boys in this photo with the black woman and why were they so important that Gram had a picture of them in her Bible?

The sandwich tasted dry as Willa took a big bite. *Oh, yeah,* she thought, *I forgot to add mayo.* So she unscrewed the lid on the Duke's Mayonnaise jar and dipped in the teaspoon her mother had provided. A teaspoon! Ha! She needed a giant serving spoon when it came to mayonnaise. Still, the teaspoon got the job done and Willa went back to eating her sandwich. Her mother had already fed Bella lunch by the time Willa and her father got back to the house, and now the little girl had gone to play with a neighbor girl. Willa was glad she had found a playmate here at Grandmom's and Granddad's.

But all during lunch, as her mother buzzed around those at the table like a bee to flowers, adding platters of fruit and sandwich meat and taking away used plates, Willa couldn't help but think about the picture she'd found. She was sure it was taken on the back stoop of her grandparents' former home. She'd spent plenty of photo "ops" positioned on the same stoop during her childhood. That would mean the two children knew or were related to her grandparents. The darker haired boy could be her father, although she was far from sure of that. But who was the blonde-haired Downs boy? And the old black woman had she worked for her grandmother?

Lunch was over soon enough and her father went to lie down for a quick afternoon nap. Willa helped her mother clear the table and put away the uneaten food. Here was her chance. Her mother had not met her father until he was 21 years old and home on leave from his Army duty, but she had been in the family for almost 50 years and knew most of her dad's growing up history. If there was anyone still alive who would know about the picture, it would be her mother.

Willa stooped to put the tea pitcher in the refrigerator and said, "Mom, Dad and I got a good bit done this morning. You'd be surprised."

"Yes, your father said you worked like a horse to get the kitchen finished. You have no idea what a burden that is off of us. We really appreciate it, hon." Her mother bent and kissed the top of Willa's head.

"Yeah, well after the kitchen, I started on that bookcase in the living room. Lots of books could be donated to your church library, Mom."

"That's a good idea, hon. I hadn't thought of that. I'll check with Pastor Gerald on Sunday."

"Well, as I was dusting the book case, I came across Gram's Bible. Dad said I could have it if it's okay with you."

"Sure, hon. I'm sure Gram would have loved for you to have it. I want you to have it. So there, that's done. What's next?"

Her mother had been kidding but Willa had a "next" in mind.

"Anyway, while I was thumbing through her Bible, look what I found. A picture! See?"

Willa's mother picked up her glasses from her chest, where they hung by a gold chain. She put the glasses on and then took the picture from her daughter's outstretched hand.

"Oh! "was all she said.

"Well, who are those kids? Is one of them Dad?" Willa asked in true, impatient fashion.

Her mother sighed. "Yes, dear. The older one is your dad. Hmmm. He looks about 4 or 5 years old."

"Who is the other one, Mom? And why would Gram have a picture of him in her Bible, of all places. That's usually reserved for family members."

"Yes, he *was* a family member, hon."

"He was?" Willa's hair stood up on the back of her neck. She had a sense she was about to find out something very important about her family.

"Yes. His name was Russell. But everyone in your Dad's family called him Buster. And he was your father's baby brother. The woman in the background took care of them when they were little. She and your grandmother apparently got very close, despite the age they lived in."

"Y...ya...you mean Dad had a little brother with...Down Syndrome? Really?" Willa was shocked.

"Yes, hon. Dad had a brother who was retarded. So, you see, this picture was in your grandmother's Bible because all three of these people were very dear to her.'"

Willa sank into a nearby chair, trying to get her mind around what she had just heard. *Why hadn't anyone ever told her about this "retarded" uncle of hers? And what other secrets had this family kept from her?*

Willa had a hard time sleeping the night she found the photo in her grandmother's Bible. She hadn't gotten very much information from her mother about this long-lost uncle before her father had come into the room and the two had stopped talking about him. She wasn't ready to ask her dad at this stage. His mother's death was still too fresh. So, she had to just lie in bed, stewing, flipping from side to side, trying to stop her thoughts from spilling into her sleep.

But that's exactly what happened. As soon as she fell asleep, she started dreaming. She dreamt she was in her grandparents' old home, staying for a visit. There was no one around, so she started for the back bedroom, where there were closets filled with old shoes, furs, hats, and jewelry for her to play dress up. She dreamed that she opened one of a series of closet doors to find nothing there.

Then she opened another and another and nothing was behind any of them. Finally she came to the last door and she became nervous, scared to turn the knob and pull it open. A lot of time seemed to pass before she finally she got up the nerve to open the door. When she did, there was a person behind it. He was tall and monsterish-looking with long, yellow teeth, yellow, brittle nails and shaggy, blonde hair. Willa screamed in fright. Suddenly her grandmother was there, dragging her away, reprimanding her and yelling at Willa to "stay away" from that closet.

Willa woke suddenly from the dream. She felt heavy and sad. She didn't need a psychologist to analyze this dream. Who was this man hiding in her family's secret closet? Was he a monster? Is that why she had never been told about him? And how could she reconcile her feelings of hurt and rejection with those of her grandparents and father, who clearly couldn't even talk about this man?

* * *

Willa sat on the floor of her grandmother's bedroom, cross-legged and surrounded by mounds of paper…newspapers, greeting cards, letters, bulletins, programs, clippings…every sort of paper imaginable. Her grandmother had lovingly held onto each piece of paper, unable to part with any of them. So now Willa was left with the task of sorting through it all.

At first it was fun to see the articles about her father's winning tennis matches in college and her distant cousin's appointment to a federal judgeship. But it soon became tedious and Willa started making quicker decisions about what should stay and what should go. Still, by noon Willa had made discouragingly little progress. She was afraid she'd throw something valuable or important away.

Just as she was about to give up, at least until after lunch, she came across a small book with a flowered, cloth cover. Opening the front cover, Willa found her grandmother's familiar scrawl, listing names, addresses and phone numbers. This could be what she'd been looking for! Willa wanted more information about her uncle…was he alive or dead? Maybe this address book would lead her somewhere.

She thumbed through the book, seeing some familiar names on the faded pages. But at first glance there was no clear lead. Then, on a second pass through the book, Willa noticed the name "Buster" listed under the "B's." Underneath the name was a series of phone numbers! One said, "Sheree—so.wker." Another said, "Whispering Pines Community." Finally, another number had the word, "dorm" next to it. She needed some time alone to call these numbers to see what she could find out.

After lunch, her father went to lie down for a rest and Willa was once again left alone with her mother. After clearing away the dishes and putting the lunchmeat back in the fridge, Willa couldn't help herself; she had to know.

"Mom?"

"Hmm?"

"Mom, I want to talk to you about Dad's brother."

"OK, hon." Her mother closed the refrigerator door and stood up, turning her full attention to Willa.

"Well, first of all, is he dead or alive?"

"He's alive, Willa. He should be in his early 70s, because he's just a little younger than your father. What else?"

"Well, where is he?"

"He's in a home. He's been institutionalized all his life."

"He has? Is he in good shape?"

"Hon, I didn't keep up with him like I should. Your grandmother was the person who knew the most about his condition. But I think he was in all right health."

"When does Dad see him? How often does he go? Can I go with him?"

"Willa, your Dad hasn't seen his brother in years. He really left that up to your grandmother."

"But Mom, Gram didn't drive. How did she get to see Buster if Dad didn't take her?"

"Well, hon, she didn't get to see him either. It got to be too emotional for her, so her doctors advised her to do as much she could over the phone."

Over the phone? Willa tried to take in all that she'd heard. If her grandmother hadn't been to see him for years, and her father hadn't seen him for years, did that mean her uncle hadn't had any visitors in years?

CHAPTER 19

Jessa was still shaking when Raymond came home early from work. He found her sitting on a chair in the kitchen, looking out into the dining room, where Buster was playing quietly on the floor with blocks. He came up behind his wife and tried to kiss her, but she pulled away, seeming distracted and agitated.

"Hey, Jessa," he said quietly. "I got here as soon as I could. What happened? Where's Danny?"

"He's down the street playing at the Jameson boys' house. He's fine."

"Good. Then, tell me what happened."

Jessa turned to Raymond and said, "I can't do this anymore. I can't do this. I can't keep him safe and you know that has always been my biggest requirement. I gotta be able to keep him safe! But Raymond, he is just so quick. He gets into stuff before I hardly know it. You know how he toppled into my mop bucket last week and just about drowned before I could get to him. I was *lucky* he pulled the bucket over and spilled all the water everywhere. Imagine, me considering that lucky. But I *was* lucky. Otherwise he would have drowned. And remember me catching him licking the rat poison out of the corners of the kitchen when we had that mouse a while back? Again, I was *lucky* he vomited so much and got that stuff up. I'm already exhausted and he is getting up more

194

and more often in the middle of the night. How am I supposed to keep him safe? And now this."

Jessa stopped for a moment and let the tears start coming. Raymond pulled up a chair next to his wife. He sat with his elbows on his knees, his head drooped from his shoulders. "Tell me what happened," he repeated.

Jessa got a tissue, blew her nose and tried again to tell her story. "I had just come in from the backyard with the laundry. I took it to our room to fold, but I'm telling you, I remembered to latch the top hook. I know I did. I remember putting the laundry basket down and reaching up to put the hook in the eye. Then I looked in on Buster in his room. He was all out of sorts because I had let Danny go outside. I tried to not let him see Danny leave, but he did and then he pitched a fit. I tried to calm him down by letting him help me get the clothes off the line, but he kept trying to run away, I guess trying to go find Danny and his friends. So I just quick, got the last of the sheets off the line and made him come in with me. He's been watching me with that hook and I just know he has figured out how it works." Jessa was jumbling up parts of the story as she went along.

"Well, then I went to our bedroom and started folding clothes, and tried to listen to the radio for a bit. There I was, just folding clothes and not thinking about too much of anything when I glanced out of the window at some movement I had seen out of the corner of my eye. It was Buster! He was outside by the edge of the road, trying to cross the street to follow Danny, I imagine.

"I dropped what I was doing and lifted up the window sash and started yelling to Buster to come back. He turned and stared at me a minute, with that determined look he gets on his face. He turned away from me and started running into the street! Mr. Maxy was coming down the street in his Chevy and had to slam on brakes to keep from hitting Buster." The tears started coming again.

"Raymond, by the time I got out of the house, he was all the way down the block to Chestnut Street! I saw him turn the corner and then heard another car slam on the brakes and my heart almost stopped! I ran as fast as I could to the corner and I turned to see a truck driver out of his truck running after Buster. You know how Buster tires quickly, so the truck driver caught up to him pretty fast. By the time I got to them, Buster was bellowing, trying to twist away from that fellow. I came up to them, crying and flustered and said, 'Thank you so much!' He was a nice fellow and helped me walk with Buster back to the house That's when I called you." Jessa buried her face in her hands and sobbed. Raymond tried his best to comfort his wife, but she was inconsolable. She felt helpless about improving the situation.

It had been eight long years since they had brought Buster home from the hospital. Sure, there had been good times, but the requirements of keeping up with Buster's needs as he got older seemed never-ending. Both parents were scared, exhausted, and out of ideas.

Jessa finally broke the silence by saying, "I don't know how I'm going to keep doing this every day. I just feel so alone and unable to keep up with Buster and still tend to the family's needs, Danny's needs. Oh, Raymond, what should we do?"

Raymond didn't like being in this position, but here was where he found himself. He felt his wife needed him to make the hard choice…a choice she just couldn't make herself. She hadn't been willing to even listen to those doctors at Duke talk about it nor had she wanted to hear what Dr. Miller had to say through the years. But *he* had listened. *He* knew, instinctively that this day would come. So he had gathered information, filled out forms and gotten their child in line. The time had come to seriously consider putting Buster in an institution.

* * *

Later that evening, after the boys were in bed, Raymond went into his bedroom to find Jessa lying on her side of the bed. At first he thought she was asleep. She'd been going to sleep earlier and earlier as Buster had started getting up in the middle of the night. But as he walked quietly around to her side of the bed he could see her eyes open, staring out the bedroom window at the pecan tree.

"Jessa?"

"Yes?"

"What are you doing?"

"Thinking."

"About what?" Raymond knew what.

She rolled over to look at him as he sat on the side of the bed next to her. "I'm thinking about how I can't watch Buster 24 hours a day. I'm thinking about how tired I am. I'm thinking about how Danny resents Buster more every day. I just don't know what to do about all this."

"Jessa, you know there is an option. You know Dr. Miller says parents of kids like Buster have done it much earlier than this. We've tried for a really long time."

"No, Raymond, I can't do it!"

"Then I'll do it for you! I don't want to send Buster away, Jessa, but we need help with him and there is no help here in Junction Point."

"Raymond, he's my baby. I can't send my baby away just because he is difficult."

"This is more than difficult. We don't know what to do for Buster! He could learn a skill or something. God knows I don't want to send my son away either! But I think we have run out of options."

"Raymond, it's so far away. All the way past Columbia, up near Jordon. How can I bear to be away from him like that? I have to be able to be with him every day."

"Being with him every day may not be possible. But we can visit him."

"Visit our own son? That's not natural. He should be with us all the time!"

"Jessa, it just may not be possible. We've put it off for a long time. I'm going to call the Asylum tomorrow to see where Buster is on the waiting list. It's time to consider all our options."

Jessa waited a moment then nodded "okay", just as she heard padded little feet hit the floor in the other bedroom.

"I'll go," Raymond said wearily. "But tomorrow I'm calling."

* * *

The Buick turned from the main road onto a long, winding gravel road. They passed under a sign that said, "SOUTH CAROLINA ASYLUM FOR IMBECILES AND THE MENTALLY INFIRM." Jessa tried not to read the sign. She just looked out the window. The road, which was really a long driveway, wound past pastures of black and white cows. Then they came to a stretch of road with newly planted crepe myrtles, maples, magnolias and other young trees. They finally came to a small, white clapboard building, marked "Office."

Jessa and Raymond sat still for a moment, neither moving to get out of the car. Neither was looking forward to what lay inside that building and what it meant for their son's future.

Suddenly, a young man in his teens came bursting around the corner of the building, walking with his fists clenched, his gait showing determination. He marched up the front steps and opened wide the door to the office. The young man had the same "look" as Buster…flat, round face, low-set ears, dangling tongue and above all, slanted eyes.

Jessa and Raymond looked at each other and when curiosity got the better of them, they got out of the car to follow the young man.

Inside the office, they came to a desk with a typewriter but the chair was empty. They could hear a loud voice coming from a back office.

"No! I do it!"

"Now, Franklin, settle down. We'll straighten all this out."

"No! I do it! It's mine!"

"What's yours?"

"My Shovel. I shovel the cow barns, not Barney."

"Okay, come with me, Franklin. Let's get to the bottom of this."

A tall, lanky, bald man in a shirt and tie, sleeves rolled up, came out of the back office first, followed by the upset young man and then an older woman with a tidy bun of hair on the back of her head. The woman said, "I'm sorry, Dr. Amos. I tried to stop Franklin from interrupting you, but he just charged right in."

"Well, can you blame him, Alice? Someone is messing with his manure shovel. That's sacred property."

About this time the group noticed Jessa and Raymond standing by the front desk, their mouths gaping open. This boy had talked! In sentences! Sure, his speech was slow and impaired, but for them to see an older version of Buster was eye-opening. This boy was upset, but he had a mission and he got his point across. For Buster to function at this level would be nothing short of miraculous, as far as they were concerned.

Dr. Amos stopped in front of the desk and said, "Sorry, folks. Just a bit of a misunderstanding here. Can I help you?"

"We're Raymond and Jessica Bland. We're here to see you, Dr. Amos."

"Ah, yes, the Blands. Well, nice to meet you." He shook Raymond's hand and nodded to Jessa.

"Doc, it's mine! You tell Barney," the young man interrupted.

"Okay, okay. I'll tell him Franklin. Can you tell the Blands hello?"

"Hullo," Franklin said shyly and even smiled, momentarily forgetting the shovel injustice.

"Tell you what, folks. Why don't you just follow along with me? It'll be the best way to get a feel for our operation here. That way you can see our layout and can ask questions as they come up."

Jessa liked this man's openness right from the start. "Okay," she said, feeling shy herself.

"All right. Alice, you hold down the fort. I'll be back, I promise."

"Yes, sir, Dr. Amos." The flustered woman looked relieved at the thought of having the office cleared out.

The group headed out the door, led by the energetic Dr. Amos. As they walked, he explained what they were seeing.

"We have 250 acres here that the state bought for the asylum back in 1921. We've come a long way in the 29 years we've been operating."

"Have *you* been here the whole time?" Raymond asked.

"Yes, I was the lucky guy the legislature tapped to head things up here. Before that, I worked at the State Hospital for the Insane. For some reason, they thought our inmates had a lot in common with the insane inmates. It's been a steep learning curve for us all.

"Anyway, we run a small dairy barn here. About 20 head of cattle. It just about pays for itself and the inmates can work in the barn, under the supervision of a couple of staff people. We also have a large vegetable garden, as you see here." The doctor waved his arm to the right to show about an acre of land plotted for a garden. It's also inmate-run. Our laundry is over there,"– again a hand motion. "And our dining hall is off to the left. Everything that happens here involves the inmates' labor. It gives them a purpose, those who are capable. And for those who aren't, they benefit from the products of our efforts here."

"Wow, it seems like it would take a whole lot of staff to watch the children here. Surely *they* aren't working yet," Jessa commented.

"Well, Mrs. Bland, we have the first generation of adult inmates who have grown up here doing much of the work. But we start training the children at a young age. It takes them longer to pick up on things than it does most children. Believe me, most of them are anxious to take part. They all can get real stubborn about things, though. Sort of like Franklin and his shovel. His work day came to a halt because he wants his shovel and nobody else's. So let's see if I can get to the bottom of this situation. You folks feel free to look around while I look into it."

Jessa and Raymond stood on a sidewalk, trying to take in the whole campus.

"It looks impressive," Raymond said hopefully.

"I don't know. It sounds like a child could get hurt doing all this work. I mean a cow could kick them in the head or something."

"Oh, Jessa," Raymond laughed a little. "No cow is going to kick Buster in the head."

"How do you know?" Jessa asked indignantly. "I was worried leaving the boys with Mrs. McGregor today, knowing how strong and fast Buster can be. How do you think he'd be here if I am not here to supervise?"

"Jessa, Dr. Amos indicated there is supervision. Just give it a chance. Let's ask to see the dorms next."

Dr. Amos had returned, having "righted" the shovel incident by moving Barney to another part of the barn for the rest of the day.

"Things usually work out," he said. "It just takes a level head to keep things from escalating," he explained.

"What happens when 'things escalate?'" Jessa asked.

"Well, I won't lie to you, Mrs. Bland. These inmates are fully grown men and women with all their hormones intact. They can be emotional and headstrong. But it's our job to discipline them when they do something wrong and reward them when they do something right. It's all part of our training. Sort of like when you're training a dog, no offense meant."

"How do you discipline them?" Jessa asked, ignoring the dog comment.

"We take away privileges, things they like. Like dessert or radio time or other things they like. Sometimes it depends on the individual. We reward the same way. Maybe they get to go on a trip into town or something. But they gotta earn it. Under no circumstances do we use corporal punishment. It's forbidden."

Jessa listened intently to everything Dr. Amos said as their tour continued. He showed them where a future hospital would be built, then took them on a tour of a dormitory. He walked them through a common area, which was furnished to look like a living room. Just off that were bedrooms with eight beds, each with a side table and a small dresser drawer. And there was a large shared bathroom for each wing.

Everything looked fine, but Jessa's heart still sank at the thought of leaving Buster here. Despite the warm "glow" painted by Dr. Amos, this still had the feel of a prison to her. Perhaps it was the tall fence and barbed wire that gave her that feeling. When she asked Dr. Amos about it he made no apologies.

"That fence is a life-saver…literally. If we didn't have it, I can't tell you the number of inmates that would wander off looking for home or whatever. Because we have the fence and lock down at 8:00 every night till 8:00 the next morning, the dorm supervisors can actually get some sleep at night. We need the fence. It's to keep the inmates safe," Dr. Amos concluded.

Jessa could believe it would take a fence like this to keep dozens of little Busters safe and contained. She just didn't want *her* baby to be behind it.

* * *

Jessa's head was swimming as she and Raymond drove the five hours back home to Junction Point. The asylum appeared to be an ideal place for a child like Buster. He'd be with his own kind, he'd have staff who were experienced in working with children like him. He'd get to learn a skill. It all just seemed so perfect. But Jessa didn't like it. It smelled of industrial cleaner, there didn't seem to be enough staff and Jessa was concerned about violence among the "inmates." Why did they use that word anyway? It even sounded like a prison.

Raymond, on the other hand, was lost in his own thoughts. He didn't like to think about institutionalizing Buster. *But let's face it,* he thought: *there is nothing for Buster in Junction Point.* If he continued the way he was going, Raymond was afraid Buster would just be "wild" and uncontrollable. He liked the idea of Buster having responsibility. He'd have to make his bed. He'd have to help out around the place. These were things Jessa and Raymond had been unsuccessful at with Buster at home.

"Jessa?" He had to broach the subject with her. He knew she would need some convincing, but at the same time, he didn't want her to ever feel like she was forced into anything.

"What?"

"We've got to talk about this. What did you think?"

"I think Buster is too young. Maybe when he's older, but right now, he's not old enough to fend for himself."

"Hon, we saw children in the Primary Program that were younger than Buster and they were doing great!"

"How do you know? How do you know they were 'great'?"

"Jessa, you know what I mean."

"Raymond, I don't know anything. I just feel like we are giving up on our child...like we are giving him away. You heard what Dr. Amos said: Buster would become a 'ward of the state.' Do we want to give him to the state to raise?"

"Jessa, I know it would be hard. But, I'm starting to think it might be the best thing for Buster."

"So you've made up your mind? You want us to give up Buster?" Jessa's voice broke as she spoke.

Raymond pulled the car over to the side of the road. He turned and put his hand on Jessa's shoulder. When she wouldn't look at him, he gently tilted her chin upward. "Jessa, I do not want to give up Buster. I wish we could do everything he needs at home. But we can't. We are having too many close calls. I don't want him hurt. We can sleep on it but in the morning, Dr. Amos will need to know our decision. He can't hold a spot open for Buster for long.

* * *

The next morning, Raymond woke to find the bed beside him empty. Jessa's pillow had not been touched. She hadn't slept in the bed at all, as far as he could tell. He grabbed his robe and walked out into the den. The boys' bedroom door was still closed, so they must both be asleep, at least for a few more minutes. He turned and quietly slipped into the living room. There, on the floor, a pillow from the sofa under her head and her bath robe the only blanket, lay Jessa...right in front of the back door.

Raymond knelt down beside her and tenderly pushed a lock of hair behind her ear. She opened her eyes.

"What time is it?" Jessa asked.

"A little before six o'clock. Have you slept out here on the floor all night?"

"Yes, I guess I have," she answered sleepily. "Right as I was about to get in bed last night I heard Buster get up. I snuck up on him and just watched. He managed to get the lock undone on the door handle and then he used a broom to push the hook open on the screen door. I couldn't believe it! When I caught him, he just laughed. He got up six more times; the last time was just about an hour ago. He tried to go in the kitchen and get himself a biscuit. The whole stove would have fallen on him if I hadn't been there. I scolded him but he just laughed. Raymond, I'm exhausted."

"I know, sweetheart." Raymond sat on the floor next to Jessa and lifted her head onto his lap.

"Jessa, I've been thinking. You're right; we shouldn't give up on our son. We shouldn't send him away."

"No, Raymond, I've been thinking too. I've always said that I was the only one who could keep Buster safe. I'm his mama and I should be able to shelter him from danger. But I have come to realize that I can't....I can't keep him safe! I am only human and when I let my guard down, when I sleep, that's when Buster gets into trouble. I have to sleep at night and you do too. So, as much as it breaks my heart to admit it, I can't keep Buster safe. I just can't"

Jessa turned her head into Raymond's chest and sobbed. She cried from exhaustion. She cried over the prospect of losing her son to an institution. She cried over possibly losing her son if he wasn't in an institution. But most of all she cried over the broken hope that had carried her this far.

CHAPTER 20

C olumbia, South Carolina is steamy and hot in July and *this* morning, Willa could already tell, was not going to disappoint. She relished her shower in her parents' bathroom. It not only washed away the night sweats Willa had been experiencing, but it also gave her time to think. Willa loved her parents very much, but she had really not had a moment to herself since the funeral. She'd either been helping at her grandmother's house or she'd been here, with her parents in their home.

Willa's mother had a doctor's appointment this morning. She had been battling back and hip pain for a couple of years now and had found that the one thing that gave her true pain relief was a steroid injection. The problem was that the relief wore off and the pain gradually returned over a period of months. So, it was time for another injection, as Willa could tell with the return of her mother's limp.

Her mother needed someone to drive her to the appointment, because she had to be sedated for the injection. Normally, Willa would have been glad to drive her mother, enjoying the time to talk one on one with her. But this morning, she had plans of her own.

"Morning, love," Willa greeted Bella as she walked into her parents' spacious kitchen. It was so nice here because her parents were early risers and so was Bella. By the time Willa finished with her morning shower, her mother had prepared a nice, hot breakfast for Bella and they'd started making plans for the day.

"Morning, Mommy. Can I go to the pool with Candee and her mom today?" Bella smiled up at Willa hopefully.

"Well, I don't see why not. There sure isn't any other logical place to spend a day like this."

"Will you come, too, Mommy?" Even though it was just Bella and Willa staying at her parents' home, and not the whole family, it seemed like Willa had been pretty busy with all the tasks at her grandmother's house. It would be nice to spend a day at the pool with Bella. But Willa had to find some quiet time by herself.

"Not today, hon. Mommy's not feeling up to sitting out in the heat. I think I 'm coming down with a cold. But you go and have fun. Dad, will you be able to drive Mom?"

"Oh sure, I was planning to anyway. Why don't you take a day off from Gram's house today and just rest? I don't want you to get run down."

"Sounds heavenly, Dad. Is that okay with you, Mom?"

"Sweetheart, I think that's just what you should do. Stay here where it's cool and quiet. Enjoy the time to yourself.

Willa poured herself some coffee and waited for her family to disperse to their different activities. When everyone had gone, Willa sat cross-legged in the middle of her bed, just as she had when she was a teenager, but this time she used her cell phone, not the house phone, to make calls.

Call number one: Joel. She missed him so much and her boys too. She *needed* to touch base. "Hi Joel," she said as she heard his voice. Even after almost 20 years of marriage she still got a flutter in her stomach when she talked to him on the phone.

"Hi, Babe! I miss you! The boys miss you. They think we are just on one big campout here at the house. We have their friends stay here overnight, if it isn't our boys who are spending the night off somewhere. They all sleep in their sleeping bags and I cook on the grill, or we roast hotdogs in the fire pit out back. We're roughing it without you. When are you coming back?"

"Oh, Joel, do you think you could spare me another couple of weeks? I've got some loose ends to tie up here."

"Loose ends? What do you mean?"

"Joel, you won't believe it! I have found a long-lost uncle I've never known about. It's unbelievable!"

Willa filled Joel in on what she'd accidently learned, which was frustratingly little.

"That's amazing! I can't believe you have an uncle who has been living 30 minutes up the road from your parents all these years. What are you going to do? Are you going to meet him or what?"

Good ol' Joel. He wanted to "cut to the chase" and get to the bottom of things.

"Well, yeah, I hope to. But there is a lot to work out first. I'm going to make some phone calls as soon as I hang up with you."

"Well, Willa, I want you to be able to see this thing through. But we miss you! I miss you! Do you think you can come home for the weekend? I just can't take off any more time from work or I'd come see you."

"Okay, sure. I know Bella's feeling a little homesick herself. She really misses y'all!"

"All right, then we'll see you this weekend. Okay?"

"Okay."

"Now, I really have to get back to work, so I'd better go. Anything else? Any other surprises?"

"Nope. I think that's it. I'll call you one more time before we come home this weekend. I love you, Joel."

"Love you too, Willa. Bye."

'Bye."

Willa hung up the phone. Second call: That was tough. Should she call the social worker, the administration or just take a chance and call the dorm directly? She decided to call the dorm. Maybe he would answer.

Her hand shook as she dialed the numbers. It rang once, then twice. A man answered the phone, "Hello, Dorm3, "

For a moment, Willa forgot who or what to ask for. "Ummm. Can I speak to Buster Bland, please?"

"Buster? We don't have no 'Buster' here."

Willa's heart sank. Then she remembered that Buster was only a nickname. What was his real name? Willa flipped back through the address book and found "Buster. But there was no other name listed.

"Do you have a student who has the last name Bland?" she tried.

"Ma'am, we don't have 'students' at this location. We got clients. If you don't have a first name, then I can't help ya. Sorry."

"All right, I'll try to find out and call back.

"Sure, ok."

She hung up, frustrated. She decided to call the social worker next. Surely she would recognize Buster's last name. Willa dialed the number.

"Hello, this is Shereé."

Willa froze. What should she ask first? "I-I am trying to get some information about a man named Buster Bland."

"Buster Bland? Do you mean Russell Bland?"

Russell! That was the name! "Yes, I'm sorry. Russell Bland."

"Well, I'm his social worker, Shereé Parks. Can I help you?"

"Yes, Ms. Parks, I—I am a relative of Mr. Bland's and I am trying to get information about him."

"Have you spoken to his mother, Jessica Bland?"

"No...I mean yes, she's my grandmother. But she recently passed away."

"Oh, I'm so sorry to hear that! I need to make a note in Russell's file. I sure will miss my monthly calls with Mrs. Bland. Such a sweet lady. And who should I put down as the contact person and decision maker for Russell from this point on?"

"I—I'm not sure. Listen, I want to talk about Buster...uh Russell, and meet him, stuff like that."

"Meet him? You mean you've never met him before now?"

"No. As a matter of fact, I just found out about his existence, right after my grandmother died. I am confused about a lot of stuff and want to find out more about him. Can you help me?"

"Well, we will see how much help I can offer you. What was your name?"

"Oh, I'm so sorry! My name is Willa Bland Grizzard. Call me Willa."

"And you can call me Shereé. Willa, Russell's annual Staffing Meeting is coming up next week. I had left a message on your grandmother's answering machine about it. If you want to come to that, you can meet with all the specialists who oversee Russell's care and find out the latest on him. He's one of our rare geriatric clients with Downs Syndrome. He's a bit medically fragile now, but you can learn all about him at the Staffing. Can I put you down on the Attendees' List?"

This sounded so official. But it did sound like a good way to get to know about her uncle. "Yes, Shereé, put me down. And can one other person attend? Can you put my father, Daniel Bland, down to attend?"

"I sure can. This is great news! No one has been able to attend Russell's staffings for several years now. To have two family members will be tremendous! I look forward to meeting you next week, Willa."

When Willa hung up, she wondered just how involved she wanted to be with this man. And had she done the right thing to include her father in all of this?

* * *

Later that evening after Willa had helped Bella shampoo the pool chlorine from her hair, read to her and put her to bed, she made a specific effort to get a conversation with her father started. The two were in the family room watching TV together.

"Dad, you need anything? I can make you some popcorn. We won't tell Mom!" Willa's mother was already in bed, taking advantage of the good rest she got whenever she'd had a steroid injection. She wouldn't approve of her husband eating "junk food" late at night.

"Okay, hon. If you'll help me eat it, I would love some popcorn."

So Willa made popcorn in the microwave and fixed the two of them drinks. When she'd finished, she balanced two small bowls of popcorn and two cups of juice as she made her way back to the family room.

"Here you go, Dad." Willa served her father.

"Good night, this looks good enough to eat," the elder gentleman joshed with his daughter.

Willa settled into her chair and started eating her snack. The only way to do this was just to do it.

"Dad, I want to talk to you about something. Something about Gram and Granddaddy and you."

"You want to talk about my brother, Buster, right?" he said hesitatingly. "Oh, don't look so surprised. Your mom told me you found a picture of us in Mother's Bible. She told me you were quite shocked to find out about Buster."

"Well, yes. To find out I have an uncle I have never known about is a little bit....shocking."

"Well, I'm a little surprised about that because you did know about him. You used to hate it when we had to make trips to Whispering Pines without you. I thought for sure you would remember that."

Willa thought for a moment and there was something familiar about all of that. "What trips are you talking about, Dad?"

"Well, for years Mother and Daddy would come over here to Columbia from Junction Point, about once a month. You were always so happy to see them because they spoiled you, mainly with attention, but they also brought you little gifts and such. The beginning of their visits was always so happy and fun for you. But somewhere in the middle, we would all three plan to go see Buster. It was a hard trip to make and one that frankly, I dreaded every month. But I knew we had to do it."

Willa blinked. She *did* remember pleading with her grandmother to take her with them on some trip. She remembered feeling instinctively that the trip made everyone sad. She remembered being confused when they told her they would be back soon but that they just had to go visit a man with the mind of a child. Willa couldn't believe it now! She had known about her uncle! At least she knew him as much as she had been allowed to know about him.

"Dad I *do* remember the trips. I also remember being confused that if he had the mind of a child, then why wouldn't I, a child, be able to come along on the trip to see him. It sounded fun and mysterious to my young mind."

"Willa, I tell you, things are so different now than they used to be. We kept things like…my brother's condition…quiet, hidden. Don't get me wrong. People in Junction Point knew I had a retarded brother. But once he went to live at Whispering Pines, we just didn't talk about him anymore. It was considered private, painful for our family, so people just didn't bring it up. My friends all just knew when I said I had to go out of town for the weekend that I was going to visit my brother. But it is not something we would talk about."

"Dad, I want to talk about him! I want to get to know him. I am going to attend his Staffing meeting next week and I want you to go with me. Will you do that? Help me get to know this uncle, this brother of yours?"

"Willa, I…I don't think you know what you're getting yourself into. I don't want you to be disappointed. It's been a while since I've seen him. I've always kinda felt like, what's the point? He doesn't even recognize me. He's been institutionalized for over 60 years! No, Willa, it's just too painful to go see him."

"Dad," Willa responded, kneeling down next to his chair, "I know this is hard. And yes, we do things differently than we used to do them. But this won't just be a visit. The main purpose will be to get an update on how Buster is doing and have some input into what happens to him over the next year."

"I don't want to go." Her dad sounded like he'd made up his mind.

"Why, Dad? Please go with me so I don't have to go alone. I don't know what to expect or what kinds of decisions I'll be asked to make."

"Listen here, Willa, you are pushing me and I don't like to be pushed. I don't want to go! I'm not going! And you have no business going either. The state has been taking care of Buster for all these years and we should just leave his care up to the team of specialists who know Buster best. You don't know him. How will you be able to help the situation at all?"

Willa looked at her father as her face started to crumple; tears started rolling down her cheeks. "Dad, you may be right. I don't know Buster, but it's not because I didn't want to know him. I was never given the chance to know him. I have spent the better part of the last year working with children who have the exact disability as Buster has! That doesn't seem like a coincidence to me. God gave me that knowledge and maybe I can use it to help make Buster's life better in some way.

"I'm going. It's Tuesday morning at 9:45 at Whispering Pines. I hope you will go with me, but if not, I'm going to go, no matter what!"

Willa tried to enjoy being home for the weekend. She'd been away over two weeks and it was good to sleep in her own bed, to see her husband and sons. But her heart was not completely with her. She still felt like she had unfinished business in South Carolina.

Bella enjoyed tussling with her brothers. She was happy as a pea in a pod to be home. She couldn't wait to go outside to play with her neighborhood friends. Willa sat on the front porch, sipping iced tea and just enjoying a quiet moment. Joel had just finished mowing the grass and came up on the porch to enjoy the shade and a cool drink of his own.

"So, Willa, how old is this uncle of yours?"

"He's 71. It's really remarkable that a man with Down Syndrome has lived so long. It's a shame it had to be in an institution."

"What are you going to do if your father refuses to go with you to the meeting? Are you still going to go?"

"Yes! I plan to go no matter what my father chooses to do."

Joel was quiet for a moment.

"What, you don't think I should go without my dad?"

"No, it's not necessarily that."

"Well, then what is it?" Willa's patience was thin on this topic, she was discovering.

"It's just…well, Willa, have you ever considered this might be a really touchy subject for your dad? You know, people back then didn't talk openly about things like they do now."

"I don't care! I can't believe my grandparents would put their son in an institution for his whole life and never take him out! And my father…why didn't he take him out when he was old enough to do something about it? Instead, it was treated as some sort of shameful secret."

"Willa, I know you are still processing all this new information you've learned about your family. But please be careful about judging people's 1940's actions by 21st century standards."

"Okay, Oprah. I won't do that!"

"No, I'm serious Willa, you don't know what times were like back then. They didn't have schools around the corner waiting to help you with education and therapy. Maybe your grandparents felt like this was their only choice."

"We both know they had another choice. Anyway, are you going to get in the shower? 'Cause I want to get in as soon as you're done."

"Okay, okay. I'm going."

Willa continued sipping her tea and watching the boys play a game of two-hand touch with their friends. Overall, it had turned out to be a beautiful summer Saturday. She only had a few weeks left before she had to head back to school. She wanted to relax and enjoy the rest of her time off. Maybe a bath would be better than a shower, she thought. So, when she heard the back door slam she knew Joel had finished with his shower.

Willa went inside, poured herself another glass of iced tea and went to her bathroom. She bent over and turned on the faucet and sprinkled a generous helping of bath salts into the tub. Then she also added a little bubble bath, because bubbles were a must.

Dropping her shirt, bra and shorts in a pile, she grabbed her towel and topped the pile off with her panties. Now where was that razor of hers? She bent over to look under the sink, but she didn't see it, so she bent even farther to see into the back of the cabinet. Oh, there it was!

Then, suddenly despite the roar of the tub water she became aware of a presence. She "felt" it more than heard it. She stood up quickly, catching her head on the corner of the counter. Slowly she turned, wincing in pain, to see her five-year old daughter standing in the doorway, looking horrified.

"Bella what are you doing? Don't you know to knock?"

"I did knock."

"What are you doing?" Willa repeated.

Bella's eyes were as wide as they could get. "Mommy, you need to get in the tub and clean yourself up. You have poo-poo all over your bottom!"

"What? Bella I don't have poo-poo on my bottom!"

"Yes you do. It's all black down there!"

Willa walked over to Bella and knelt down, careful to keep the towel tight around her. "Bella, honey, that's not poo-poo. It's hair."

It seemed unlikely that Bella's face could register any more disgust, but somehow, it did. "Mom! Ewww, hair?"

"That's right, Bella. Grown women grow a small amount of hair around their bottom area. One day you'll have some too."

It was more than a girl could take. Bella made a gagging sound and turned to leave. Willa stood there wondering if she had scarred her child forever. But before Bella got far, she turned around and said, "Oh, yeah, mom. Here's the phone. It's Aunt Cora."

Willa took the phone and gave Bella the stretched eyeball look that said, "Beat it!" Then she pulled the door shut firmly behind her and turned off the running water. She then decided to climb into the tub for the call, making a body-sized opening in the bubbles.

"Cora, hi! Sorry that took so long. I…"

"Yes, I heard what you were up to. You do know that she's going to share that scene with at least a friend or two."

Willa groaned.

"And don't be surprised if all her Barbies end up with anatomically correct drawings between their legs."

Another groan. "I was caught off guard. I didn't know what to say."

The two chatted casually for a few more minutes, and then Cora said, "Lora is flipping out at Mom and Dad's."

"What? Why? I think we got a lot done. They should be ready for the estate sale by the time I get through there."

"It's not Gram's house that has Lora so flustered. She talked to Mom and Dad right when she got there yesterday and they told her you are determined to meet Dad's brother. We just want to know, 'Why?'"

"Why? Well because we have a close relative that none of us has ever met and I can't stand the thought of him being closed up in that institution for all those years. You should see all the services we give to our students at school. Nowadays, he could have speech therapy, physical therapy, occupational therapy. All sorts of assistance is available…"

"Willa, let me stop you right there. We don't know anything about this man. He could be violent or deranged. But mostly Willa, it's the sadness Lora says she sees in Dad's eyes. I just can't condone hurting our father! You need to let go of this 'rescue mission' you seem to be on. Dad's brother has survived just fine so far."

"See? He's 'Dad's brother' to you, not 'my uncle.' This man is related to us, Cora! He is Gram's son! He's not just some man somewhere. He's our uncle and he's locked up in an institution! I, for one, can't stand the thought of it."

"Willa, you are so stubborn and I know you have made up your mind. But me and Lora, we don't want anything to do with all of this. You need to think about Dad and all he's done for us and try not to tread all over his feelings. Try to be patient and understanding. That's all I really called to say."

The two hung up after a little longer and Willa was left with an uneasy feeling. She was used to her sisters standing by her side in almost every situation. But not this one. She could tell this one would be a lonely, emotional journey she would take alone. But that was okay. She was determined to take it, no matter what.

Chapter 21

D anny tried to put his head against the car window in the backseat of his parents' Buick and sleep. But he couldn't. Still, he kept his eyes shut because Buster would try to engage Danny in some sort of play if he gave any hint of being awake. And Danny didn't feel like playing. Not today.

They'd been in the car for hours and were almost to the new "school" Buster was going to go to. Danny had watched as his mother had taken down a little black suitcase from the closet shelf and had packed Buster's underwear and undershirts. She'd bought two new pairs of dungarees for Buster and four shirts with long sleeves, buttons down the front and button-down collars. *Buster is sure gonna need help with all those buttons,* Danny thought.

His mother put all that into the suitcase. She had included Pete, the old stuffed bear Danny used to drag around but now it belonged to Buster. Danny didn't need a stuffed bear any more. Then she put in two of Buster's favorite books and a blanket with satin trim that Buster loved to sleep with. Finally, she included a picture of the family at Danny's last birthday party. His mother had acted all sad and teary-eyed as she packed the items, but Danny didn't buy it. This was going to make life so much easier for all of them.

The suitcase held just enough items to get Buster started at the new school. They would have clothes and stuff for Buster when he got there, his mother had explained…sort of like a uniform, Danny guessed.

As they'd left their home, Mrs. McGraff had come out and hugged Buster tight. She had cried and so had his mother. Not Danny though. This was for the best. His father just kept a tight-lipped, grim face during all the packing. Danny and his parents had brought suitcases so they could stay in a motel, near the school for the night. It was like going on vacation. But Buster was staying and they were not.

The car turned off the main road and onto a gravel road. Danny could see the front gate of the school. Buster reached up and tapped his mother on the shoulder and said, "Maw, Co-cola."

"Not now, Buster. We'll get a drink in just a minute," she replied. His mother had explained to Danny how the people at the school would help Buster talk better, so that others could understand him. But there was very little to misinterpret now. Buster kept saying with urgency, "Co-cola. Co-cola."

The road wound through some pasture land and finally came up to a landscaped area in front of a white building. His dad parked the car and looked over at his wife, the same tight-lipped expression on his face. Both parents opened their doors and got out of the car. Buster quickly opened his door and slid out too. Danny noticed his mother slipping her gloved hand into Buster's. How silly, Danny thought. Buster is eight-years-old and doesn't need to hold his mother's hand any more. Danny quickly walked past the two of them, with his own hands shoved deep into his pants pockets.

Inside the building, an older lady smiled at them all and inquired politely about their drive. Then she showed them to the restrooms and promised drinks for them all when they returned. "Co-cola," Buster said loudly.

"Okay, Russell, fine. A Co-cola it will be. Same for all the rest of you?"

"Yes, that'll be just fine," Danny's mother said.

When they emerged from the restrooms, the cold drinks were waiting, and so was some paperwork, which Danny's father sat down and got to work on. His mother stayed close to Buster, helping him manage his drink. Danny walked along the walls, looking at pictures. One showed a bunch of children who looked surprisingly like Buster, dressed in costumes and dancing. They were surrounded by adults dressed in their Sunday best, applauding and smiling. Danny liked the picture. It made him feel happy. This place would be a lot of fun. *It isn't fair that Buster gets to come here and I don't,* Danny thought.

As his father was finishing the paperwork, a man named Dr. Amos came out of a back office to meet with them. First, he looked at Buster and said, "Hello Russell. How are you today?" He bent from his waist to be more at eye level and reached for Buster's hand. Buster grasped Dr. Amos' hand very clumsily, his big, fat fingers curling around Dr. Amos' in an attempt to shake hands.

"Doctor, his name is Russell, but all he's ever been called is 'Buster,'" Danny's mother said.

"Mrs. Bland, all of our records will list his given name. No one will know to call him by a nick name. He'll get used to it soon enough." Danny's mother's eyes fluttered down. He'd seen her do her eyes like this to keep from crying.

Danny wasn't going to cry like his mother. He was a big boy now and all of this was no reason to cry. His parents had explained that Buster needed a special school to help him learn better. But Danny knew the real reason Buster was being sent away. It was his party. Buster had just been so bad at his party and Danny had let his parents know, this time, that he was really mad about it. Buster should be sent away to learn how to behave at birthday parties. This would be a good thing for Buster.

Dr. Amos instructed the Blands to get back into their car and drive around to the dorm where Buster would be staying. Dr. Amos would meet them there.

The dorm had linoleum floors, perfect for running and skidding on, Danny thought. There were two men who introduced themselves to the Blands as the dorm monitors. Buster would share a bedroom with seven other boys, ranging in age from five to 15. The bathroom had four sinks and two shower stalls with plastic shower curtains. Back in the bedroom, one of the dorm monitors was trying to help Danny's mother get Buster settled in.

"Here...Russell. Here is *your* bed. You can put Pete on the pillow to keep you company." His mother's voice quivered. The man then showed her the dresser for Buster's clothes. She quickly emptied the few items neatly into the drawers and shut the suitcase.

"Won't you need to leave the suitcase for Buster, Mother? For when he comes back home?" Danny asked and immediately wished he hadn't. Her eyes did that flutter thing again.

Danny's father was largely silent during the whole process. He walked around and looked at everything, followed rambunctious Buster and spoke to him more tersely than usual about keeping his hands off of everything.

In the common room, two boys, both older than Buster, were picking up toys and putting them in a basket. One of the dorm monitors reminded the boys that they were needed in the "mess" hall to prepare for the evening meal, so the three of them left the dorm. Buster spied a small ball in the toy basket and immediately sat down in the floor to roll the ball around. Danny stood a good distance away and watched as his parents asked Dr. Amos a few more questions. It looked to Danny like everything had been said and that it was time to leave, but his parents lingered longer. His mother sat on a sofa and pulled Buster onto her lap, trying to snuggle with him, but he kept pulling away, distracted by the ball. Danny's father kept looking at his watch and then walking back and forth between the rooms, inspecting again and again.

Dr. Amos made small talk and patiently waited for the Blands to come to their own decision about when to depart. He had obviously witnessed this same scene many times before and was in no rush to make the Blands leave.

Finally, after Jessa had smoothed Buster's hair for the hundredth time, and Raymond had paced back and forth between the rooms a hundred times, he looked at his wife and said, "Hon, it's time to go."

She looked up at her husband, this time not even trying to hide her rush of tears. "Oh, Raymond, I can't!" she said and kissed Buster on the top of his blonde head. Then she turned and ran out of the room, to their car.

Raymond looked helplessly at Dr. Amos, as if asking what to do next. "Sometimes it's best to make a quick exit," Dr. Amos offered.

Raymond held out his hand to Danny, who looked at his father and then back to his brother. None of them had been in this situation ever before, so they didn't know what to do, or how to act. Danny went over to Buster and knelt down and picked up the ball. Buster immediately became possessive and reached to snatch the ball from Danny. Danny offered no resistance, which seemed mildly surprising to Buster. But he quickly went back to rolling the ball between his two, outstretched legs. Danny smiled to try and keep the tears from coming. This was his brother. "Good-bye, Buster."

Buster looked up from his ball and smiled at Danny. "Bye-bye Dan-ee," he said, his eyes a kaleidoscope of blues and greens, punctuated by the strange, white slivers in the irises. Danny looked down at the ball, stood up and walked out to the car.

Raymond tussled his son's blonde hair knelt down and asked for a kiss and a hug, and Buster gave him both, all the while smiling about the ball. "Ball, Dad-ee, ball." Raymond held the ball up and looked at it through a blur of tears. This would make his son happy while they slipped away, this simple object. What a relief that he was so easily distracted. Raymond didn't know what would happen when Buster noticed they were gone. He didn't know what would happen when bedtime came. How would his son process all of this? Would he be frightened? Would he cry? Scream? Or worse of all reactions, would Buster just seamlessly fall into the routine here and not really be able to recall those nice people who lived in the blue house with the pecan trees in front?

It was all so confusing, so hard. Why couldn't anything be simple with Buster? Since that night in the hospital waiting room eight years ago, Raymond had been trying to take this situation and make it better. He had wanted so badly to be able to make it better. He'd tried so many things and they had all been the wrong things. Now he was reduced to having to abandon his child to strangers. Who knew if this was the right decision? If he went by his feelings, he would jerk this little boy up from the floor and run out the door with him.

But when they got home, things wouldn't be right there either. Jessa was exhausted, Buster was only getting bigger, stronger and more belligerent. There was no school to take him to and there was very little information available to help them know what to do with Buster. He required so much time and attention that Danny's needs had been pushed to the back burner for years now.

Logically, leaving Buster here made good sense. But when it came to his heart, his wife's and other son's hearts, it felt so wrong. It felt like he, the man of the family, was actually tearing the family apart.

Raymond handed the ball back to Buster and stood up. Dr. Amos came over to him and said, "I know this is hard. I've seen it happen dozens of times and still it's never easy to watch. We have a really nice grandmotherly lady, Nancy Smith, who we will put with Buster these next few nights. She'll help comfort him through the transition."

"Do...do you think he will miss us, Doctor? I mean I don't know how much he understands."

"Yes, Mr. Bland, he will miss you. He will be sad, sometimes on the inside and sometimes outwardly, too. We will watch him very carefully and you feel free to call us any time you want an update."

"We will be back next weekend to see him." Raymond didn't know how they would be able to afford the gas, the motel room, he just knew that's what they'd all want to do."

"Mr. Bland, I know you will feel like coming back immediately to visit Russell. But in our experience, it is best for both the inmate and the family if you give it some time. You'll all need to adjust to a new 'normal.'"

"How much time, Doctor? I don't know how long I will be able to keep my wife away."

"We recommend six-weeks at least. That way Russell will have adjusted to our routine here. And you all will have been able to establish a life without Russell."

A life without Buster. Raymond could hold back his emotions no longer. He shook Dr. Amos' hand, mumbling a few parting words. Then he turned to the little boy in the floor. "Good-bye, Buster." He forced a smile, and turned to leave.

As he walked down the corridor, he heard Buster's feet slapping against the linoleum. He heard the dorm manager and Dr. Amos try to distract him with the ball again, but this time Buster was having none of it.

"Dad-ee? Dad-ee?" At first Buster's calls were calm, questioning. But as he saw his father walk further down the hall without turning back, he started yelling. "DAD-EE!"

By the time Raymond walked through the glass door he could hear his son crying and sobbing, working into hysterics. He took one look back to see that Buster had gotten away from the two men briefly and was doing his best to run after Raymond. The dorm manager caught him and Raymond turned away. He walked across the parking lot towards the car but stopped halfway to bury his face in his hands. After briefly composing himself, Raymond made his way to the car to try and comfort Jessa and Danny.

Jessa stayed in bed a lot those weeks after taking Buster to the State Asylum. Danny was 10 and he didn't need her to watch over him every second anymore. And with Buster gone, she felt she had no real purpose to fulfill on a daily basis. So she slept. All the years of exhaustion seemed to come upon her at once, swallowing her up, like Jonah's whale. She just couldn't bear to hear the silence, to miss the mess, to touch his sheets, but not him, to smell the stench of desertion. So, her bed is where she took refuge.

Raymond grieved silently, stoically. He barely noticed Jessa's disappearance into her covers. He couldn't stand to hear her whimper in her sleep, to see the dark circles under her eyes, to feel the bag of bones she had become, to taste the palpable sense of loss.

As for Danny, he played with his friends uninterrupted, worked on puzzles unbothered, ate his dessert without having to share with a pesky brother. That was during the day. But at night, he couldn't sleep. He tossed and turned, often expecting to hear a hoarse whisper from the bed next to his, asking, "Wrong, Dan-ee?

His heart physically hurt him. He gurgled up the backwash from his stomach, often swallowing it back down and sometimes throwing it all up. But he did all this silently, so as not to bother his mother and father. They were sick too. No use in bothering everybody with his feeble condition.

And sometimes, when he just couldn't stand the pain, the emptiness, the loneliness, he would put his face in his pillow and scream until he himself was hoarse. It was the only way he knew to let it all out without bothering anyone.

* * *

The first visit the family paid to see Buster came about 10 weeks after they had dropped him off. None of them felt strong enough to make the trip before then. Jessa and Raymond had started talking about going at the six week mark, but just felt the overwhelming sadness was too much. After another month, they all were anxiously waiting to see their son, their brother.

Turning up the driveway to the asylum seemed different than the last time. For one, it felt like spring was coming on them, even though it was only early March. Some of the young trees had tiny buds forming on them. So it seemed less gloomy than it had in January.

They could see some young men in the distant fields, trying to work a few head of cattle toward a barn. Passing the laundry they saw young women pinning sheets to a line. The thought of all the laundry produced here gave Jessa a shudder.

Finally, they pulled up to the dorm where they had last seen Buster. There was a real buzz of excitement amongst the three as they got out of the car and prepared to see him again.

Raymond knocked on the front door of the dorm and waited. An older man, who looked in his face just like Buster, except for his darker hair, waved them all in. Immediately a dorm manager came over to greet them.

"Hi, folks! I hear you're here to see Russell Bland. Is that right?"

"Yes, that's right," Raymond responded. "Is he here?"

"Oh, he's here. He's helping with the trash right now. Saturdays are our clean up days. I'll go get him." Jessa and Raymond wandered into the common room and then looked in the door to the bedroom to which Buster had been assigned. Jessa noticed right away that Pete wasn't sitting on Buster's bed.

"Here we go, folks. Here's Russell." The dorm manager came walking into the common room, leading Buster by the hand.

"Buster!" Jessa cried. "Buster, come here to Mama!"

Buster just stared off into space, in the direction the dorm manager had left him pointing, working his tongue in and out of his mouth, fiddling with his fingers and acting as if he had not heard his name.

"Buster!" Jessa said again and she walked up beside him, knelt and turned his body to face her. "Buster," she said gently. "It's me, Mama."

He finally looked at her, made eye contact and smiled slightly. That was all the encouragement Jessa needed. She threw her arms around Buster and hugged him tight. After a moment, he pushed back from her and she awkwardly stood up.

Raymond and Danny got the same cool reception. They were all surprised and more than a little hurt.

"Buster, look honey, Mama brought you some homemade cookies." She opened a handkerchief with a dozen cookies folded in the middle. He looked at the cookies and gave a big grin. She offered him one and he took it, greedily putting almost the whole thing in his mouth at once.

Danny tried to connect with Buster next. "Buster, I got some neat cars that I brought from home. Wanna play?" Danny held out the cars in one palm. Buster took just one, the way they always played at home. The two boys sat on the floor of the common room and began to roll the cars, making motor noises. This glimpse of something so "normal" made Jessa catch her breath. She hadn't seen her boys play like this in weeks and it did her good to see it now. As the two of them occupied each other, Jessa and Raymond tried to find the dorm manager. They wanted to talk to him about how Buster was doing. They found him eating his lunch at a counter in a makeshift office/kitchen off the common room.

"Well, I'm just here for the weekends, Friday evenings through Sunday evenings. But as far as I know, Russell is doing fine," the manager explained. Not exactly the detailed accounting Jessa and Raymond had hoped for. "He gets his message across, even though he can't talk. He points and gestures and we get his point."

"But he can talk! He says dozens of words. Doesn't he say anything here?" Raymond asked.

"No, I can't say that I've ever heard Russell say any words. Just gestures, like I said," he responded.

"Well, what about his name? Does anyone call him Buster, like we do at home?" Raymond continued.

"No, sir. We just say what's written on his chart. Around here, he's Russell."

"Does he respond to that name?" Jessa asked.

"Come to think of it, he doesn't really respond much at all when we speak to him. He just smiles and stares off into space."

Jessa felt sick. She had hoped to come here and find that Buster had made great strides. After all, that was one of the big reasons they moved him here in the first place. To hear that he'd stopped talking for all these weeks was very distressing.

Just then, a crowd of boys came in with another dorm manager. He called out to the first manager, "They are really wild today! That means no dessert for them. Ted didn't come when I called him and David actually ran in the opposite direc…." He stopped when he walked in and saw the Blands. "Oh, sorry folks. Just giving my recess report to John here. I'll let y'all finish."

"We were pretty much finished. May we take Buster…I mean Russell…outside for a walk?" Jessa asked. It felt so odd to ask for permission to do something with her own son.

"Sure thing, Mrs. Bland. You can take him down to the playground and walk along the trail that circles the gardens if you want. It's a beautiful day. I'll be along with the rest of the boys from his group just as soon as I can finish my sandwich." John said.

"Okay, sounds great," Raymond responded as he stood up. He held his wife's chair as she stood too. When they returned to the common room, they found Buster rolling his car along and lying with his face to the floor, watching the wheels spin. Danny, in turn, was watching Buster.

"How's it going in here?" Raymond asked. "Are you two having fun?"

"I guess," Danny replied.

"What's the matter Danny?" Jessa asked.

"Oh, nothing. It's just, Buster wants to play with his car alone, I guess. He didn't want to play with me," Danny replied.

Jessa knelt next to the boys and smoothed Danny's hair. "Oh, honey, he is just excited about the new toy. Let's walk down to the playground and see what there is to do there," Jessa suggested. She knew their time today was short. They couldn't afford to drive here *and* rent a motel room, so it would be a tough 12 hours, with them leaving the house at 7:00 am and not returning home until 7:00 in the evening.

"Okay," Danny said.

Jessa stroked Buster's hair now and asked, "Buster want to go for a walk? Want to go play outside?"

Buster looked up at her and smiled. The family made its way down to the playground, not more than 100 yards behind the dorm building. Jessa chattered the whole way down, referring to the trees, the squirrels, the daffodils blooming. When they got to the playground, they found a set of four swings on one side, a slide with a sand box at the bottom, a monkey bars next to a push merry-go-round. On the other side there was another set of swings. *Nice equipment*, Jessa thought.

She watched as Buster passed up the first set of swings, all the other equipment and came to the second set of swings. He stopped in front of the third swing, shoved his toy car into his pants' pocket and lay across the swing on his stomach, pushing the dirt with the tip toes of his shoes and managing a nice back and forth movement.

"Oh, Buster, here is how we swing. Sit up and I'll push you," Jessa said. She walked over and tried to get Buster up off of his stomach. No such luck. He clung stubbornly to the rubber seat and wouldn't stand up as Jessa fussed over him. Then Raymond jumped in.

"Buster, now stand up son, right now. You're getting your shoes all dirty." No response. "Buster, Daddy said to stand up!" Still nothing. "Young man, you still have to listen to me! I'm still your Daddy. Now stand up!" Raymond walked over and picked Buster up, swing seat and all, and tried to disentangle the two.

"Buster," he started almost yelling, "let go of that seat or I will have to spank you! Let go, right now!"

Jessa pulled on the swing and on Raymond at the same time, not wanting him to be so harsh with Buster. Danny pulled on Jessa's waist, for no reason other than he was caught up in the family fracas. The four, or really the three, because Buster was just holding on silently to the swing, made quite the noise, with Raymond hollering at Buster and Jessa and Danny hollering, "No, no Daddy, don't spank him!" Suddenly, the group became aware of the presence of others. They turned and saw a dorm manager and eight boys looking at them.

Raymond spoke first. "We were just trying to get Buster to swing sitting up so he can have more fun."

"Well, Mr. Bland, I hate to contradict a father. That's not normally my way. But don't beat the boy. We teach them to swing themselves on their stomachs. There just aren't enough of us to push all of them on the swings. He's doing exactly what we have taught him to do."

"Oh!" Jessa's hand went up to her mouth. Raymond silently put Buster down, and the boy promptly started pushing his toes in the dirt again. This time it was Raymond who walked back to the car first.

Jessa and Danny stayed and watched the whole group play and Danny even joined in. All too quickly, it was time for the boys to go back to their dorm and to prepare for an afternoon snack. Jessa and Danny said a tearful good bye to Buster and were even more affected because Buster was so unmoved by the parting this time. He just stared off in the same impersonal way he had when they had first arrived. All that marked the visit was that Buster was left with a handkerchief full of cookies and the rest of the Blands were left emotionally exhausted and confused, with hundreds of miles to drive home.

CHAPTER 22

It was the morning of the meeting about Buster, or a "staffing" as it was known. As it was explained to Willa, it gave all interested parties...family, physicians, social workers and therapists...a chance to discuss the client's progress over the past year and make a plan for addressing his specific needs for the next year. All well and good, but Willa had some hard questions about what was best for her uncle. She'd listen to the so-called "experts" but then she was going to have her say.

Willa dressed quickly that morning and went down to fix Bella her breakfast. The two had arrived back at Willa's parents just after nightfall last night, so it had been a quick turnaround. Willa had barely had time to talk with her parents before bedtime, so, she was surprised to come down to the breakfast table to find her father dressed in his suit pants and a dress shirt and tie.

"Morning, Mom, Dad. How are you all? I feel like all we did last night was get here, unpack and fall into bed."

"You're right," Willa's mother said. "That's about how it was. I don't like you driving in the dark. I wish you'd gotten here a little bit earlier."

"I know, Mom, but Ray and Daniel had softball games and I really felt like I should go to the games after church. I haven't seen them play at all this summer. Little did I know that both games would go into extra innings. I agree, though. It did put us here too late."

Willa turned to try and distract her mother from stewing about her arrival time. "Dad, what's a retired guy like you doing dressed like that on a Monday morning?"

"Well, sweetheart," he began. "I've done a lot of thinking about it and I've decided to go with you to Buster's staffing this morning. I think it would be best to have two sets of eyes and ears there to witness the proceedings. It's always hard to go to these things. But Buster is getting older now and we need to make sure his care is suited to his changing needs."

"You're going? Well...that's...great!" Willa enthused. Truthfully, she wasn't sure how she felt now about her dad being there. After the talk with her sister, she had kind of mentally prepared for being the only family member present.

But there was something else. Her father seemed tense and very solemn this morning, not at all like his normal energetic, sunny disposition. Would she have to "take care" of her father emotionally while trying to get familiar with the staffing process, not to mention meeting Buster for the first time? She had to admit to suffering from her own case of nerves this morning.

Bella came down to join the family for breakfast. She was still all sleepy-headed and drowsy-eyed, and immediately wanted to curl up in her mother's lap for a long hug while she continued to "wake up." But Willa's nerves didn't allow her to sit for a long snuggle. Instead, she passed her daughter off to her mother, who did more than a fine job of filling in in the cuddling department. Bella didn't seem to mind.

Willa went upstairs and finished getting ready. She wanted to leave plenty of time for the drive up to Whispering Pines.

* * *

The car ride was quiet, except for the easy listening music playing on the radio satellite system. Willa's father had insisted on driving, as he always did. It gave him a sense of control in a rather uncontrollable situation, Willa thought. And he did know his way there, turning on back roads to shorten the trip. That was his specialty, when it came to car trips. He liked to find little ways to save time by taking less direct routes. He was pretty good at it, as Willa remembered, from car trips of her youth.

The two didn't chatter or exchange jokes like they usually did. They just sat quietly, until finally Willa's father broke the silence.

"Willa, I want to thank you for insisting on attending this staffing. I haven't been to one in over 10-years. It will be good to hear what they have to say. And it's always good to see Buster. It's also sad to see him, in a strange sort of way. Hon, I will completely understand if you have changed your mind and do not want to go through with this. I'll step up to the plate and take on this duty so you don't have to."

Not go? Willa felt like she had come this far and now no one was going to stand in her way. She wanted to meet this mysterious uncle of hers. She wanted to know what life was like for him all these years in an institution. She wanted to ask questions and use her newfound "expertise" to help her uncle in any way she could. Not go? That simply wasn't an option.

"Thanks, Dad. But I plan to attend the meeting. I'll be okay." She added the last part because she realized her father wasn't trying to be evasive. No, he was feeling protective toward her with all of this.

The car finally arrived at the gates of Whispering Pines. The name was professionally painted on a board that spanned the archway over the driveway. It was set in wrought iron, which curled and wound all around the sign and down the sides of the brick posts holding it up. Willa noticed in much smaller letters it said, "A South Carolina State facility for the mentally disabled."

They turned up the driveway and followed it for about a quarter of a mile without seeing much except open fields on both sides. But soon they came to a landscaped portion of the drive, showcasing huge magnolias, crape myrtles and ornamental shrubs and perennials. Finally, there were patches of flowering annuals; petunias, begonias, ageratum, vincas, marigolds, salvia, all layered and presented in a colorful display. The property became deeply shaded with towering pine trees waving above the rooftops of the brick buildings. Dappled sunlight lit their way.

Willa's father brought the car to a stop in front of a building marked "Administration." The two got out and walked inside. A cheerful reception area was surrounded by a half dozen private offices. The woman at the front desk smiled and said, "May I help you?"

"Yes, we're here for a staffing meeting. It's for Russell Bland."

"Oh yes. Are you Mr. Daniel Bland and Mrs. Willa Grizzard? I have your name tags right here."

She handed them the badges and Willa wondered how they'd known who was coming.

"Yes, I called to let Mrs. Parks, the social worker, know we would be here," her father said.

Oh, that's how they knew. Willa was suddenly glad her father was here to guide her through the unfamiliar process.

After getting directions to the meeting location they got back in the car and drove deeper into the campus. As they drove, they passed old brick buildings with wheelchair ramps and air conditioning units hanging outside the windows. All around them were huge, old oak trees, shading the drive with their fingertips. Her father stopped in front of yet another building, this one two stories tall and marked with an "F" on one bricked corner. So this is where the staffing would be held.

"Are you ready?" her father asked. He said it more as a statement than a question. Willa could clearly tell this was not an experience her father relished. Leading worship at church…

he loved. Golfing with friends…he looked forward to. But this… her father's weathered face wore a tense expression rather than its normally warm smile.

He lifted his tall frame out of the car and walked around to let Willa out of her door. As they walked toward the building, he threw his arm around her shoulders and said, "We'll get through this together." Willa's nerves were soothed by her father's touch.

They entered a building that was obviously set up as an office building, but one could tell from the awkward layout that the rooms had once been used for a more home-type environment. They stopped at a desk and waited for the woman behind it to get off of a call.

Finally, she asked politely, "May I help you?"

"Yes, we're here for the Russell Bland staffing."

"Okay, right this way. They're gathering for the meeting right now." The short, round woman lead them down a hallway, her pantyhose swishing together as she walked.

"Here we are." The woman stepped into a wood-paneled room, centered by a conference table. Settling around the table were three men and three women. The air conditioning window unit hummed in the corner, blowing out cold, stale air.

Willa's heart stopped and her ears went silent for a moment as she looked around the room for a sign of her uncle. And then, suddenly, there he was, being escorted into a chair by a man in hospital scrubs. He and the woman who had brought them back both left and the room seemed less stuffy.

Willa wasn't sure what she had expected, but she was somewhat shocked by her uncle's appearance. He was diminutive in stature, only about 5-feet, 3-inches tall, hardly bigger than some of her students. He probably weighed less than 100 pounds. His thinning hair was light grey and cut in a standard men's hair style. His once startling blue eyes were clouded. But the one thing that stood out most was that this old gentleman had his tongue hanging out. He seemed completely unaware of his surroundings and remained seated where he had been placed.

Willa's father walked stiffly over to her uncle and gave his shoulders a side hug. "Hey, there, Buster. It's been a long time, brother." Her uncle didn't respond and continued looking forward and slightly down, not really focusing on anything.

"Hello, Russell. Welcome, Mr. Bland and Mrs...." one of the men started.

"Grizzard." Willa quickly filled in.

"Yes, Mrs. Grizzard. Have you ever been to one of these staffings before, Mrs. Grizzard?"

"No," she almost peeped. "This is my first one."

"Okay, well, let me tell you how it usually goes. First of all, I'm Dr. Gerald Balding, a staff psychiatrist here at Whispering Pines." Then he indicated each of the people around the table as he introduced them. "This is Shereé Parks, Russell's social worker. Next to her is Dr. Evan Saunders, head of our on-site hospital. Then there is Vivian Smith, a speech and language pathologist, and Olive Newton, a physical therapist. Occupational therapist, Sam Davis, is our last member of the team of professionals that works with Russell. He also is serviced by a team of house assistants, headed by house managers. They help Russell tend to his daily needs. We have a few formalities to state into the record and then we can begin."

Willa listened intently to all that was said and watched as the speech therapist took notes. Still, she was glad she was seated across from her uncle because he was the one that fascinated her. She could hardly take her eyes off him. Just like Willa had seen several of her students do in parent/teacher conferences, her uncle sat oblivious to the lofty proceedings happening around him. He watched his fingers, twiddling them and thrusting his tongue in and out of his mouth. Willa marveled at how much he looked like a miniature version of her grandfather.

"Now we will begin our reports," Dr. Balding said. Mrs. Dawson, you can go first and give an overview of how things have gone for Russell over the past year. Then each of the others can fill in more details about their area of expertise."

"Okay," Mrs. Dawson said. "This has been an eventful year for Russell, medically speaking. He has had pneumonia twice, being hospitalized here on campus both times. Because of that, he was moved from his longtime bed in Hall C to one for our more medically-fragile residents inside the Banner Medical facility. He suffered some lacerations and bruising at the hands of another inmate shortly after his move, but has been relatively fine since then.

"He has become more withdrawn since the move. Attempts to get him to interact with staff, therapists and other residents are met with the kind of behavior you see here.

"The one thing Russell does continue to enjoy is eating. He is very familiar with the times for meals and the routines leading up to meals. If things go out of sequence, he becomes agitated, which for him just means he paces and wrings his hands. The Housing Staff reports that food is the only motivator they can use anymore to get him to complete long-mastered tasks, such as dressing himself…although they must fasten the buttons…pulling his blanket up on his bed and standing still for grooming.

"Russell has lost most of his interest in exercises like walking, pushing a laundry cart, throwing a ball, etcetera. The Housing Staff is instructed to try and get him moving twice a day through various methods like playing music to get him to dance or walking outside when the weather is nice. But Russell still has a hyper-sensitivity to weather, meaning he hates the feeling of rain falling on his skin or of wind blowing on him. So we don't attempt to take him out unless the weather is really pleasant.

"Russell is a quiet, overall cooperative resident who tends to keep to himself. He really is a pleasure to work with. He could benefit from short outings with family and from visits as well."

With this, Mrs. Dawson sat down. Dr. Balding looked at Willa and could tell she had questions so he said, "Mrs. Grizzard, if it's all right, let's hear from the others in attendance and then we will take questions at the end."

"All right," she agreed.

Next, the medical doctor gave his report. "Russell is experiencing steadily deteriorating health, as can be expected with someone of his age and disability. That being said, he is really in remarkable health, again for his age and disability. He has normal blood pressure, his heart problems were corrected in 1954 and his heart remains strong. Our main concern with Russell is his tendency to aspirate while eating. That means he breathes in small amounts of liquid and food while eating. We believe this is what caused his two cases of pneumonia this year. We feel that another bout could be fatal for Russell and we are proposing a feeding tube be installed to provide him nourishment while eliminating the risk for aspiration…"

"Wait a minute," Willa interrupted. "Are you saying you think you should put in a feeding tube and take away the one thing he still enjoys…the act of eating, tasting his food and feeling its textures as it goes down?" Willa had behaved herself for as long as she could.

"Well, I don't know about textures, Mrs. Grizzard. As you can see, Russell had all of his teeth removed several years ago, due to decay, so all of his food has to be puréed anyway. He was not a candidate for dentures due to his tongue thrust."

"I see. So, to be clear, you think the tradeoff for losing his ability to eat is medically necessary?" Willa asked.

Dr. Saunders hesitated a moment, looking a bit uncomfortable with the choice himself. Then he said, "I do, Mrs. Grizzard. I know it seems cruel, but if he incurs another case of pneumonia any time soon, his lungs will be too weak to recover. We also believe Russell's esophagus was damaged many years ago, when he accidently ingested some cleaning fluid. He's had many cases of pneumonia over the years. It's a hard choice, but one I believe is medically necessary."

So, the rest of the reports were made and Willa did her best to wait for questions until the end. Then she had her say, wanting to know about the "incident" with the other inmate, where her uncle was harmed. She even required them to go back and read the original report about him drinking cleaning fluid, which took them a while to find. Come to find out, there were *two* incidents where Buster had drunk cleaning fluid.

Willa finally noticed that all the time she peppered the staff with questions, her father sat back in uncharacteristic fashion. He listened intently but didn't join the conversation. What was wrong with him? This was their one chance this year to catch up on her uncle's treatment and her father was being so passive.

Finally, Willa ran out of questions to ask and the group sat and looked at one another for an instant. Then Mrs. Parks, Buster's social worker said, "Will you be taking Russell on an outing today?" It caught Willa off guard. So it was her father who replied. "Yes. He likes to go to the Dairy Queen. Is it still on the Highway 321 Bypass?"

"Yes," Mrs. Parks answered. "He'll enjoy that. It's been years since he left this campus."

Willa was a bit in shock. She hadn't realized they would be left alone to care for her uncle. But after a moment she decided she was up for it.

The group stood around, talking politely to each other. Willa just followed her father's lead. He walked over and helped slide back the chair Buster was sitting in. Then he put his hands on Buster's shoulders and helped guide him to his feet. Buster stood up automatically in response to the touch.

How easy he was to maneuver. Willa wondered if this was the result of years of practice in walking in lines like the ones she tried to lead in her school.

Mrs. Parks walked them out. "Just turn right as you leave the campus and continue straight for 4 miles. You'll come to the Dairy Queen on your left."

"Okay, thank you, Mrs. Parks," her father replied as he continued to guide Buster towards the parking lot.

"Where are all the residents?" Willa asked, looking around at the quiet buildings and empty fields surrounding them.

"Oh, we don't have that many residents anymore. And this hasn't been a working dairy since the 1970's. So that's why you don't see many of our clients. It's mainly older folks like your uncle now. These days, most families keep their children with disabilities at home. There're so many services available in the community now, that they don't really have much use for full time institutionalizing. Back when your uncle first came here, there were no therapists and specially-trained teachers in local schools. Families with disabled children were on their own. We've really come a long way."

Willa's dad had her uncle by the elbow and was guiding him to the back seat of the car. Willa said a quick good bye to Mrs. Parks and walked around to help her father. After he got Buster into the car, Willa leaned in to buckle the back seatbelt across her uncle's lap.

She paused a moment and marveled at how he was going along with things without so much as a peep. He didn't know where they were going. He showed no signs of recognizing her father, yet he was so cooperative. Willa couldn't help wondering if her uncle had been subject to beatings or other forms of force to get him to comply with the requests of others so readily. Or was this just his personality? She shook her head and chose not to think about this too long.

"Okay, here we go!" Willa tried to sound excited rather than nervous.

Her father smiled from the driver's seat.

"Do we have to sign him out or anything?" Willa questioned.

"Mrs. Parks will take care of that. We just have to sign him into his dorm when we get back," her father said.

And so, they were off. Willa left her window down so they could all enjoy the smells of the trees and flowers on campus. But when her father turned onto the steaming asphalt road she rolled up the window so the air conditioning could circulate.

Things were quiet. Willa didn't know what to say to her father and certainly not to her uncle. She glanced behind her and saw her uncle looking out the window at the farm land rolling by. Years! It had been years since this man had enjoyed the simple pleasure of a car ride. How could this be? She looked at her father and felt anger and frustration with him over the matter.

Eventually they came to the Dairy Queen. Willa's father started toward the drive through and she quickly said, "Oh, let's go inside to order."

"Ok," her father agreed quietly.

So, they parked and Willa, feeling bolder now, marched straight to the backseat to unbuckle her uncle. He complied with her gesture to get out of the car. Then suddenly, the old man reached out for her hand, almost automatically. Willa felt a warm rush as she grabbed her uncle's hand and started across the parking lot, her father right behind them.

When they got inside, Willa asked, "Buster, what do you want? A Blizzard? Or a sundae?"

He just continued to look straight ahead, his tongue rubbing along his bottom lip.

"Oh, he'll have a vanilla ice cream cone, won't you, Buster?" her father interjected.

Willa bristled at the lack of choices, but gave in, knowing her father had more experience with her uncle than she did…although not much.

They ordered the cone and one for Willa and her father as well. Then they guided her uncle to a nearby table. When he saw the ice cream cone, his eyes finally lit up and when Willa offered it to him, he took it and greedily started to eat it.

Willa smiled at the enthusiasm her uncle showed. How could the doctors think it would be all right to take this pleasure away from him?

The three sat quietly, eating their cones. When her uncle was finished, his face and chin were dripping with vanilla ice cream. Willa took a napkin from the holder and handed it to him. He just held it, as if he didn't know what to do. So Willa took the napkin back and used it to wipe her uncle's face. She tried to be extra careful around the lower lip and chin area because they were so chapped. Her uncle turned his face disagreeably, letting Willa know she'd wiped enough.

The ride back to the facility was quiet. The little man stared out the window, watching the scenery pass by and Willa sat up front, feeling a knot in her throat. She hadn't anticipated how difficult dropping her uncle off was going to be. But her father had. His mouth set in a grim line let her know he was not looking forward to this any more than she was.

When he parked the car, Willa went to unbuckle her uncle and motioned him out of the car. This time, he shook his head "no" and stayed put. He even grunted in protest. He reached to close the door. *What in the world? Did he not want to go back to the dorm? What if he had been mistreated there,* Willa wondered? *Why didn't he want to get out of the car?*

Willa finally stood in the doorway so her uncle couldn't shut himself up in the car in the sweltering heat. Her father talked gently to his brother, trying to coax him from the backseat. He wouldn't budge.

"Willa, you stay here. I'm going to get one of the house attendants."

"All right," Willa agreed. She maintained her stance and kept coaxing her uncle, to no avail.

Her father came back with an attendant, who asked Willa to step out of the way. He then reached in and went to lift her uncle out of his seat. Her uncle let out a howl in protest and even kicked his feet.

Willa couldn't stand it. "Put him down! Leave him alone!" But the attendant continued walking. Her uncle looked extra small next to the man and his bulky muscles. "I can't stop," the attendant called out over his shoulder. He walked up the front steps and into the dorm, with Willa and her father in tow.

The minute they were inside, the attendant gently put him down and said, "See, Russell? Everything's going to be all right." Her uncle stopped wailing and in fact appeared to be completely fine again. Willa looked at the attendant and said, "What was that all about?"

"Well, as best as I can tell, it was the hot wind that was blowing so hard out there. Russell doesn't like wind or rain. You're lucky he didn't shut down on y'all while you were out. He didn't, did he?"

Willa relaxed and let her guard down. "No, he was so good for us. So you think the wind was what did it?"

"Yes. I've been working with Russell for eight years now. They moved me with him to his new dorm. That's why they don't take Russell out on car rides more often. They almost always end up with him upset, so it's really not worth it."

"Well, thank you for explaining," Willa said. "What is your name?"

"I'm Dexter. Just an attendant around here."

"You're more than an attendant to us. We didn't know what to do," Willa remarked. She looked over at her uncle, who was once again calm and thrusting his tongue out. So this was home to him. It was a place where he felt most comfortable, not a place of abuse, at least not from appearances.

She looked around while her father signed her uncle back into the dorm. Other mentally disabled individuals were watching TV in a large room with sofas. Some were coming and going. Two other attendants were perched in chairs, looking rather bored. They both perked up when they saw Willa come into the room.

It was so hard to tell. Was this a good place or a bad one for her uncle? Willa guessed the answer wasn't so simple.

It was time to leave. When Willa turned to say good bye to her uncle, she found him seated on the sofa, staring at the TV. She knelt in front of him and tried to make eye contact. "Bye for now, Buster," she began. She could tell he wasn't engaged with her, so she just gave him a quick hug. Her father did the same.

As they drove off, Willa felt a sense of relief. She hadn't realized she'd been so tense. She leaned back into the leather seat and closed her eyes. It had been a long morning…for all three of them. And Willa, for one, was glad it was over.

CHAPTER 23

The years after the Blands took Buster to the institution were generally happy ones for Jessa. She watched proudly as Danny grew from his primary grade school years to his high school years. He was a good boy, attending a new independent Bible church with his mother every Sunday.

Raymond stayed home on these mornings, still not seeing the point of such religious rituals. The whole experience with Buster had left him hardened to life in general and God specifically. Like many people who have experienced hardship of some kind, he blamed God…he asked, "Why?" And not receiving an obvious answer, he hardened inside, just so he could function.

The family went to see Buster at least two times a year. With Raymond's work schedule, that was as frequently as they could make the long drive. It usually involved driving until almost midnight to get back home without the expense of staying in a motel.

Danny had always accompanied his parents on these trips, even though a lot of conflicting emotions rose up in him during the visits. He could feel sad, angry, bored or frustrated on any given trip, sometimes even a mixture of them all. He'd figured out a long time ago that Buster didn't remember him, at least not like one brother should remember another brother. And Danny tried to understand it. After all, Buster was at an institution for imbeciles. Didn't that mean Buster was an imbecile? So no wonder Buster didn't talk to him like he used to or seem interested in Danny at all.

Danny had just graduated from high school and this summer, he was spending eight blazing hours picking cotton, peanuts and other crops to earn money for college. He also was planning to date…a lot. He and Mary Ann Brewer were a couple and he couldn't wait for Friday nights to get to see her. He usually took her to the local hamburger drive-in where he could also meet up with some of his friends. There might be a dance at the armory or a special social at church.

That's what he had done last night. He worked all day, came straight home and took a shower, then dashed off to Mary Ann's house to pick her up. Then the two were invited to the home of a couple from church. They lived on the lake and had a bonfire in the yard for roasting marshmallows and had cleared the patio for dancing to the record player. He had dropped Mary Ann off by her 11:00 curfew and had gotten home about 11:30 himself.

Dropping in the bed exhausted, it seemed like only a moment before his Daddy was waking him. It was 4:30am and the two had plans to go fishing. His father always woke him by pulling his toe so he could quietly slip out of bed and get dressed. They grabbed the picnic lunch his mother had made for them last night and hit the road….with Danny doing the driving.

It was about an hour's drive to Galavant's Ferry. They were headed to the black waters of the Little Pee Dee River. Father and son spoke sporadically; most often about fishing.

"Let's start under the big oak near the bridge. Then you can go your way and I'll go mine," his father said. "We can meet up by the same tree at noon to eat lunch."

"Aww, Daddy, can't we eat any earlier than that? I'm starving now!" Danny protested. He had enjoyed these fishing excursions when he was younger, but now he just felt overly tired and had other things he wanted to do with his free time.

"Pull over at Leonard's store and I'll buy you an egg biscuit and some milk."

"Make it coffee and you're on," Danny replied.

They stopped at a little store near the lake and got their breakfast, along with two sodas to drink later. They'd brought their own crickets and some fat, green worms taken from under the leaves of the fig tree in the backyard, so they didn't need bait.

The two always parked near the old ferry depot. The ferry had long stopped running here. The store and the large barn next to it had developed into a political campaign meeting place that no serious candidate for office neglected to attend. They literally let the candidates stand up on an old stump of a large oak tree to make their speeches, thus the term "stump meeting" really applied here.

Danny and his father sometimes borrowed a small johnboat to fish the river, but this morning they were fishing from the shore. They started, silently baiting their hooks and casting into the calm-looking, black water, known for offering up some of the best game fish caught anywhere in the area. Largemouth bass, catfish and brim were favorites. Danny went for brim, leaving the more difficult fish to his skilled father.

The morning passed slowly. First the full moon slipped behind the trees. Then the sun rose in its place. A serpent of some sort slipped off an overhanging tree branch and slithered away in the water. Cicadas started their incessant drone and Danny could feel the sweat beading on his brow. He glanced at his watch. It wasn't even 8:00 yet and already, he was nodding off between casts.

He knew his father would expect a respectable catch from him for supper for the next night or two. But there was plenty of time. Now he needed some shuteye.

* * *

Danny woke with a start. He was propped up under a large, overhanging tree, resting in its shade. A quick check of his watch told him he had less than an hour to catch his share of the fish. That was tight. He would have to hit a honey hole if he was going to make it. He looked around, assessing the situation. Seeing some bramble and bushes growing right under the bridge, Danny instinctively knew there could be fish bedding underneath. How could he best get to it? Casting into the bushes could get his line bird nested. So, he would have to climb up on the bridge, lean out, cast and then let the current carry his hook to the fish.

The old, wooden bridge stood about 40 feet above the water. Danny had to scramble up a steep bank to the road, and then make his way to the bridge's ledge. It was just wide enough to allow workmen to repair the bridge without having to do it from the road. This was the country and traffic was normally slow, but you still didn't want to make a practice of standing in the middle of the road.

Danny walked, one foot over the other, to the very middle of the bridge. Then, turning to face the water, he had to hook himself to the wooden railing with one arm. He used his other arm to hold onto his pole. When he had gotten his balance, he drew the pole back over his left shoulder and cast out in front of him. Just as he had expected, the current started pulling his line back toward the bridge. But it missed the bushes completely.

Danny had to let go of the bridge to reel in his line, so he stood perched in a precarious position, reeling slowly. Now he was going to cast out even farther so he would have time to guide the line toward the bushes. He flung the line out as far as he could. Then he started reeling in and dragging the line to the position he wanted. He leaned out a little farther than the ledge allowed and before he knew it, he was tumbling toward the water. He landed with a loud splash in the inky water. The swift, underlying current quickly caught him and started pulling him down the river. Danny was a strong swimmer, and was doing his best to work his way over to the bank when an underwater log bumped his ribcage hard, knocking all of Danny's breath out. Being unable to grab a breath caused him to panic and he flailed in the water. Suddenly, a strong hand reached out from shore and gripped Danny by the wrist. The hand started pulling hard and managed to drag him out of the water and onto the sandy bank.

Danny sputtered and coughed as he looked up into his father's worried eyes. "Danny!" the older man said. "Are you all right? Are you okay?"

All Danny could do was gasp.

"Danny, I saw you go off the bridge and my heart stopped. What happened? Are you okay?"

Danny nodded.

"Okay, then just lay back, son. Catch your breath." Then Raymond turned away and buried his sweaty face in his hands.

Danny watched and rose up on his elbows to try and reassure his father, only to collapse back onto the ground.

Raymond turned back around. The fear in his eyes had been replaced by anger. "What were you doing up on that bridge? Are you crazy? You could have been killed! I don't know how I'm going to tell your mother about this. She won't ever want you to go fishing with me again. Do you understand how dangerous that was? Do you?"

For a moment, Danny was afraid his father was going to grab him by the collar and shake him. But instead, his dad just plopped down on the sand himself, trying to calm down. After a few minutes of silence between the two, he eventually felt he owed Danny an explanation for his outburst.

"Son, I'm sorry I got so angry. It was pure fear talking. I was so worried when I saw you go under that log, that you'd drowned. I had a vision of you all blue and dead up here on the bank. I just couldn't stand it. Do you hear me? " The father turned toward the son. "Do you understand? I couldn't stand to lose another son. Your brother's situation is bad enough. But it would break your mother's and my hearts to lose you too. That's all."

Raymond stood up and reached a hand out to his son. Pulling Danny to his feet, he threw an arm around his boy and started walking back up river. Danny winced at his tender ribs. He couldn't believe how far down stream they were. His daddy would have had to run, full speed, to catch up with Danny in the river. It seemed like they'd both come a long way. A very long way indeed.

* * *

Jessa looked at the dirty breakfast dishes in the sink before her. She groaned slightly and then just plunged her hands into the soapy water and started scrubbing bits of egg and marmalade off the plates. She never loved doing the dishes, but this morning she was particularly distracted and wishing to be elsewhere.

She and Raymond had driven to Columbia last night when Danny had called them and said Lila was about to give birth to their first grandchild. Jessa was so excited she could hardly stand it! The elder Bland couple had let themselves into the small house that Danny and Lila had moved into just a year ago. They had been waiting on the call for the last two weeks at least. When they arrived this evening, Jessa went straight to the nursery and saw that it still had bear walls and the crib was without sheets. She guessed Lila was waiting to see if she had a boy or a girl.

Danny had said over the phone last night that they had arrived at the hospital at about 6:00 p.m. He said Lila was fine and had been whisked away by a few nurses to the labor room. It was now 8:30 the next morning and Jessa was sure the baby had to have been born. Why hadn't Danny called them? Was something wrong?

Just then the phone rang. Jessa ran to answer it and Raymond ran into the kitchen from the other room.

"Hello?"

"Mom?"

"Yes Danny. Is everything all right?"

"Mom, the doctor says everything is fine. Lila had the baby about an hour ago. It's a girl!"

"A girl! Oh how exciting! We can't wait to meet her, son. Have you settled on a name?"

"Well, Lila wants to name her after her grandmother. Her name is Willamina Ann. She weighs 6 pounds 7 ounces."

"Oh, that's a good weight," Jessa enthused. "How is Lila?"

"She's good. Tired but good. She's in recovery right now. But Mom...I'm worried."

"Why, what's wrong?" Jessa asked with alarm.

"It's the baby...her head...her face. They're all smashed in. She's bruised and looks terrible. Mom, I wonder..." Danny's voice broke. "I-I wonder. What if she turns out like Buster?"

Jessa thought of her 24-year-old son standing alone in the hospital, trying to process all that had happened behind closed doors to his baby. She couldn't stand it.

"We'll be right there."

* * *

Jessa and Raymond peered through the nursery glass at their new granddaughter. Danny was right. Her head and face were a mess. Right now Danny was with the doctor who delivered the baby and the pediatrician. He had cornered them in the hallway and they had ushered him into a nearby office. He wasn't gone long.

As he walked toward them he looked as if the weight of the world had been lifted off his shoulders.

"They both agree. She's fine. Her head just looks smashed in because they had to use forceps to pull her out. But they say her head will round out over the next few days and that we'll never know a difference in her and other children. So she's going to be fine," Danny finished with a big grin.

"Oh, praise God," Jessa said. Raymond was so choked up he couldn't say anything so he just smiled.

The three of them uniquely understood how things could have gone very differently. The relief was palpable as they huddled together in an awkward hug. The baby was fine...this time.

* * *

Jessa sipped her cup of tea and admired the flowers outside her kitchen window. One of her granddaughters had come over and planted them for her to enjoy. They were beautiful! She had always loved flowers but now she was just too old to get down and put them in the ground. It was all she could do to stay in this house all alone, now that Raymond was gone.

He had passed away 18 months ago from cancer and Jessa's world had changed dramatically. She had decided to stay in the small, patio home Danny had helped them purchase, just around the corner from him. But the lonesomeness was her new companion. She stayed in the house, many times refusing invitations to dinner with Danny's family. She felt more comfortable being among her familiar things.

She and Raymond had moved to this home ten years ago and had brought all their furnishings and knickknacks from their Junction Point home. They had enjoyed some good years together here, especially while Raymond was still driving. He would take her to the Piggly Wiggly or to the hair dresser. They did everything together.

Raymond acted protective over Jessa, but Jessa was no less protective of Raymond. She repeated what strangers said in the grocery store so that he could hear. She light-heartedly explained his gruff responses to questions from family members and she tried to interpret when he spoke a few phrases of broken Chinese, which he remembered from active duty, to his Asian dermatologist.

The last two years had been really tough. Raymond's hands and feet grew increasingly numb and his coordination was off, so he had to stop driving altogether. This depressed him, even more than he was already depressed as his body continued to deteriorate with age. This strong, tough, former Marine now had to have all his food mashed up in order to be able to chew it. He followed the lawn care workers around his tiny yard, using his walker for balance. He liked to correct them and fuss at them for not grooming his yard the way he used to when he was able. And there were times Jessa thought she would lose her mind as Raymond turned the television volume up louder and louder. There was nowhere in the house that she could escape from the blaring gunfire from the Westerns he liked to watch.

Now she wished so badly that she could hear him bellow from the TV room for the remote control. She missed him so! But there were things to be happy about. Her son and his family were close by and good to her. She had good neighbors who helped her get to the grocery store and hairdresser. And most of all, she had the Lord Jesus as her constant companion. Their relationship had grown stronger, sweeter and more meaningful every year. She talked constantly to him in prayer and he in turn would speak to her heart through scripture she had either memorized or read recently. It was this relationship, above all else, that kept her going, here at the end of her days.

The phone rang, interrupting Jessa's thoughts. She got up and shuffled to answer it, expecting a sales person to congratulate her on having "won" a free vacation to beautiful Cozumel, or some such place.

Instead, she heard a pleasant-sounding, female voice on the phone. "Mrs. Bland?"

"Yes. This is she."

"Hi, Mrs. Bland. This is Shereé Parks from Whispering Pines. How are you today?"

"Well, I guess I'm okay. About as good as you could expect for a lady in her 80s."

"I'm sure you are, I'm sure you are."

Pause.

"Well Mrs. Bland, I was wondering when you think the next time you might be coming up here to visit Russell…I mean Buster."

"Oh Shereé, I'm not sure when I will be able to get there. My husband is deceased you know and I don't drive."

"What about other family members. Any way one of them could bring you here to see him?"

"I just don't know, Shereé. I have another son, but he is very busy with work and all."

"Well, maybe he wouldn't mind bringing you up for a little visit. He could see Buster too."

"Yes, well the thing is, he gets very, very sad when we come to visit Buster. It seems to be just too much for him."

"Well, I can understand that. It's just that Buster is facing some medical procedures that we thought you both might want to be apprised of. Can he join you for a phone call do you think? Sometime soon?"

"I'll have to check with him to see when he is available. Then can I call you with the time?"

"Sure, sure. That will work."

Pause.

"Mrs. Bland? I just wanted to tell you that Buster is now considered a senior resident. He's in his early sixties. You know, he has lived a long time for a person with Down Syndrome. He really is an unusual case."

"Yes, Mrs. Parks. I know exactly how old Buster is. Why do you mention that?"

"Well, I just wanted to prepare you that his condition has deteriorated over the last year or so. I don't want it to come as a complete surprise."

"Oh." Jessa's voice broke.

"I don't want to upset you Mrs. Bland, really I don't. I just wanted you to prepare yourself for the difficult decisions that are coming up soon with Buster."

That's just what Jessa did not *want* to do. She had nearly exhausted herself with making difficult decisions the last month or so of Raymond's life. She just didn't think she could handle making such decisions for a child of hers.

"Listen, Shereé, I have to run. I've got something boiling over on the stove. I'll be in touch with you about when Danny and I can be on a phone call together."

"Okay Mrs. Bland. I'll wait to hear from you."

"Thank you Shereé. Goodbye."

Jessa hung up the phone and stared around her quiet kitchen. She'd go lie down for a while. Then maybe she'd feel like talking to Danny about all of this. She'd just have to see how she felt when she got up.

As she shuffled to her bedside, she automatically picked up her Bible from the nightstand. The cover was leather, but it was cracked from use. The once gold page edges were worn away and her name was barely visible on the lower corner of the cover. She had read this Bible since she was a little girl. It was truly her most prized possession.

Jessa leaned back against the pillows on her bed and opened the book. Out fell a familiar picture, one that seemed so far away, so long ago. She held it up and examined it for the thousandth time. It was black and white. There were two little boys pictured along with a colored woman. Queenie. Dear Queenie. She had been the best friend Jessa had ever had. It was odd to think about in some ways and yet perfectly natural in others. Queenie had helped Jessa to regain her faith when Jessa thought she'd lost it forever. For that, Jessa would be eternally grateful.

Next her eyes fell on Danny, her beautiful, good little boy. Even in the picture he had his arm around his brother, trying to keep him still for the photograph. He'd grown up to be a fine man and Jessa couldn't be prouder.

Lastly, she looked at Buster. His blonde hair was white in the photo. Even with Danny's arm around him, Jessa could tell

Buster was ready to bolt and run. He always did like to run. It was a game for him.

It occurred to Jessa as she looked at the photograph that there really had been a few good years where they were a family. It had been hard, but they had made a few years work with the four of them together under one roof. Why hadn't they been able to continue? That was the question that had haunted her for all these years. Willa, her granddaughter, was now working with children like Buster. They lived at home with their parents, went to school with the other boys and girls and had a normal life. If she had just tried harder, not been so weak, maybe Buster could have stayed home with her. The guilt made her nauseous, as it usually did, when she allowed herself to "go there."

Jessa was tired, too tired to read the scriptures. She'd have to quote them in her mind instead. "He who dwelleth in the shelter of the Most High shall abide in the shadow of the Almighty. I shall say of the Lord, 'He is my refuge and my fortress, my God, in whom I shall trust.'"

And with that, Jessa closed her eyes and went to her rest.

CHAPTER 24

The new school year had started off with some changes. Maleeke had moved away and Jack and Jared had both been mainstreamed into a kindergarten classroom. But the biggest change for Callie and Willa was the addition of a blind student, a girl, who also had autism. This was a whole new level of disability for them and a one-on-one parapro was assigned to Chelsea to help her get around school and the classroom. This meant a new personality to get used to on the teaching team and another student with very specific needs who had to receive the best education possible.

Tracy Peters made a good addition to the team, being a patient, capable helper to Chelsea, her main charge. But both Callie and Willa realized this job could be trying, so they tried to give Tracy breaks and also let her do some of the paperwork and classroom wall decorations.

Chelsea was eight-years-old and had been blind from birth. She had other health issues and over the years of struggling to raise her daughter past the age of all medical predictions, Chelsea's mother, Meredith, had developed into a no-nonsense, heavy-hitting protector for her daughter. So Callie, Willa, and Tracy were warned by the administration to be extra attentive and careful not to raise this mother bear's ire. Special Education in general was fraught with lawsuits from vigilant parents who felt it their duty to push all educational limits and barriers for their child. Deerfield County had had some lawsuits in the past and people with the county office were extra careful not to tempt fate in this area.

Willa tried to ease into the new school year and largely forget her misgivings about her uncle's situation, but of course, she couldn't. Each day as she worked with her students, especially those with Down Syndrome, she imagined how things could have been so different for her uncle if he had been born a few decades later. It was impossible not to wish that he could have had all the therapies and educational assistance that is available in modern times. Willa sometimes dreamed about Buster being able to talk to her and help her around the house....*her* house. It was funny, but Buster was always at her house with her family in her dreams. And this planted a seed. What if she could arrange to take custody of her uncle and have him come live with her?

The idea grew. Willa thought about how she could help feed him so he could continue eating by mouth. She had done it with her babies, who all had bad reflux. They had to be fed slowly and kept upright after eating to prevent them from spitting everything back up. Willa couldn't bear to think of Buster with a feeding tube. Taking away this last pleasure seemed particularly cruel.

It was September before she had the nerve to bring the idea up to Joel.

"What? Are you joking? That would never work." Joel was propped up in bed reading.

"It could too work, if everybody was in on it...if everybody was in agreement. I know I could make it work," Willa replied stubbornly from the other side of the bed.

"Don't you mean 'we' could make it work?" Joel had her on this one. He was normally so positive and supportive of her endeavors. This time, he was downright negative.

Willa let it go and didn't bring it up again for a week. And then a few days later. And a few more days after that. She just kept mentioning it to Joel to help him get used to the idea. But the appeal became more urgent as Willa was notified that Buster's surgery for the feeding tube implant was quickly approaching.

"Joel, we've got to do something! You just don't know how devastating this will be for Buster. He gets all of his enjoyment out of eating. You should see him! You'd feel the same way I do."

"I know he enjoys eating, Willa. But I just can't see us taking an elderly, infirm man who has been institutionalized his whole life to live with us! It's just impossible! I bet his handlers wouldn't think that was the best idea either."

"His 'team' not his 'handlers.' He's not a trained animal!"

"Willa, I know he's not, but this is one of your big ideas that I have to say 'no' to for the sake of our family as well as your uncle. It's just not practical."

Willa looked defeated. "When have I ever been accused of being practical?"

*   *   *

It was several weeks later and Willa was at a hospital in Columbia, South Carolina. She was waiting with her father to see her uncle when he arrived at the hospital. Willa had paced the waiting room and had sat browsing through a magazine and was on the verge of complaining that the Department of Mental Retardation's van was late. Then, all of a sudden, there was her uncle, being wheeled in by his social worker.

Willa had forgotten in the few short months since she'd seen her uncle just how small and fragile he was. He sat in the wheelchair, uninterested in his surroundings…just staring off into the distance. He was wearing a South Carolina Electric and Gas baseball cap, a striped shirt, a windbreaker, and some jeans.

Willa went immediately to hug Buster and felt nothing in return. "Hi, Buster," she said quietly as the social worker talked to a nurse. "How are you?" No response.

Her father, who had also been holding back, leaned down to hug his brother. He received the same reaction Willa had.

Willa pulled up a chair to see her uncle eye-to-eye. She again noticed his tongue thrusting had left his mouth area chapped and red. She tried to get Buster to look at her, but he wouldn't. He just stared absently out the window.

"Look, Buster," Willa pulled out a purple, stuffed bear she'd brought for him. "Look, here's a bear. He's real soft. His name is Cloudy," she said, reading the tag around the bear's neck. He's for you. She put the bear at eye level with Buster. Her uncle sat there staring, working his tongue in and out of his mouth, his gold flecked eyes focusing on the bear's face. He didn't reach out for the bear, so Willa gently tucked it under Buster's arm.

Willa tried to concentrate on what the nurse was saying to the social worker about the surgery. But she couldn't help but be distracted by her uncle's thrusting tongue. Sometimes it would move in and out and sometimes it would hang out like a dog's. Willa watched the red, cracked area and thought about how dependent she was on lip balm. She had to have something on her mouth at all times or she felt naked. How did Buster feel with the sore, chafed area around his chin and mouth?

She couldn't help it. She quickly dug through her pocket book and found her round, little tub of lip balm. It was her favorite… strawberry flavored and medicated to help heal chapped lips. She screwed the lid off the tub and pressed her manicured finger into the goo. Without giving it a second thought about the germs she might contract, or might give him for that matter, Willa took her finger and smoothed the balm over Buster's chin, upper and lower lips. Buster smiled briefly at the sensation and taste of the gloss but then went right back to thrusting his tongue in and out. *Oh, well, at least he had one last flavor to enjoy before he never tastes again,* Willa thought sadly.

* * *

It was mid-morning and Willa helped the students get their snacks open. Most of them brought Jello cups or a banana or crackers with juice. But little Jeff's mother always packed a full lunch, with a sandwich, pudding, cheese sticks and more. She was trying to fatten him up, Willa reasoned.

Caleigh was sitting at her desk enjoying her own snack. "Mrs. Grizzard, come here a minute," she said with a sly smile. "I want to tell you something."

Willa grabbed her yogurt and pulled up a chair. "What's going on?"

"Well, you know I was on the phone with Jason's mom earlier. They had quite the weekend."

"What happened?" Willa's curiosity was piqued.

"They have been working with Jason and his phobia of trees. You know how he is around trees."

Willa knew all too well. Her back bore the results of carrying the large boy when he became hysterical around trees. No one understood it. It didn't make any sense. The family said they couldn't think of anything that would make him so fearful of trees and all their parts. But he was afraid, nonetheless.

The class enjoyed eating lunch out in the courtyard when the weather was nice. There were tables and some nice shade trees in containers around the walls. Jason would whimper when they walked outside but was usually okay once he got to the table. He was one who was very motivated by food, so he would usually focus on his plate. Everything would be fine unless the wind stirred. Then leaves would scatter across the cement ground. Jason would start screaming, "Oh, no, trees!" and, without warning, would almost tackle the closest teacher and start to climb up her. The other students were so accustomed to this that they would just casually continue eating. Jason would be inconsolable. He would cry and bury his face in his teacher's chest, runny nose and all, and would moan, "No trees." Caleigh had started trying to desensitize Jason by actually getting a leaf or a piece of bark and putting it on the child's leg or arm. Of course he would scream hysterically at first, but the longer it was held there, and nothing happened, the more the he would calm down. It was all very fascinating to Willa.

"They decided to take Jason camping! In the woods...with trees! They thought that they could show Jason how fun it was to be in the great outdoors. Well, guess what happened?"

"What?" Willa replied.

"He was so stricken with fear that his dad had to hold him the whole time...all 80 pounds of him! He screamed and cried most of the time and finally they decided to go to sleep early to see if a new day would bring relief.

"Well, in the middle of the night, in the still darkness, Jason would croak out, 'Trees!' So they finally decided to pack up and leave at about midnight. Isn't that crazy?"

"That's our boy!" Willa responded. "None of us understands it but his fear is very real to him. All we can do is try to console him, but he doesn't understand reason, so there's really very little we can do."

"That's right. Now if we could just get him to be a little afraid of food..." Caleigh smiled and nodded toward Jason, who was double-fisting pretzels and raisins into his mouth as fast as he could.

Ain't that they truth? Willa thought as she headed to the closet to get the broom.

* * *

When Willa got the word that her uncle had passed away, she didn't cry. She knew he truly was better off. No more feeding tubes, no more life in an institution. No more Down Syndrome. It felt good to actually allow herself to imagine Buster in Heaven. *What would he be like without all the constraints of his disability? What would he do first? Would he recognize Jesus right away?*

Willa felt a sense of relief. Even though she had not known him for very long, she had felt a responsibility towards him. She wondered how her father was feeling. She was glad her grandmother didn't have to go through this loss. Even though Willa knew her grandmother did the best she could at the time, Willa still had a hard time imagining what would have driven her grandmother to let her younger son go. It was all too much for her to grasp.

The funeral was a private one, with just her parents, her sisters and their families, and Willa and her family. Willa listened quietly as her father spoke a few words at the graveside. His voice cracked, raw with emotion. It occurred to her just how much her father must have loved his only brother. It must have been so hard to love someone who didn't return the love. Buster was just not capable, although the Down Syndrome children she knew were very loving. She guessed it really was a matter of individual differences and most importantly, their environment, which determined how loving the children were.

That night in bed, as Willa thought more about her grandparents and their decision to send Buster to an institution, she couldn't help but talk to Joel through the dark.

"Why do you think they did it, Joel? What could make a parent give away their child?"

"Willa, I don't know for sure. But I think it could be love that caused them to do what they did."

"Love? That's not a loving thing to do, Joel."

"Not on the surface. But what if they thought it was the absolute best thing for Buster? What if they felt they had no choice? I mean, we're talking more than a half a century ago. They didn't have schools and therapists. They didn't have the technology we have today, the medical advice we have or anything else like we have. They just had themselves. There was a whole lot of ignorance about Down Syndrome children and children with other disabilities for that matter. I think they did the most loving thing they knew how...They sent Buster where they thought he could get some help. That doesn't mean that at some point they didn't realize they had made a mistake, if in fact it was a mistake. But by then it was too late. Buster was used to his surroundings and didn't really recognize his family any more. What could they do?"

"I guess," Willa replied. "I still wish I could do something to bring attention to Buster's life. I mean he was here on this earth for over 60 years! Shouldn't he get even a gravestone to prove he existed?"

"Willa, I don't know what we can do about it now. Your father meant well. He just wanted to get things over with. I think he is really hurting over all of this. It's been his life, you know."

"No, it has been Buster's life. And now he's gone."

Things got silent and Joel almost drifted off to sleep when Willa sat up in bed and said, "I've got it. I know how we can remember Buster!"

* * *

It was a cold, blustery day in Deerfield County. A small group of people huddled together on the grounds of Goshen Community Church, with their backs to the wind. More people were coming from the parking lot. This was a moment that the church had been waiting for…. Breaking ground on a brand new children's wing. The existing classrooms were overflowing on Sunday mornings and it was either expand the building or turn people away.

The Grizzard family stood with the group, waiting for the pastor to start the ceremony.

"Gather in everyone, gather in. Maybe we can form a human wall against that wind," the pastor joked. "We want to get started now though, so let me have your attention, please. As you can see, this expansion project means a lot to a lot of people. We have been squeezing children into our small Sunday School wing and we just can't squeeze any more. But turning them away is unthinkable. Jesus said, 'Let the little children come unto me.' And that is just what we want to do. But building wings costs money. Lots of money. And a few months ago it looked like we wouldn't be able to break ground for years. That's when my dear friend, Willa Grizzard, came in. She had a heart for growing this church and she especially wanted to help grow the children's ministry here. She took on the fund-raising for this expansion and now, today, largely because of her, we can say that this wing will be paid for in full by the time it is completed this summer."

The crowd broke out in applause.

"She and her husband Joel won't like me saying so, but they have made personal donations that have come from huge sacrifices on their part."

The crowd clapped again as Willa blushed and looked down bashfully.

"Willa knew that we needed this new space and she even had special ideas about how we could use some of the classrooms. But I can't do it justice. We will just have to hear from her. Willa, come on up here."

Willa tried to move toward the pastor, but her heels were stuck in the cold, hard ground. So she started out with a little stumble.

"Always graceful, that's my motto," she said self-deprecatingly. The crowd laughed and then grew quiet.

"I have had a small passion growing inside of me. I have seen a segment of our population here in Deerfield County that has been left out of our church community. We see these people every day and yet we haven't made a dedicated space for them to join us.

"You see, they may walk a little slower or look a little different, but they are children of God, just the same. I am talking about children with intellectual and physical disabilities. They need classrooms where they can feel included. They need a playground where they can participate. Their families need to be able to leave their children and know they are safe and happy while they attend the service. There is a whole segment of our population that may not feel welcomed at churches in our community because they have different needs from the rest of us. But they aren't really so different from us. A higher counter allows a child in a wheelchair to pull right under the table for coloring time. Large, chunky Bible figures will allow children with fine motor issues to grasp and act out Bible stories. Lower swings and slides give all children access to playground fun.

"So with the elders' blessings, we are constructing a building that will be accessible to all children. We will have extra volunteers in classrooms just to work with children with disabilities so they can attend Sunday School right alongside all the other children. We will have equipment, training, and expertise from Special Education teachers who already attend Goshen Community Church.

"With these things in place, we will be able to welcome any parent with children with special needs and know we will offer the best to these families. Thank you."

Willa walked back to join Joel. She glanced over her shoulder and saw Caleigh applauding with the rest of the crowd. The pastor again spoke.

"Willa is selling herself short here. She is playing a big role in doing the research we need to construct a building that will welcome all. The only thing I've ever heard her ask for in return is that she'd like to choose the name of the new wing. Willa, what's it going to be called?"

"The Russell Bland Children's Wing," Willa said with a smile. "In honor of my uncle who had Down Syndrome."

www.ingramcontent.com/pod-product-compliance
Lightning Source LLC
Chambersburg PA
CBHW021714120626
46545CB00004B/1553

* 9 781961 250567 *